MW01104261

RoboHelp®
for the Web

John Hedtke
and Brenda Huettner

Wordware Publishing, Inc.

Library of Congress Cataloging-in-Publication Data

Hedtke, John V.
    RoboHelp for the Web / by John Hedtke and Brenda Huettner.
        p.   cm.
    Includes index.
    ISBN 1-55622-954-2
    1. RoboHelp (Computer file).   2. Online data processing.   3.
    Question-answering systems.   4. Web site development.   I. Huettner,
    Brenda.   II. Title.
    QA76.55 .H43 2002
    005.2'76--dc21   2002009385
                                                            CIP

© 2003, Wordware Publishing, Inc.

All Rights Reserved

2320 Los Rios Boulevard
Plano, Texas 75074

No part of this book may be reproduced in any form or by
any means without permission in writing from
Wordware Publishing, Inc.

Printed in the United States of America

ISBN 1-55622-954-2
10 9 8 7 6 5 4 3 2 1
0207

All inquiries for volume purchases of this book should be addressed to Wordware Publishing, Inc., at the
above address. Telephone inquiries may be made by calling:

(972) 423-0090

Dedication

To Richard Rogers, for songs sung, stories told, and always making sure my drinking horn was filled. Thanks, old friend.
    —John

For Paula and Lynn, who gave me a chance when I was just getting started.
    —Brenda

Contents

Contents

Contents

About the Authors

John Hedtke is an international award-winning author with over two decades in technical communications and computing, including five years as a programmer/analyst and seven years in technical publications management. He has written 23 books on a wide variety of topics, including RoboHelp 2000, MP3 files, Washington trivia, and Windows shareware. John has also written more than 70 manuals and online help systems and has published close to 100 articles in such magazines as *Windows*, *Publish!*, *PC Magazine*, and *Accounting Technology*. (A complete list of books, articles, projects, and awards can be found at his web site, www.hedtke.com.) John does frequent speaking appearances and consults on business processes, IT, and how to set up Technical Publications departments. John is also very active in the Society for Technical Communication, of which he is an Associate Fellow and a member of the society's Nominating Committee. When not engaged at the computer, John cooks, plays the banjo, and loses at backgammon to his wife, Marilyn. They live in Fort Wayne, Indiana.

Brenda Huettner is a writer, speaker, and consultant with 18 years of experience in the technical publications field, ten of those years in documentation department management. She has written manuals, help systems, procedures, and proposals for a wide variety of corporate clients and has published articles in magazines as diverse as *Career Woman* and *American Window Cleaner*. She is active in the Society for Technical Communication at both local and international levels and is a member of the IEEE Professional Communications Society. A regular presenter at conferences across the country, Brenda speaks on documentation, management, and career issues. Brenda lives in Arizona with her husband and two children, not far from the Arizona-Sonora Desert Museum.

Acknowledgments

This book would not have been possible without the gracious assistance of the following people:

Neil Salkind and all the wonderful folks at Studio B.

Julie Revell Benjamin, our diligent technical reviewer.

A whole bunch of people at eHelp who were very helpful, including Stephanie Ballabio, Silkie Fleischer, Alisa Popolizio, Mike Hamilton, Michael Pinard, Christa Bailey, Suzanne Smith, Suzanne Hardy, Sherri Jackson, Marvin Stompler, Jorgen Lien, Ron Linyard, and Tim Wood. The eHelp Technical Support team—Vartouhi Galpchian, Charles Jeter, David Beck, Gerry Palmer, Jason Eberwein, Raul Ramos, Steve Rossell, and Teri Browne—-are also richly deserving of recognition.

And Marilyn who was, as always, a delight.

To all these and many more, our thanks.

John Hedtke
john@hedtke.com

Brenda Huettner
brenda@p-ndesigns.com

Introduction

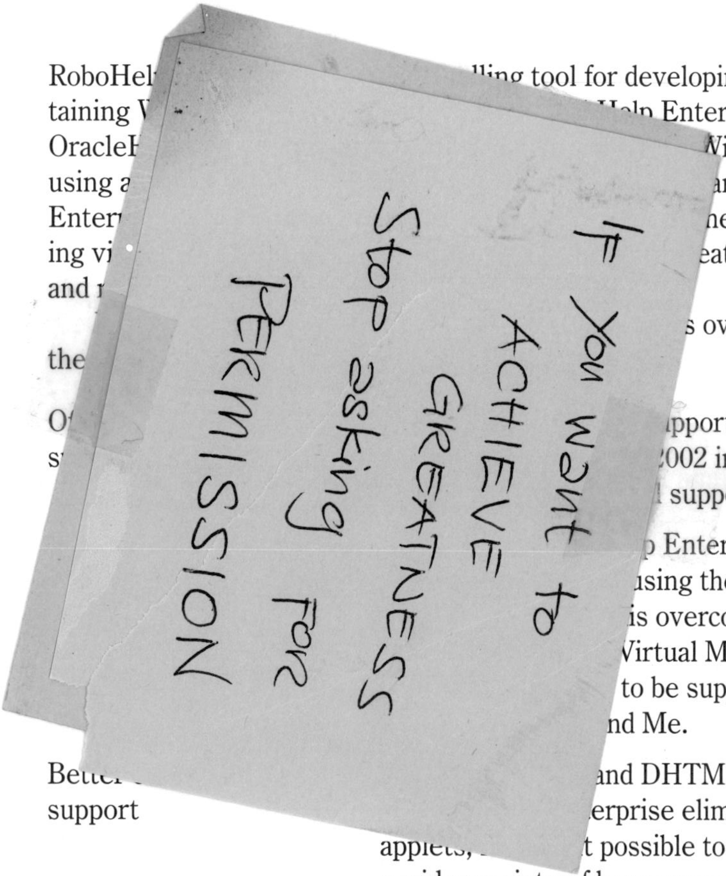

RoboHel... ...lling tool for developing, creating, and maintaining ... ...elp Enterprise, JavaHelp, and
OracleH... ...WinHelp and HTML Help
using a... ...and compilers, RoboHelp
Enter... ...hent process by automat-
ing vi... ...eating topics to testing
and ...

the... ...s over previous versions of

O... ...pports the latest version of
s... ...2002 in Office XP. (Word 95,
... ...l supported.)

... ...p Enterprise can be generated
... ...ising the Pure HTML and
... ...is overcomes Microsoft's
... ...Virtual Machine on Windows XP.
... ...to be supported on Windows 95,
... ...nd Me.

Bette... ...and DHTML options in WebHelp
support ... ...erprise eliminate the need for Java
applets, ...t possible to display online help on
a wider variety of browsers and platforms.

Improved Netscape support	In addition to eliminating the need for Java for WebHelp and WebHelp Enterprise, RoboHelp has improved popup and table support for Netscape.
Direct FrameMaker® import (MIF)	You can directly import FrameMaker documents into RoboHelp—including tables of contents, indexes, and glossaries—and turn them into a complete help project. It's not necessary to have FrameMaker installed on your computer.

[Handwritten note: "If you want to ACHIEVE GREATNESS stop asking for PERMISSION"]

Smart Word Import	The Smart Word Import feature automatically separates a Word document into multiple help topics based on their styles. It also preserves the document's table of contents and index.
Natural language search	The natural language search feature lets the users ask questions in plain English. You can also generate reports that show the kinds of questions being asked.
Team development support	RoboHelp Enterprise lets you merge help projects (including tables of contents and indexes) at run time, making parallel development of project modules easier.
Customizable look and feel	You can use skins to customize the look and feel of the finished product, including icons, fonts, buttons, navigation panes, and toolbars.
Improved cross-firewall support	The WebHelp DHTML and Pure HTML options can eliminate the need for Java applets, making for easier access to online help from behind a firewall.
Section 508-compliant WebHelp	WebHelp is compliant with Section 508 regulations so that your online help is appropriately accessible to people with disabilities.
Enhanced multimedia support	You can now include Microsoft Media Player, QuickTime, Real, and Flash files in online help.
Spell-checking the table of contents, index, and glossary	RoboHelp now lets you spell check the table of contents, index, and glossary.
Context-sensitive help API	The context-sensitive help API lets you invoke your online help using topic IDs, context IDs, map IDs, or URLs. The API supports C/C++, Java, JavaScript (HTML), and VB functions.

End user feedback reports	RoboHelp Enterprise provides reports on how the online help is being used, including reports on which questions are being asked most often and which questions are not being answered, which topics are viewed most frequently, and when the online help is being accessed. Questions can now be grouped on reports to make it easier to identify areas that need improvement.

In addition, there are a number of other improvements to the product, including the following:

Glossary tab	WebHelp and WebHelp Enterprise let you add a glossary so end users can look up defined terms.
Topic headers and footers	Help topics can have headers and footers. You can include help section or contact information, copyright declarations, or company logos.
Topic templates	Topic templates are models for topics that can include cascading style sheets (CSS), boilerplate text, and headers and footers. Topic templates can speed up topic development as well as standardize topic look and feel.
Changes to links	Alinks are now called See Also links. RoboHelp remembers the settings for Related Topics, See Also, and Keyword links.
Exact window positioning	The API lets you specify the exact position and size for the WebHelp windows to appear on the end user's screen.
International support	You can change the user interface text of your online help to another language. Users can also use the full-text search capabilities in their native language.
XML navigation	WebHelp and WebHelp Enterprise projects now utilize XML for navigation, which makes them load faster.
External document search	External documents can be searched as if they are part of an online help project. You can include Word documents, Excel spreadsheets, HTML files, PowerPoint presentations, and PDF files.

Other improvements   There are many other improvements, including:
- Video tutorials of common tasks
- Tip boxes describing help development processes step by step
- Better hyperlink and frameset handling
- More robust MPJ file handling
- Customizable popups

Why You Should Read This Book

This book shows you how to use RoboHelp Enterprise. It tells the beginning user of RoboHelp Enterprise how to install and configure the product and how to create HTML Help and WebHelp projects. The book also shows intermediate and advanced users how to create and maintain WebHelp Enterprise projects and how to develop help in teams most effectively. Appendixes provide additional information on topics such as file extensions and RoboHelp reports.

How This Book is Organized

There are 17 chapters and 2 appendices in this book. The following describes what you'll find in each section:

Chapter 1: Installing RoboHelp

This chapter tells how to install and configure RoboHelp. It shows what the various product features look like and how to use the tutorials. It also describes many of the new features.

Chapter 2: Understanding Online Help

This chapter is a general introduction to the various "flavors" of help, such as what it is, how it works, and when you would choose/use each one. It also describes how to plan your online help projects for maximum efficiency.

Chapter 3: Getting Started with RoboHelp HTML

This chapter introduces you to the basics of RoboHelp HTML. You'll learn how to use the various features in RoboHelp HTML and how RoboHelp treats the various project files.

Chapter 4: Creating Your First RoboHelp HTML Project

This chapter shows you how to start a new online help project in RoboHelp HTML. You see how to add topics and keywords and compile and test your help project.

Chapter 5: Linking Topics Together

This chapter shows how to enhance your RoboHelp HTML by adding more topics, jumps, popups, and links.

Chapter 6: Formatting Text, Paragraphs, and Topic Pages

This chapter teaches you how to enhance the appearance of the RoboHelp HTML files by adding color, formatting, and different fonts.

Chapter 7: Using Lists and Tables

This chapter addresses the subject of using tables and lists. You'll learn to add a simple table, add and merge rows and columns, embed tables within other tables, and format information. The chapter also shows you how to create and maintain numbered lists, bulleted lists, and directory lists.

Chapter 8: Adding Images and Special Effects to RoboHelp HTML Files

This chapter teaches you how to insert graphics into RoboHelp HTML files. You'll also see how to link graphics as hotspots, add buttons and image maps, and use the Graphics Locator tool to find graphics on your system.

Chapter 9: Getting Organized Using Folders, Tables of Contents, and Indexing Tools

This chapter shows you how to create a variety of navigation tools in your online help, including tables of contents and indexes.

Chapter 10: Maintaining Consistency with Templates and Skins

This chapter demonstrates how to use styles in RoboHelp HTML to create consistent, easily maintained online help. You'll learn about linked, embedded, and inline styles, style tabs, dynamic styles using DHTML, cascading style sheets, and topic templates.

Chapter 11: Using Windows in RoboHelp HTML

This chapter discusses ways in which you can create and customize windows to improve the display of your online help. You'll also see how to link customized windows to topics.

Chapter 12: Creating Context-Sensitive Help

This chapter teaches you to create and maintain context-sensitive help. You'll learn how context-sensitive help works, how to use map IDs and aliases, and how to test your online help. You'll also see how to create What's This? Help.

Chapter 13: Creating Forms

This chapter describes how to create interactive forms for gathering information from end users. You'll also see how to use CGI scripts to add power to your forms.

Chapter 14: Using Frames and Framesets

This chapter shows you how to create, use, and customize frames in your online help.

Chapter 15: Using Other RoboHelp Tools

This chapter describes how to use many of the tools included with RoboHelp.

Chapter 16: Creating WebHelp Enterprise

This chapter shows you how to create WebHelp Enterprise. You'll learn how to generate and publish WebHelp Enterprise projects, how to view them and use the natural language search features, how to copy WebHelp and WebHelp Enterprise projects to other locations, and how to fine-tune the RoboEngine for best results. You'll also learn about the various WebHelp Enterprise reports.

Chapter 17: Developing Large Online Help Projects

This chapter describes how to use build tags and browse sequences to develop large online help projects.

Appendix A: File Extensions

This appendix lists the various types of files and their extensions.

Appendix B: Reports

This appendix describes the various RoboHelp reports.

Conventions Used in This Book

There are a number of standard conventions used in this book. The following list describes these conventions.

- Boldface type in procedures designates a keypress, typed text, or a clicked button or option selection.

Example	*Meaning*
Type **ABC** and press **Enter**.	Type the text "ABC" and press the Enter key.
Press **Esc**.	Press the Esc key.
Click **OK**.	Select and click the OK button.
Use the **File|Save As** menu selection.	Pick Save As in the File menu.
Select the **AutoSave** option button.	Click the AutoSave option button so it is black.
Check the **Standard toolbar** check box.	Put a check in the Standard toolbar check box.

- Combination key sequences are connected with a + symbol. A series of keypresses is connected with commas.

Press **Alt+F**.	Press and hold Alt while typing the letter F.

 TIP: *A tip provides a helpful hint or a useful technique.*

 NOTE: *A note contains brief information that is worth mentioning in connection with the current discussion.*

 CAUTION: *A caution indicates a condition or procedure that may potentially cause data loss or corruption.*

Sidebar

A sidebar provides extensive additional information on a topic or procedure.

Contacting the Authors

We've done everything we can to make this book complete and accurate, but it's possible that we've left something out or made an error (who, us?). If you find an error or have a suggestion for something that can be improved in the next edition, pleased drop us email at john@hedtke.com and brenda@p-ndesigns.com. Be sure to check out the online help resources at www.hedtke.com, too.

Chapter 1

Installing RoboHelp

This chapter introduces you to RoboHelp and tells you how to install RoboHelp on your system. You'll first be introduced to the products in the RoboHelp family. You'll also read about the new features in RoboHelp Enterprise 2002. Next, you'll learn how to install RoboHelp Office and RoboHelp Enterprise Author on the computer being used to create online help, how to install RoboEngine on a network server, and how to do the basic RoboEngine web site configuration using the RoboEngine Configuration Manager. Along the way, you'll see what you need in the way of hardware and software for the client and server computers.

Which RoboHelp Do You Need?

RoboHelp isn't a single product. There are actually several different varieties of RoboHelp. All of them will help you create high-quality online help while substantially reducing development time, but which RoboHelp product you should use depends on what you need to create. Table 1-1 describes the various RoboHelp products currently available.

Table 1-1: The RoboHelp family

RoboHelp version	Description
RoboHelp for WinHelp	Creates WinHelp (also known as "classic help") only. Use this for creating help systems that will be used exclusively on Windows independent of an Internet browser.
RoboHelp for Microsoft HTML Help	Creates Microsoft HTML Help only. Use this for creating help systems that will be used on computers running Microsoft Internet Explorer.
RoboHelp Office	An integrated package that has all the features of RoboHelp for WinHelp and RoboHelp for Microsoft HTML Help as well as the ability to create WebHelp and other types of HTML-based help. Use this for creating the complete range of help systems.
RoboHelp Enterprise	In addition to all the features in RoboHelp Office, RoboHelp Enterprise provides exciting server-based features for WebHelp projects, including natural language search, feedback reports, and support for development of large help projects by teams.

Both RoboHelp Office and RoboHelp Enterprise offer a complete help development environment for all popular types of online help, but only RoboHelp Enterprise has the natural language search and team development features.

 NOTE: *A complete 15-day demo version of RoboHelp Office appears on the CD included with this book.*

What's New in RoboHelp 2002?

Both RoboHelp Enterprise 2002 and RoboHelp Office 2002 have a number of exciting new features and product enhancements, as shown in Table 1-2.

Table 1-2: New features in RoboHelp Enterprise 2002 and RoboHelp Office 2002

Feature	Description
MIF (FrameMaker®) file import	RoboHelp can import FrameMaker documents (including TOCs, index, and glossary) from an MIF file. It's not necessary to have FrameMaker installed on the computer doing the import.
Customizable look and feel	You can change the way RoboHelp looks by using *skins*, theme files containing information on how to display the RoboHelp toolbar, icons, fonts, navigation panes, buttons, and help system colors. You can even apply skins to WebHelp Enterprise projects so a help project can be customized with the company colors and look and feel.
Glossary tab	WebHelp projects now have a glossary tab for quick reference to glossary items in the help file.
Topic templates	You can create topic templates to standardize topic formatting and save time.
Headers and footers in topics	Topics can now have headers and footers, such as copyright information, section information, or logos.
Java is no longer required for WebHelp	WebHelp and WebHelp Enterprise are no longer dependent on Java, the Java Virtual Machine, or ActiveX controls to work, thereby supporting WebHelp projects on Windows XP (which eliminated the Java Virtual Machine). The current releases of RoboHelp have DHTML and Pure HTML options that let you release WebHelp projects that will work on any browser. In addition, there is enhanced popup and table display features for Netscape.

Feature	Description
Continuing support for Windows	The DHTML and Pure HTML options let you use WebHelp and WebHelp Enterprise projects on Windows XP computers (which do not ship with the Java Virtual Machine as part of the operating system). Previous versions of Windows, including Windows 95, 98, 98SE, 2000, and ME, are all supported.
Enhanced spell-checking	Spell-checking now works on TOC, index, and glossary text, as well as on topic and heading text in help projects.
Multimedia enhancements	QuickTime, Flash, Real, and Microsoft Media Player files can now be included in help projects.
New help API	A new context-sensitive help API lets you call help topics using a context, topic, or map ID or the topic's URL. The API also has VB, JavaScript (HTML), Java, and C/C++ functions. The API also lets you define the exact location and size of topic windows in the finished help project.
Enhanced popups	You can manually size the popup windows in the finished help project.
Enhanced hyperlinks	Hyperlinks that are part of drop-down hotspots now retain relative path information.
Increased stability	Framesets are more stable and easier to create and edit; MPJ (master project file) handling has also been improved.
Section 508 compliance	You can create Section 508-compliant WebHelp projects. (Section 508 specifies how help projects should be accessible for those with disabilities.)

In addition to these features for RoboHelp Office and RoboHelp Enterprise, there are some specific features that appear only in RoboHelp Enterprise, shown in Table 1-3.

Table 1-3: New features in RoboHelp Enterprise 2002

Feature	Description
Natural language search	One of the most powerful features of RoboHelp Enterprise, natural language search lets end-users enter questions in plain English rather than using more traditional help navigation tools.
Feedback reports	As part of the natural language search features, RoboHelp has reports to show how the help is being used, when, and what types of questions are being asked. The reports also group similar questions even though they're phrased differently.
Team development features	Merge help projects at run time for increased team productivity.

Installing RoboHelp

This section shows you how to install RoboHelp Office and RoboHelp Enterprise.

Installing RoboHelp Office and RoboHelp Enterprise Author

RoboHelp Office is shipped on a single CD that you install on the computer on which you intend to use it. RoboHelp Enterprise comes on two CDs: the RoboHelp Enterprise Author, which is approximately the same as RoboHelp Office, and the RoboEngine, the server component of RoboHelp Enterprise. The basic procedure for installing RoboHelp Office and the RoboHelp Enterprise Author is identical.

The system requirements for both products are shown in Table 1-4.

Table 1-4: System requirements for RoboHelp Office and RoboHelp Enterprise Author

Feature	Requirements
Hardware	At least a 300 MHz Pentium II with 128 MB of RAM and 200 MB of available disk space for the software.
Software	At least Windows 95/98/ME/NT 4.0/2000/XP and Internet Explorer v4.0. (Internet Explorer 6.0 is including on the RoboHelp Office and RoboHelp Enterprise Author CDs.)

Uninstalling Old Versions

If you have an earlier version of RoboHelp Office or RoboHelp Enterprise on your system, it's a good idea to uninstall the old version before installing the new version. Running multiple versions of the software on the same computer is not supported and may cause substantial problems. Follow this procedure:

1. Copy any help project files that may be in the RoboHelp Office folder. (These might be erased with the other files in the RoboHelp Office folder.)
2. Save the RoboHelp templates. (This is only necessary if you made any changes to the standard RoboHelp templates; if not, you can skip this step.)
3. Use the Add/Remove Program feature in the Windows Control Panel to remove the old RoboHelp software.

To install RoboHelp Office or RoboHelp Enterprise Author, do the following:

1. Close any unnecessary programs.
2. Insert the RoboHelp Office or the RoboHelp Enterprise Author CD in your CD-ROM drive. If you have the autorun feature enabled on the drive, the installation program will start automatically. If not, start the installation yourself by

choosing **Start | Run** and entering *d*:**setup** (where *d* is the drive letter for the CD-ROM drive).

NOTE: *Both RoboHelp Office and RoboHelp Enterprise Author need to be installed appropriately for your licensing agreement. If you have a single-user license, you can install the software on a network, but only one person can use the software at a time. Multiple-license agreements are available; check with your eHelp sales representative for more information.*

The installation procedure starts and displays the Software License Agreement screen (shown in Figure 1-1).

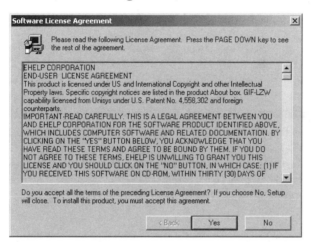

Figure 1-1: The Software License Agreement screen

3. Click **Yes** to accept the terms of the agreement. The Installation Welcome screen appears.

Figure 1-2: The Installation Welcome screen

4. If you haven't already closed other Windows programs, do so now, and then click **OK**. The User Information screen appears.

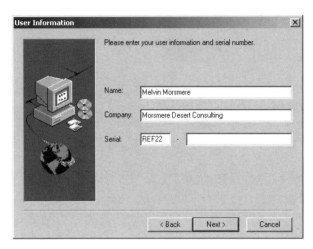

Figure 1-3: The User Information screen

5. Make any corrections to the information appearing in the fields. Enter the last part of the serial number in the second serial number field and click **Next**. (The serial number appears on the sticker on the CD sleeve for the RoboHelp Office or RoboHelp Enterprise Author.) The User Information Confirmation screen (shown in Figure 1-4) appears.

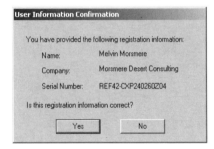

Figure 1-4: The User Information Confirmation screen

6. Check the information that appears in the screen. If there are any corrections to the name, company name, or serial number, click **No**, and the installation procedure will display the User Information screen again so you can make changes. When you are satisfied with the information as it appears on the User Information Confirmation screen, click **Yes**. The Select Version screen appears, as shown in Figure 1-5.

NOTE: *Be sure that the name and company name appear exactly as you wish them to be. You won't be able to change them subsequently unless you uninstall and reinstall the software.*

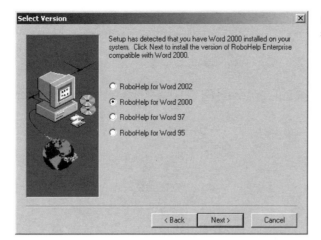

Figure 1-5: The Select Version screen

7. Make sure that the installation program has detected the right version of Microsoft Word. (This will likely be a problem only if you have multiple versions of Word on your computer.) When you are satisfied with your selection, click **Next**. The Word Location screen (shown in Figure 1-6) appears.

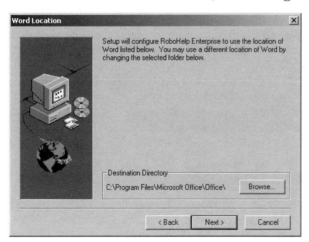

Figure 1-6: The Word Location screen

8. The installation program will install the RoboHelp templates in the Microsoft Office directory where Word is installed. You can specify a different directory by clicking Browse and identifying a new directory, which will then be displayed in the Destination Directory field on the screen. When you are satisfied with the destination directory, click **Next**. The installation program will check the installation information, after which it displays the Setup Type screen, shown in Figure 1-7.

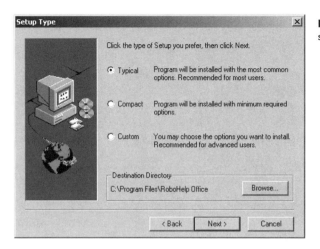

Figure 1-7: The Setup Type screen

9. Select one of the three options (described in Table 1-5) from the Setup Type screen.

Table 1-5: Installation options

Option	Description
Typical	The installation program will install RoboHelp Office or RoboHelp Enterprise Author with the most common user options. If you don't have any reason to do otherwise, you'll probably want to select this.
Compact	The installation program will install the absolute minimum necessary for RoboHelp Office or RoboHelp Enterprise Author to run. Use this option if you have space limitations.
Custom	The installation program will let you install the RoboHelp Office or RoboHelp Enterprise Author options you specify.

If you select **Custom**, clicking **Next** displays the Select Components screen, shown in Figure 1-8.

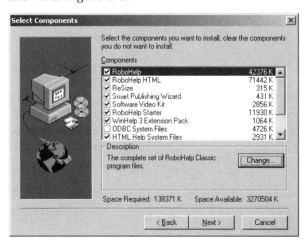

Figure 1-8: The Select Components screen

You can select the various components you wish to install. (The default options are the ones installed when you select Typical from the Setup Type screen.) Note that Internet Explorer v6.0 (at the bottom of the list) is not automatically selected for installation.

The installation program will install the RoboHelp software in the directory specified in the Destination Directory field. You can specify a different directory by clicking **Browse** and identifying a new directory, which will then be displayed in the Destination Directory field on this screen.

Many of the options in the Select Components screen will have sub-components that you can select individually. To see a list of sub-components, click **Change**. The Select Sub-components screen for the highlighted option appears (shown in Figure 1-9 with the sub-components for the RoboHelp option).

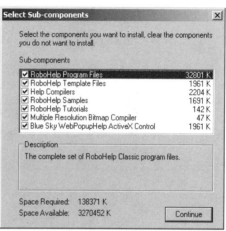

Figure 1-9: The Select Sub-components screen

When you are satisfied with your selections of sub-components, click **Continue** to return to the Select Components screen. When you have selected the components you want to install, click **Next**. The Select Program Folder appears, as shown in Figure 1-10.

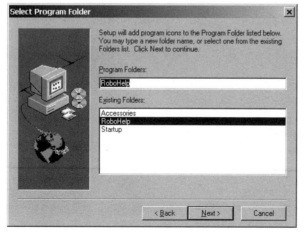

Figure 1-10: The Select Program Folder screen

10. Select the program folder in which to install the program icons. The default selection is RoboHelp, but you can specify an existing folder or create a new one. When you are satisfied with the destination, click **Next**. The installation program starts installing the components you've selected. A process monitor

(shown in Figure 1-11) appears to show you how much of the installation process is completed.

Figure 1-11: The installation process monitor screen

When the components have been installed, the Product Registration screen appears.

Figure 1-12: The Product Registration screen

11. If you click **Next** with the registration box checked, the installation program will open your default browser and attempt to register you via the eHelp web registration screen (shown in Figure 1-13 with sample data already entered).

Figure 1-13: The eHelp web registration screen

12. Fill in the fields and click **Register Now** at the bottom of the web page. The web site will register your software. When you complete the web registration, close your browser and click **Next** again to continue the installation. The Setup Complete screen appears, as shown in Figure 1-14.

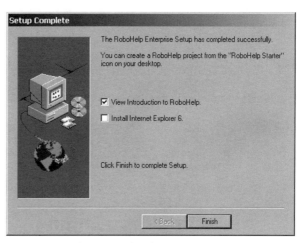

If you have not already done so, you can install Internet Explorer v6.0 by checking the appropriate box. When you

Figure 1-14: The Setup Complete screen

click **Finish**, the introduction to RoboHelp appears (this is the default option). The introduction will appear in the default browser (part of the main page appears in Figure 1-15).

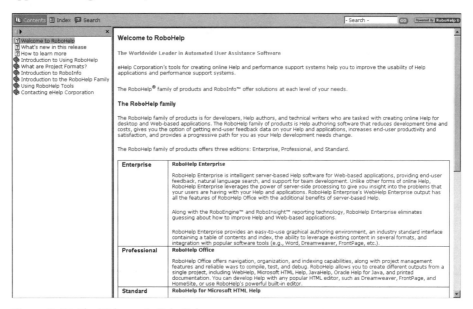

Figure 1-15: The Welcome to RoboHelp screen

Congratulations! The installation is complete. As part of the process, the installation program adds the RoboHelp Starter icon to the desktop.

TIP: *Although the icons are installed in a folder and added to the Programs section of the Start menu, you may find it useful to add the various RoboHelp icons to the desktop. The fastest and easiest way to do this is to display the folder, hold down Ctrl, and then click and drag each icon to the desktop. (Holding down Ctrl drags a copy of the icon rather than the icon itself.) Figure 1-16 shows the four RoboHelp icons added to the desktop.*

Introduction   RoboHelp   RoboHelp   RoboHelp
to RoboHelp   Starter   Classic   HTML

Figure 1-16: The RoboHelp program icons

Installing RoboEngine

If you're using RoboHelp Office, you won't need to do anything further to install RoboHelp software. If you're installing RoboHelp Enterprise, you'll now need to install the RoboEngine portion on the server.

Before you start the installation procedure for RoboEngine, make sure that the server will run the software. The system requirements for RoboEngine are shown in Table 1-6.

Table 1-6: System requirements for RoboEngine

Feature	Requirements
Hardware	At least a 450 MHz Pentium III with 128 MB of RAM, 50 MB of available disk space for the software, and an additional 200 MB of available disk space after the installation.
Software	Windows NT 4.0 Server and Microsoft Internet Information Server (IIS) 4.0 or Windows 2000 Server and Microsoft Internet Information Server (IIS) 5.0. In addition, you should have the latest service packs installed for your version of Windows. (Windows NT and Windows 2000 Professional are not robust enough to adequately support a server-based system in production, although it is possible that you may be able to use such a configuration for testing. However, installing RoboEngine on these operating systems is neither recommended nor supported by eHelp.)

CAUTION: *Be sure to install the latest security patches for your version of Windows and for Microsoft IIS. Without the security patches, IIS is susceptible to a number of security problems including the Code Red virus. Check the Microsoft web site (www.microsoft.com) for information on the latest security and product patches.*

To install RoboEngine, do the following:

1. Close any unnecessary programs.
2. Insert the RoboEngine CD in your CD-ROM drive. If you have the autorun feature enabled on the drive, the installation program will start automatically. If not,

start the installation yourself by choosing **Start | Run** and entering *d*:\setup (where *d* is the drive letter for the CD-ROM drive).

The installation procedure starts and displays the RoboEngine License Agreement screen.

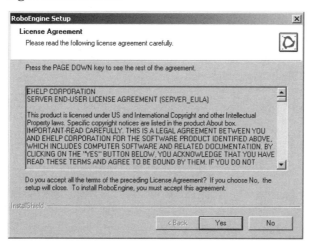

Figure 1-17: The RoboEngine License Agreement screen

3.   Click **Yes** to accept the terms of the agreement. The Customer Information screen appears.

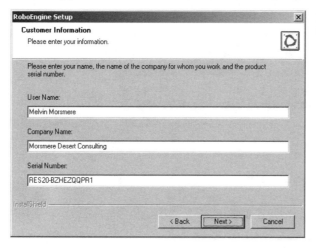

Figure 1-18: The Customer Information screen

4.   Make any corrections to the information appearing in the fields. Enter the Serial Number in the serial number field and click **Next**. (The serial number appears on a sticker on the CD sleeve for the RoboEngine CD.) The Choose Destination Location screen (shown in Figure 1-19) appears.

 NOTE: *Be sure that the name and company name appear exactly as you wish them to be. You won't be able to change them subsequently unless you uninstall and reinstall the software.*

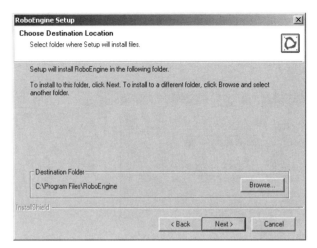

Figure 1-19: The Choose Destination Location screen

5. The installation program will install the RoboEngine software in the directory specified in the Destination Folder field. You can specify a different directory by clicking **Browse** and identifying a new directory, which will then be displayed in the Destination Folder field on this screen. When you are satisfied with the location to install files, click **Next**.

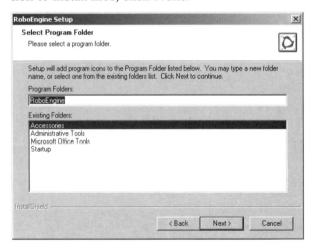

Figure 1-20: The Select Program Folder screen

6. Select the program folder in which to install the program icons. The default selection is RoboEngine, but you can specify an existing folder or create a new one. When you are satisfied with the destination, click **Next**. The installation program starts installing the components you've selected. A process monitor (shown in Figure 1-21) appears to show you how much of the installation process is completed.

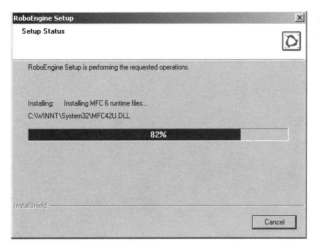

Figure 1-21: The installation process monitor screen

When the components have been installed, the InstallShield Wizard Complete screen appears, as shown in Figure 1-22.

Figure 1-22: The InstallShield Wizard Complete screen

7. Click **Finish** to reboot the computer to complete the installation process. (If you don't want to reboot the computer at this time, select No on the screen and click Finish.) When you reboot the computer, the RoboEngine Configuration Wizard will start and step you through the process of creating a new help engine. The opening RoboEngine Configuration Wizard screen is shown in Figure 1-23.

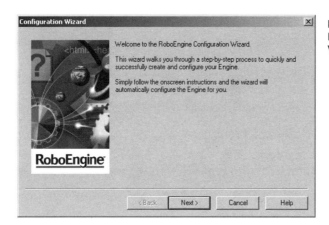

Figure 1-23: The opening RoboEngine Configuration Wizard screen

8.   Click **Next**. The Select Web Site screen appears, as shown in Figure 1-24.

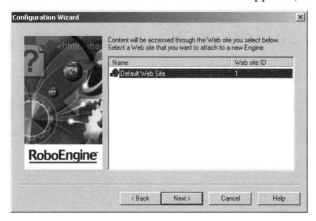

Figure 1-24: The Select Web Site screen

9.   Select the web site to which you want to attach the new engine.

Understanding Server Web Sites

You can have multiple web sites on Windows NT4 and Windows 2000 servers. When you first install RoboEngine, there is a single default web site, which is the computer identification. For example, if the computer is named "SHEBA," the default web site would be \\SHEBA. While this will work okay for the basic RoboEngine functions, it can present security problems—users will be logging directly into the shared volumes of SHEBA. In addition, if the computer identification is more esoteric (such as PRH002A1), the users will have a hard time remembering how to reach the help server. As a result, you're likely to want to create at least one new web site, which you or the server administrator can set up using the Internet Service Manager included with IIS.

There are some rules for creating and running multiple web sites on the server:

- If the web sites are both port 80, the web sites must have different IP addresses assigned to them, or they must have different host header names if the IP addresses for the web sites are flagged as "All Unassigned." You can use the Internet Service Manager to set the IP address and the host header name for the web sites.

- If you're using the machine for internal testing, the host header name you assign can be any internal domain name, but once a system is in production, you'll need to use a registered domain name. (If you've configured the internal domain to be *abcdefghij.com* and there's also a registered domain on the Internet with the same name, the results will be unpredictable as to which web address will be found and displayed in the browser.) Be sure to update the server's HOSTS file as well as the HOSTS files for all machines connecting to the server.

- You must have one product license for each web site you're configuring.

- Only properly configured web sites will appear in the Select Web Site screen.

When you are satisfied with the web site selection, click Next. The Configure Database screen appears, as shown in Figure 1-25.

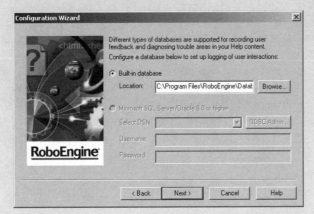

Figure 1-25: The Configure Database screen

10. RoboEngine records feedback and other information in a database. The default database is a built-in Microsoft Access database, but if you also have the RoboEngine Connectivity Pack (purchased separately) installed on the server, you can use another Microsoft Access database as well as a Microsoft SQL Server or Oracle 8.0 database. If you want to use a Microsoft SQL Server or Oracle 8.0 database, you'll need to enter the database's DSN, the username, and the database password.

What's the Difference between Database Options?

The built-in Microsoft Access database works okay, but, frankly, it's not very robust. If you're just going to be running a small intranet-based system for 30 days at a time between server reboots with a couple hundred users and not a lot of traffic, it's fine. It's also good for testing, where you usually won't have much load on the database. But the built-in database is just not durable enough to handle real production loads for hundreds or thousands of users. So, if you're planning on releasing online help via the Internet or you have a very large intranet with lots of users and a high-traffic environment, you should seriously consider getting the RoboEngine Connectivity Pack and using a Microsoft SQL Server or Oracle database.

While Microsoft SQL Server and Oracle are very robust, using either one for your database also has some drawbacks. You must have someone create and configure the database, which will probably require you to get someone outside your department involved. If an SQL Server or Oracle data source doesn't already exist, you'll need to use the ODBC Administrator to create a system data source. (Because RoboHelp Enterprise won't be logged into a user account, you can't use a user data source nor can you use NT Authentication.) Also, the database user name/password should have permission to create tables.

In addition, you must have someone administer the database: backing it up regularly, cleaning and compressing database information, and possibly even doing database tuning and load balancing. All of this, while not a large job, still requires a certain amount of time for an IT person. Consider your RoboHelp Enterprise needs and requirements carefully and weigh them against the options afforded by each type of database.

When you are satisfied with your selections, click **Next**. The Configuration Wizard creates the engine for the selected web site. Progress is shown in the Creating Engine screen.

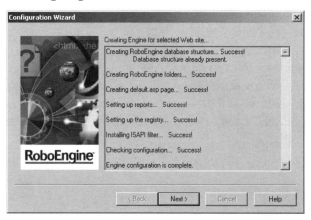

Figure 1-26: The Creating Engine screen

11. When the engine has been created, click **Next**. The Configuration Wizard displays the Summary screen.

Figure 1-27: The Summary screen

12. Click **Finish** to complete the engine creation process.

You've now successfully configured the web site. The Database options you selected in step 9 appear on the RoboEngine Configuration Manager main screen.

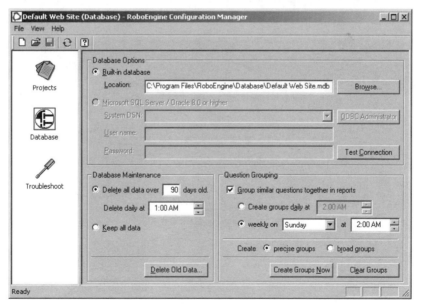

Figure 1-28: The RoboEngine Configuration Manager main screen

You'll learn more about using the RoboEngine Configuration Manager as part of creating WebHelp Enterprise projects in Chapter 16, "Creating WebHelp Enterprise." You won't need to have the RoboEngine Configuration Manager running to create basic HTML Help or WebHelp projects, but it's a good idea to set up RoboEngine and configure it early as there are many potential configuration issues that will take time to resolve.

Using the Tutorials

Once you have installed RoboHelp on your system, you can take advantage of the tutorials included with the product. The most important tutorial is the introduction to RoboHelp (shown in Figure 1-15), which will introduce you to using RoboHelp, RoboInfo, other products in the RoboHelp family, and the RoboHelp tools.

Another resource that will be of great help to you is the eHelp RoboHelp Community web site, http://www.helpcommunity.ehelp.com/robohelp/. (The opening screen for the eHelp RoboHelp Community is shown in Figure 1-29.) From this web site, you can access several areas that provide help and information for help developers, including the following:

- Developer and Help Author forums, message boards where you can post questions and information about specific issues with RoboHelp and help development

- eHelp Knowledge Base for information on specific problems and techniques

- Sample files you can download for WebHelp Enterprise, HTML Help, JavaHelp, WebHelp, and WinHelp

- Various publications, including articles, the eHelp "Help Corner," and assorted tips and tricks

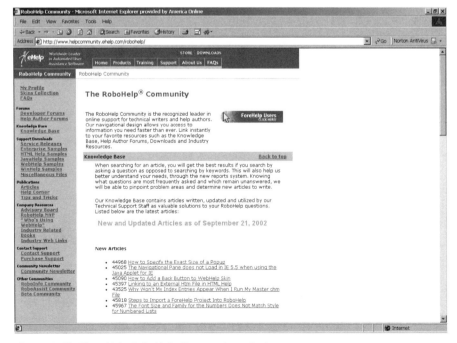

Figure 1-29: The eHelp RoboHelp Community web site

Summary

In this chapter, you learned the new features in RoboHelp Enterprise 2002. You also saw how to install RoboHelp Office and RoboHelp Enterprise Author, as well as RoboEngine. As part of this, you learned the hardware and software requirements for the client and server computers and saw how to do the basic RoboEngine web site configuration using the RoboEngine Configuration Manager.

In the next chapter, you'll learn about the types of help you can create with RoboHelp Office and RoboHelp Enterprise Author and how to plan your help system.

Chapter 2

Understanding Online Help

This chapter discusses what online help is and shows you the types of online help you can create with the family of RoboHelp products. You'll also learn how to plan an online help project.

What is Online Help?

In its simplest form, online help is a collection of text-based topics with some method for navigating them, such as a table of contents. With the advent of WinHelp ("classic help") for Windows systems, the basic expectations for online help have grown to include the following:

- Text is arranged into *topics*, each of which appears on a single screen (which may or may not need to be scrolled). Topics are not merely ASCII text displayed on a monochromatic screen; they can be formatted with a wide variety of options, including colors, fonts, styles, and other attributes such as the location of a specific help window.

- *Hyperlinks* (or just *links*) provide a way to get from one topic to another and are a method of navigating separate from other methods of navigation, such as the table of contents and the index.

- A *table of contents* (or *TOC*), very much like the table of contents in a book or manual, lists the topics in online help in a logical order. Because the topics can appear in the actual online help files in any order, the table of contents provides a logical organization for the order and groups in which topics are arranged.

- An *index* in online help is composed of *keywords*, which are similar to the index entries in a printed book. Online help has options for looking up keywords and looking at the relevant topics. There are also many full-text search options supported by most popular forms of online help so you can search for information that doesn't have a keyword assigned. In addition, the new natural language search features in RoboHelp Enterprise let you expand this concept to include asking questions in standard English.

Depending on the type, online help may also be *compiled* (just like software) from source files. The compilation process is done with a help compiler. Depending on the type of online help being created, the compiled help may be turned into a single file, or it may remain in individual files of each topic.

Compiling online help files lets you do extensive error checking before releasing the help. It also optimizes the help files so that they run faster. Some types of online help are *interpreted*—that is, the files are never compiled but are always opened and run on the fly—but interpreted help runs slower than compiled help because of the overhead of opening and interpreting the information in the source files each time.

Most users are familiar with the online help that accompanies a program and tells you how to use it, but you can also have stand-alone help files that distribute information on some topic, such as product information files, white papers, general background information, and training materials.

Advantages to Using Online Help

There are many reasons for using online help instead of printed manuals and documentation.

Versus printed manuals and documentation, online help...

...**is more accessible.** Hyperlinks, keywords, and full-text search make finding specific topics quick. In combination with such navigational aids as See Also links and browse sequences, online help is perfect for a variety of reference applications.

...**is easier to use.** To be effective, manuals must be organized in a logical, sequential fashion. You can thumb through a manual to find information, but the order in which topics are presented is predetermined. Online help has a similar feature—the table of contents—that presents a linear, hierarchical organization to the online help. However, in addition, the topics and sections in online help can be navigated in almost any order with basic navigational tools like keywords, browse sequences, and See Also links. For more advanced applications (such as self-paced training written in an online help format), you can create online help that prompts for input of various kinds to determine what information should be presented and in what order.

...**is a richer communications medium.** Printed manuals can be well-formatted and even colorful, but the information on the page will not change. In contrast, online help can use colors for emphasis easily (and at no extra cost). Online help also offers the whole range of software techniques to enhance the message. You can include jumps, popups, pictures, sound effects, video files, links to programs and web sites, hyperlinks, buttons, and browse sequences. Furthermore, you can make these links and effects conditional on such things as information the users have entered or the type of computer they are using. Finally, users can copy and paste information from online help to other documents, making it easy to transmit blocks of text, command strings, scripts, macros, and sample code.

…communicates more effectively. The average retention rate for new material is 10 to 20% of the material three days later if you show or tell the information. If you use multimedia with text to combine showing and telling, the average retention rate for new material after three days goes up to 65%. Because of the additional richness of online help over printed documentation, it's possible to create multimedia presentations and procedures that will greatly improve the retention rate for new material.

…is faster to create. Even for a small run of cheap offset printing, printed manuals take up to a week to print and bind. For larger print runs (or printing that requires color), printing and binding can require up to one month. As a result, there is invariably a delta between the information in the printed manual about the product and the final product. Most software products have significant changes in the last month of development; some of them have drastic changes to their look and feel shortly before they're shipped. Because online help requires no printing time, help can be developed roughly in parallel to the software. While the product itself is in final testing, the online help can be edited and tested. Information about last-minute changes to the software can be added on the fly as necessary.

…is cheaper to create. Printed manuals are expensive compared to the other materials in a software product box. If the manual is of reasonable size, the cost for the printed manual is usually greater than the cost of everything else in the software product box (including the box). If you switch to a printed manual that's a guide for installation and then shift to online help for the bulk of the documentation, you can reduce the cost of goods by up to 50%. You can also reduce other costs, too; product boxes don't need to be as big and shipping costs will go down. A typical product box with minimal printed documentation weighs less than 2 pounds, while similar products with comprehensive printed documentation can easily weigh twice as much. (One classic product some years ago weighed 35 pounds, 30 pounds of which were manuals.)

…is easier to maintain. Changing printed manuals is expensive and difficult. New pages need to be desktop-published, interpolated, and printed. You may have to consider repagination (and changes to the manual's table of contents, index, and internal page references). You then have the time and the cost of shipping the updated manual (or at least, the updated page if the manual is in a loose-leaf binder) to your users or customers. And, if there is an inventory of old manuals, it may not even be possible or practical to update printed documentation quickly. In contrast, online help is easy to change. Updating online help is simply a matter of inserting the new text or topics, fixing browse sequences, and recompiling. Minor changes can be made in a matter of minutes. The online help can then be distributed directly via the company's web site.

…is easier to customize. Creating customized printed manuals is almost always difficult and unpleasant. The best solutions usually involve modularized chapters and sections that can be assembled relatively easily to omit information about specific topics or features, but adding custom logos, screens, or formatting requires a complete reworking of the manual. Online help, on the other hand, can be customized to any level necessary by modifying company names, logos, and other information. You can remove references to topics, commands, or features that aren't shipped with the customized version of the product. RoboHelp Enterprise 2002 also has *topic templates* that let you change the formatting and *skins* that change the look and feel of the help itself.

…is easier to distribute. As discussed earlier, online help weighs nothing. It can be distributed on the same CD containing the product for no extra charge. Updates can be released electronically (with almost no distribution costs) using your company's web site or intranet. You could even email small help files (or a link to a site) as part of an automatic update service to provide your customers with immediate access to updated online help.

…reaches more people. Everyone ends up looking for the one last copy of the product manual in the office sooner or later. This takes time and effort and isn't very effective. If a company made a site purchase of a product, it's entirely likely that they didn't buy an adequate number of manuals, making it all the more likely that there won't be enough to go around. Shipping online help as part of the product ensures that the users will always have a copy of the documentation.

…is easier to integrate with the product. Online help can be tied directly to the software through context-sensitive links and What's This? Help. With RoboHelp Enterprise's skins, you can match the look and feel of the online help to the product. By designing a "knowledge-based" help system or using the natural language search feature in RoboHelp Enterprise, you can anticipate user questions and product needs.

In general, the advantages of online help are dramatic cost reductions for documentation development, product, and support. Good online help can also help users find information faster and even improve customer satisfaction with the product.

Disadvantages to Using Online Help

Online help isn't a perfect, one-size-fits-all solution for documenting products. Some of the reasons you should consider not using online help are…

…**online help must be used at a computer.** You can read printed manuals anywhere: while watching TV, on the subway, or in the bathroom. On the other hand, online help requires a computer. While this may be effective if the online help is addressing specific product issues, more general documentation (such as understanding basic accounting before setting up a home accounting program) may be something that your customers will want to read away from the computer. You may want to print information like this in a separate manual.

…**you have to install it before you can use it.** Online help is typically installed along with the product. As a result, unless you have a separate online help file for pre-installation or configuration information, the users will need a simple booklet of installation instructions. Having a booklet also has the advantage of giving the users a place to write down installation-specific configuration information, such as user IDs, directory names, and IP addresses.

…**online help is harder to create than printed manuals.** To write good printed manuals, you must be a good writer who can communicate technical concepts clearly. To create online help, you must also know how to use the various help creation tools and work very closely with the product developers. Creating online help also requires an understanding of a new set of usability issues.

…**online help looks and reads differently than printed manuals.** The amount of information you can effectively put on a screen is about one-third of the amount of information that will fit on a standard 7" x 10" printed manual page. The amount of information is further reduced because it's best to keep the information in a topic to a single screen (whereas the information for a single topic in a printed manual can be spread over two pages). In addition, the online help may not be able to take advantage of high screen resolutions; if the online help is going out to a variety of users, you may need to design help for the lowest common screen resolution.

…**you use online help differently from printed manuals.** To find something in a printed manual, you usually will pick it up and thumb through it to skim for phrases or headings that look relevant. You may repeat this process a few times, narrowing in on the information you want. However, you can't thumb online help: the topics may not appear in the online help files in order and thumbing a book can be sped up, slowed down, or even paused as you see things you want to look at.

...online help is harder to read than printed manuals. Printed text and graphics can be very detailed, with up to 2400 dpi resolution. Text and graphics on a screen are displayed at much lower resolutions, which tend to tire the eyes quicker. Because online help must also be read at the computer, you have to sit in one position without much latitude for shifting around (as when reading a manual). In addition, online help almost always feels more fragmented than printed documentation because the topics are smaller to accommodate the different usability requirements.

...online help takes up space on the computer. With 100+ GB hard drives available at price clubs, it's a rare online help file that will take up a significant amount of space; nevertheless, online help files that include a substantial amount of video and audio information can take up 10 or 20 MB, which may still be meaningful for the size of the overall distributed product.

Online help is exciting and powerful stuff, with new features being added to it all the time, but it's not going to completely replace printed manuals. It's not as flexible in some ways, it's harder to read, and it's used differently. For the best results, you should consider using both printed manuals and online help together. How much of each and how much overlap of subject matter is dependent on factors such as the type of product, the audience you are writing for, and what you hope to accomplish with each type of documentation. The "Creating a Documentation Plan" section later in this chapter shows you how to identify the requirements for your documentation—both online and printed—and how to craft a plan for creating and maintaining your online help.

Ways You Can Use Online Help

Despite the shortcomings mentioned in the previous section, online help is profoundly helpful in many situations. Foremost of these is providing documentation of some kind for software, certainly the primary purpose for which online help is created. It's fair to say that no program of any significance is released these days without some amount of online help. Moreover, with the percentage of programs being distributed via the Internet, an increasing number of programs are shipping with online help exclusively.

Online help for software generally takes the form of tutorial and reference information. Online help for software is almost always context-sensitive, which lets you query for information about a specific screen, option, field, or command.

Another use for online help is to put a variety of internal documents online, including manuals, product handbooks, reference materials, and white papers. This practice has some distinct advantages. You can distribute new and updated releases of various documents quickly without lead time for printing. Distributing documents online saves paper, too. And by distributing updates through a company intranet, employees can have the latest information immediately. For example, one large cell phone company maintains HR documents, announcements, policies, and other company information of timely interest to employees on an internal web site. Creating web-based online help can help you distribute such information in your company as well.

Another use for online help is in the creation of reference and technical documentation used in the field. Many organizations that use field support personnel have libraries of technical documentation on a CD that can be accessed quickly on a field engineer's laptop computer. This lets staff carry an extensive array of documentation—even documentation for the company's entire product line—on field assignments.

Online help can be used at other levels of the company as well. You can use online help to help the sales staff sell the company's products. In addition to the typical canned sales pitches with PowerPoint presentations, you can provide sales-oriented online help presentations that can be left with potential clients or even available for downloading from a company's web site. This type of online help file might have information on one or more of the company's products, service information, product demos using multimedia files or even work with a stand-alone version of the product, contact information for the salesperson, links to programs, the salesperson's email address, and the company's or other web sites that would be of interest to the client. You can also create online help versions of product pricing information and product catalogs for the salesperson's laptop.

Marketing departments can also benefit from online help in the form of newsletters, product one-sheets and catalogs, brochures, company information, and other marketing materials. Web-based marketing materials can be distributed on the company web site along with other press materials.

One area that's a natural for using online help is the technical support department. One way in which online help can save money is to provide each tech support person with the complete range of product manuals online instead of printed. Depending on the size and quantity of manuals, this can easily save $100 or more per person. In addition, having online versions of the manual will make it easier to get the right information to customers calling in for support.

Training is still a somewhat underdeveloped arena for online help. You can create self-paced tutorials, background materials, and computer-based training (CBT) systems with online help. As with other applications of online help, online training materials can be made available to users via a web site or company intranet. They can also be updated quickly and done by the users without a trainer or a specialized classroom. Self-paced training materials are also good for longer term reference—the students can repeat sections as needed and easily refer to the course materials later on. By adding more advanced features, you can also make the training materials interactive by asking for information from the student for personalization, exercises, and quick review tests. In addition, you can add audio or video clips to clarify or enhance particular sections.

Which Type of Online Help Should You Use?

RoboHelp Office and RoboHelp Enterprise let you create online help in a wide variety of formats. This section describes the types of help you should consider for your projects.

 NOTE: *Although you can create online help in one format and then convert it to almost any other format in RoboHelp, it's best to start working in the primary format you want to use for your finished online help. This will let you create online help that uses all the features available to you in that format while avoiding potential shortcomings of the conversion process later.*

WinHelp

WinHelp (also known as "classic" help) is the first version of Windows help. Although early versions of WinHelp appeared in Windows 1.0 and 2.0, it was not released to the public until Windows 3.0, when it appeared in the Windows 3.0 Software Development Kit (SDK). Since then, WinHelp has developed from very limited GUI-based hypertext into a comprehensive, full-featured help system that can display text, graphics, sound, video, and multimedia, link to other WinHelp files, URLs, and programs, and even interact directly with users through dialog boxes and prompts.

WinHelp is still the best-known and most popular version of online help. It still has many advantages—it's a compiled help format, it's stable, it's feature-rich, and it works on any version of Windows back to Windows 3.1—but it will only run on Windows and it's not web-compatible. The most likely use of WinHelp is for developing online help for applications that run exclusively on Windows computers.

A typical WinHelp screen appears in Figure 2-1.

 NOTE: *Although RoboHelp Office and RoboHelp Enterprise will create WinHelp files, WinHelp is not covered in this book. For more information on how to create and maintain WinHelp files, look at The RoboHelp 2000 Bible by John Hedtke and Elisabeth Knottingham.*

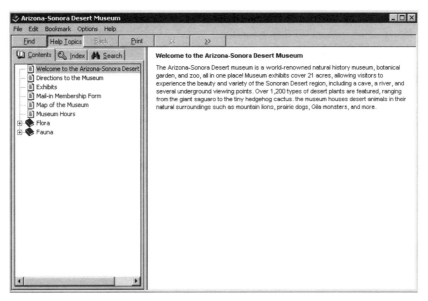

Figure 2-1: A typical WinHelp screen

HTML Help

HTML Help is a compiled help format introduced as part of Windows 98. Microsoft declared HTML Help the standard help format for Windows and Windows applications starting with Windows 98.

While HTML Help is broadly similar to WinHelp, there are significant differences. First, HTML Help is written like a web page; information is laid out and formatted using standard HTML (Hypertext Markup Language). Second, where WinHelp uses the built-in WinHelp viewer, HTML Help can be displayed on any system with Microsoft Internet Explorer 4.0 or later. Because HTML Help is written using HTML and displayed in Internet Explorer, it looks a lot like a web page.

The biggest advantage of HTML Help is that it's HTML-based, so you can create online help that can also be used directly on a web site without the necessity of converting or recoding your help. You can also use Java and other standard web-based techniques to expand the capabilities of the web pages to link to other files and programs and add a full range of features. The biggest disadvantage of HTML Help is that it only runs on Internet Explorer, so if your users are using Netscape or another browser or don't have Internet Explorer available to them, HTML Help won't work. Because HTML Help relies on a browser, it's not quite as stable as WinHelp (all browsers, because they're large and complex, will crash occasionally). And, much like the pages in a web site, HTML Help topics are in individual files. For a large online help system, this can mean hundreds or even thousands of individual topic files, which can be a nuisance when maintaining and installing HTML Help systems.

The most likely use of HTML Help is for developing online help for 100%-Microsoft-compatible applications. HTML Help is covered starting in Chapter 3, "Getting Started with RoboHelp HTML." A typical HTML Help screen appears in Figure 2-2.

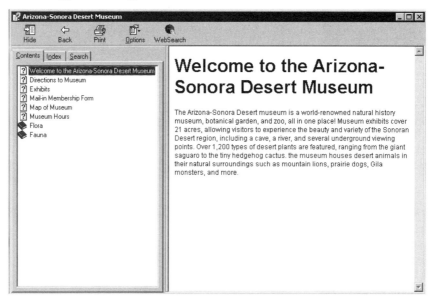

Figure 2-2: A typical HTML Help screen

WebHelp and WebHelp Enterprise

WebHelp is a compiled web-based online help system developed by Blue Sky (now eHelp). WebHelp is very similar to HTML Help in many ways. Both use HTML for laying out and formatting information. You can also use Java and other techniques to add features and functions to the online help. WebHelp looks very much like HTML Help. In fact, you usually will develop HTML Help and then convert the online help to WebHelp.

The significant difference of WebHelp with respect to HTML Help is that WebHelp runs on virtually any Internet browser on any operating system (as opposed to HTML Help, which is limited to running on Internet Explorer). The compiled WebHelp file tends to be a single large file (like WinHelp) rather than a collection of individual topic files, as is the case with HTML Help. WebHelp can be used under Windows, Macintosh, Linux, Solaris, and a number of Unix varieties. The most likely use of WebHelp is for developing HTML-based online help that requires a wide platform and/or browser compatibility.

A typical WebHelp screen appears in Figure 2-3.

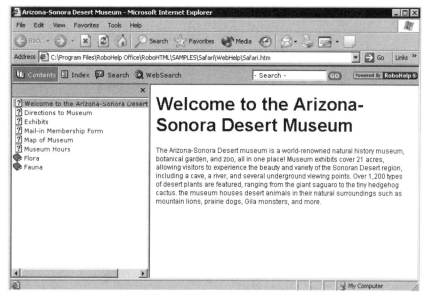

Figure 2-3: A typical WebHelp screen

WebHelp Enterprise uses the same help files as WebHelp, but they are published to the WebHelp Enterprise server, which provides a number of additional powerful features, including natural language search, help reports, and team development features. WebHelp Enterprise is covered in detail starting in Chapter 16, "Creating WebHelp Enterprise."

What's This? Help

What's This? Help provides quick, popup help for individual program elements. It's context-sensitive, so that you can get information about things like a screen, a field, or a button. Although What's This? Help first appeared in Windows 3.1, it was hard to create and difficult to maintain. It was refined and simplified in the version that appeared in Windows 95.

What's This? Help is used exclusively on Windows computers. It can be used by itself to document features in an application or it can be used in combination with WinHelp or HTML Help. A typical What's This? Help screen appears in Figure 2-4.

NOTE: *What's This? Help is covered in Chapter 12. For additional information on What's This? Help files, see The RoboHelp 2000 Bible by John Hedtke and Elisabeth Knottingham.*

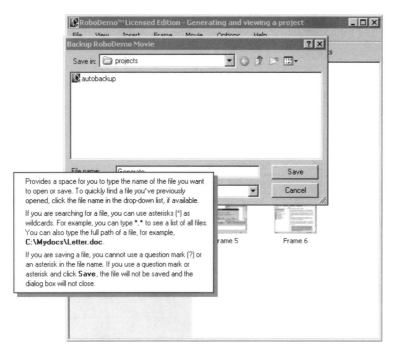

Figure 2-4: A typical What's This? Help screen

JavaHelp

JavaHelp from Sun Microsystems is an online help format for use with Java applications. Both Java applications and JavaHelp will run on a broad range of platforms and browsers using a JavaHelp Viewer. You compile JavaHelp from HTML files in RoboHelp. It looks like HTML Help but is not as close a visual match as WebHelp.

RoboHelp Office and RoboHelp Enterprise support JavaHelp 1.0. It includes a wide variety of Java-based and HTML-based features that include tables of contents, full-text search, dynamic index, navigation controls, popup windows, browse sequencing, Java applets, and See Also features. JavaHelp files can be compressed to make them easier to distribute.

The advantage of JavaHelp is that it is fully integrated with Java applications, making it compatible with almost any operating system and browser. The disadvantages of JavaHelp are that it's not as feature-rich as WinHelp, HTML Help, or WebHelp. Moreover, it's fairly slow to load and run. Use JavaHelp if you're developing Java applications; otherwise, use WebHelp. A typical JavaHelp screen appears in Figure 2-5.

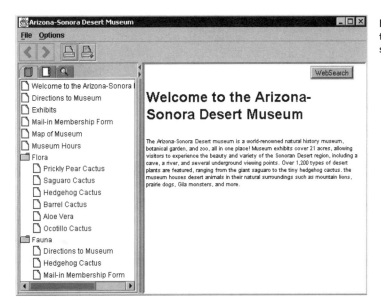

Figure 2-5: A typical JavaHelp screen

Oracle Help

Oracle Help is an online help format from Oracle that uses the JavaHelp standard developed by Sun Microsystems. It can be used with applications written in any language, although it was designed primarily for use with Java applications. Like JavaHelp, Oracle Help will run on a broad range of platforms and browsers and includes a wide variety of Java-based and HTML-based features. Oracle Help files can also be compressed to make them easier to distribute.

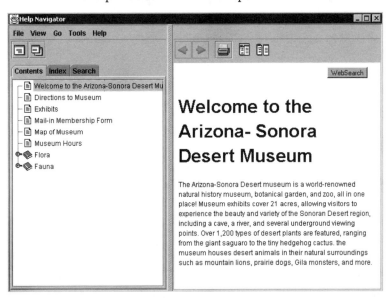

The advantage to Oracle Help is that it offers the features of JavaHelp and can be used with applications written in languages other than Java. As with JavaHelp, it's not as feature-rich as WinHelp, HTML Help, or WebHelp, and it's slow to load and run. Use Oracle Help if you're developing help for Java or mixed-code applications. A typical Oracle Help screen appears in Figure 2-6.

Figure 2-6: A typical Oracle Help screen

Other Types of Online Help

Earlier versions of RoboHelp would create several other types of online help that are not currently in wide use. These forms of online help include Windows CE help, Netscape NetHelp, and Netscape NetHelp2. If you need to develop help in any of these formats, you may want to obtain a copy of RoboHelp Office 2000 or RoboHelp Office 9.

Planning Your Online Help System

One of the real pleasures of creating online help is playing with the RoboHelp software and seeing topics appear on the screen. Your end result will almost certainly be better if you allow some time to plan the outcome. It's important to map out the goals and methods for the project. Some of the things you should consider are:

- What are you writing?
- Why is this online help needed?
- Who will use this document?
- What kind of online help do you need to use?
- How do you want to create the online help?
- Who will write the online help?
- Where will the online help be written and maintained?
- When will the online help be written, reviewed, tested, and released?

As with any writing project, you should create a comprehensive documentation plan that answers all of these questions and provides a plan of action for creating the online help.

Why is It Important to Plan Your Online Help?

Building a documentation plan is vital to your success in any writing project, whether it's a printed manual, an online help system, a CD, or some combination of all of these. The primary reason for creating a documentation plan is to state what is being created and how it will be created. This statement of work will then form the basis for planning writing, editing, and production resources and schedules. Furthermore, without a clear statement of work, you won't be able to verify that the online help you're creating will use the most effective methods or formats or even meet its goals.

A documentation plan also establishes your credibility as a writer. A comprehensive plan that shows what you're doing, for whom, when, how, and why underscores your professional credibility. In addition, because very few developers create effective working specifications for their projects (if any specs at all), a detailed documentation plan will make you look even better.

A documentation plan provides information about the audience for the online help. Most online help files are created with more than one type of user in mind, even if it's only to reflect the needs of the same user as he grows and develops in his ability to use the program. Because the online help will almost certainly be used by other people in the company or by the company's customers as part of the product, you must be able to communicate what you plan to create. A documentation plan not only states what the finished online help will look like, it is also a helpful tool for identifying tasks that must be done by other groups and departments.

The final reason to create documentation plans is that they are political documents. They state what your expectations, assumptions, and methods for a project are. Getting approval from other department heads and your boss will help prevent "scope creep," wherein additional features, options, and requirements are added on the fly to the project, but the resources and schedule are unchanged. With an approved documentation plan in hand, you have an excellent tool to renegotiate terms, conditions, and resources should you need to. The documentation plan becomes a contract: you're agreeing to create a specified online help system by a given date with a certain number of resources. If scope, purpose, and goals of the contract get changed midway through the project, the documentation plan will provide you with a way to measure the changes you must make to accommodate the new contract terms.

Creating a Documentation Plan

There are two parts of a typical documentation plan, the Executive part and the Detailed part. These are broken into the following subsections:

- **Executive Summary**
  The Executive Summary is a brief (one-page) description of the scope and purpose of the project. (Executive section)

- **Executive Outline**
  The Executive Outline is an outline of the first-level headings in the topics. (Executive section)

- **Overview**
  The Overview describes the scope, purpose, and goals for the finished project, a description of the audience, information about the responsibilities of each group, and the assumptions on which the documentation plan is based. (Detailed section)

- **Marketing Information**
  The Marketing Information section contains information about marketing strategies, relationship to other products, and even information about competitive products or documents. (Detailed section)

- **Production Information**
  The Production Information section states the format and standards to be used. (Detailed section)

- **Staffing**
  The Staffing section says who will write, edit, review, and approve the online help. (Detailed section)

- **Schedule**
  The Schedule lists the project schedule as well as the assumptions that went into creating the schedule. (Detailed section)

- **Detailed Outline**
  The Detailed Outline is a full-blown outline of the modules, sections, and topics in the online help to whatever level of detail seems appropriate. (Detailed section)

The best way to get information for the documentation plan is to talk to the various people who have input on the project: the VP or director of product development, product development managers, testing managers, product managers, and other marketing people. In addition, you need to interview as many individual developers, testers, and marketers as possible. The view of the product from the trenches is usually different from the view from the tower, but both views need to be considered in the documentation plan.

TIP: *Some people will be clearer than others about their goals for the product. As you interview people, make notes for your own reference of who has the strongest and most articulate vision of what the online help should be. This information will help you weigh review comments later in the project.*

Executive Summary

The Executive Summary is intended for quick review by executives who may not want to read the entire documentation plan (which can easily run to 15 or 20 pages). You should introduce the project and a brief statement of scope and purpose as well as the product(s) the documentation is designed to support. Keep the Executive Summary to a single page.

Executive Outline

Like the Executive Summary, the Executive Outline is a high-level view of the project. List the module and section names for the online help, but don't show detailed headings. The Detailed Outline will provide this information if the reader wants more detail.

Overview

The Overview is the most important section in the documentation plan. It tells
you what you're writing, who you're writing it for, and what the reader will get
out of the online help when they're done reading it. The Overview typically provides answers to the following questions:

■ **What is the name of the online help or document?** The name of the project will focus the writing effort, so it's important that product development
and marketing managers buy in to the project name from the start. (Surpris-
ingly, agreeing on a name can be as much of a political football as anything
else.) If you're working on several related online help projects simultaneously, a good name is also important for distinguishing which project is
which. Listing the project name in *italics* whenever it appears in the documentation plan will emphasize the name.

■ **What is the type of online help or document?** State the type of documentation, such as end-user tutorial, advanced tutorial, reference guide,
stand-alone white paper or marketing piece, or some combination of these.
Identify if there's a relationship between the online help and an application.
Will it provide general help or will there be context-sensitive help and, if so,
to what level of detail (screen, field, option)?

■ **What is the scope of the online help?** Identify the project's scope: what
the online help will cover, in what detail, and (equally important) what it
won't cover. As an example, the statement of project scope for online help
that documents an online stock trading and financial system might look
something like this:

"The online help starts by presenting the philosophy and background of the
system, how it came about, and what its goals are. The next section will
present a brief primer of basic stock market concepts: stocks, bonds, IPOs,
mutual funds, calls, puts, options, the Dow, NASDAQ, NYSE, and so on. The
online help then shows how to sign on for the first time, how to configure
your basic account, and how to access the online product tour. The online
help will continue with sections on major features of the system: purchasing
stocks, getting information on upcoming IPOs, buying and researching
mutual funds, and trading bonds. You'll also see how to use the system's
portfolio manager to quickly monitor the activity in your account. The final
sections in the online help will cover the various financial services for bank-
ing, insurance, and taxes, as well as mortgage brokering and retirement
planning.

For intermediate and advanced users, the online help will discuss how to
do research online using the system's knowledge base and research library
features, as well as the many options for information bulletins, alerts, and so
on. There will also be a section describing how to take part in the user community through the system's chat and discussion group features and

scheduled live system events, such as featured speakers. The online help will conclude with information on system features not otherwise covered, such as the online bookstore and shopping center and the stock trading game."

■ **What is the purpose of the online help?** Identify the project's purpose. State the goals for the online help and why the reader should use it. To continue the previous example, the purpose statement for an online stock trading system might look something like this:

"The online help provides the beginning user of the system with an introduction to the features and options of the system and shows the user how to get started using it with the most efficiency. This beginning section is designed to familiarize the user with the basic system and provide a basic vocabulary of concepts, rather than make the user an instant stock market maven. The online help will also show intermediate and advanced users how to get the most out of the system by taking advantage of some of the more complex and broad-reaching features. Online appendices and reference material will give the most advanced users information on how to do complex, long-range financial planning."

■ **Who will use the online help?** Identify the intended user of the online help. State who the online help is written for. This might be company employees (for an intranet system), customers, salespeople, executives, tech support staff, or developers. These users can be novice, intermediate, or power users, system administrators, trainers, professionals, or students.

The more information you have about the people who will be using the online help, the more accurately you can write to fulfill their needs. Talk to Product Development, Marketing, and Technical Support for information on how they perceive the audience for the online help. (And don't be surprised if their visions of the audience differ radically—this is one of the best examples of why you want to create a comprehensive documentation plan.)

There may be more than one audience for the online help. For example, you might have a statement like:

"The primary audience for this online help is the beginning or intermediate user with no previous experience in stock trading of any kind and who has little or no previous experience with using web-based business applications. The secondary audience is the advanced user who has had some experience with online stock trading but is not familiar with this particular system."

■ **What will the user need to know to begin with?** To write online help that meets the needs of the user, you must write to their beginning level of understanding. You need to determine the minimum prerequisite skills and experience the user will need to get the most from the online help. You'll need to do this for each class of user. For example:

"The primary audience for this online help must know the following:

- Basic computer concepts
- How to use a computer
- Basic Windows or Macintosh concepts
- Basic Internet and web concepts
- How to use a browser

The primary audience is not expected to know anything at the outset about stock trading, financial analysis, or performing financial transactions online.

The secondary audience for this online help will have all the skills and experiences of the primary audience, as well as some knowledge of stock trading (whether online or through a broker) and performing financial transactions online. The secondary reader is not expected initially to know anything about financial analysis and long-term planning, although it's likely that they will have some skills in this area."

■ **What are the goals for the online help?** Identify what the reader will get out of the online help when they complete the online help. A set of goals for the online stock trading system might look like this:

"The online help should help the user learn how to do the following specific tasks:

- Log on to the system web site
- Register as a new user and configure one's personal information
- Take the system online tour
- Get help using the system's quick-tip help
- Research a specific stock, bond, option, IPO, or mutual fund
- Buy and sell a stock or option online
- Get information on upcoming IPOs and make conditional offers on IPOs
- Research, buy, and sell shares in mutual funds
- Research, buy, and sell bonds
- Get credit ratings on companies
- Use the power system to save on commissions and charges
- Use the system's portfolio manager to track your portfolio
- Research and use the tele-banking services
- Research and plan retirement strategies
- Shop for mortgage rates online
- Shop for rates for auto, life, and home insurance online
- Research and plan for tax abatement using IRAs, tax-free munis and muni bond funds, and other techniques
- Set up and use a system email account to send and receive email

◆ Read and use the system message boards

◆ Chat with other system users

◆ Find and participate in live events on specific topics of interest

◆ Perform general market research using a variety of online tools

◆ Get more information on the system from other resources, such as online user forums and technical support"

■ **What are the responsibilities for each group or department?** As was mentioned earlier, one of the functions of a documentation plan is to identify the responsibilities for the various players.

 NOTE: *Most responsibility statements tend to be boilerplate with only minor variations from documentation plan to documentation plan.*

A typical statement of responsibilities looks like this:

"Technical Publications' responsibilities on this project are:

◆ Creating a documentation plan that states:

  ☐ Scope, purpose, target audience, and goals

  ☐ Applicable standards

  ☐ Production standards and information

  ☐ Project staffing

  ☐ Schedule and benchmarks

  ☐ Proposed outline

◆ Writing and revising the text, appendices, and index

◆ Working with reviewers and editors to revise and refine material

◆ Creating screen shots

◆ Coordinating with designer for any necessary graphic work for logo and the like

◆ Working with technical reviewers to review submitted material for technical accuracy, content, and style, and providing appropriate comments for changing the submitted material as necessary

Product Development's responsibilities on this project are:

◆ Providing technical reviewers to completely review submitted material for technical accuracy, content, and style, and providing appropriate comments for changing the submitted material as necessary

◆ Providing adequate technical resources and accurate information about the context-sensitive sections of the program

◆ Providing timely information about changes to the scope and purpose of the project, distribution and marketing, or the target audience that may affect the technical accuracy, content, or style of the online help

◆ Coordinating inclusion of the online help with the released product

Technical Support's responsibilities on this project are:

◆ Providing technical reviewers to completely review submitted material for technical accuracy, clarity, and completeness, and providing appropriate comments for changing the submitted material as necessary

◆ Providing timely information about changes to the scope and purpose of the project, distribution and marketing, or the target audience that may affect the technical accuracy, content, or style of the online help

Testing's responsibilities on this project are:

◆ Providing technical reviewers to completely review submitted material for technical accuracy, clarity, and completeness, and providing appropriate comments for changing the submitted material as necessary

◆ Testing context-sensitive help features for accuracy and completeness

◆ Providing timely information about changes to the scope and purpose of the project, distribution and marketing, or the target audience that may affect the technical accuracy, content, or style of the online help

Marketing's responsibilities on this project are:

◆ Providing technical reviewers to completely review submitted material for presentation, scope, and style, and providing appropriate comments for changing the submitted material as necessary

◆ Providing timely information about changes to the scope and purpose of the project, distribution and marketing, or the target audience that may affect the technical accuracy, content, or style of the online help"

■ **What are the assumptions on which the documentation plan was created?** List the assumptions used to create the documentation plan. A typical set of assumptions looks like this:

"The estimates and proposed outline presented in this plan are based on the following assumptions:

◆ All the information in the Overview section of this plan is complete and correct.

◆ The first, second, and final drafts will each be reviewed once, with acceptance occurring with delivery of the gold master.

◆ The context-sensitive numbering used in the program will not be changed once development on the context-sensitive help has begun.

◆ Any proposed changes to the format and contents will not add significantly to the writing and editing time."

NOTE: *Like the information about responsibilities, the assumptions will tend to be boilerplate text. The inclusion of the assumptions is a political measure to protect against sudden course changes that would affect your ability to meet the deadlines with the given resources. These assumptions provide an escape clause that allow you to renegotiate the schedule and resources without being unilaterally held to a commitment that may not be kept by Development or Marketing.*

Marketing Information

The Marketing Information section is not always required for an online help project. For example, if the online help is being created for internal use only to support a new company HR web site, marketing information may not be necessary. However, you might be creating a suite of online help that will complement the company's new product line, in which case marketing considerations are vital to meeting the company's goals for the online help.

The Marketing Information section typically provides answers to the following questions:

■ **Are there related documentation projects?** Identify the relationship (if any) of this online help to any other online help, documentation projects, or software projects, past, present, or future. This can be valuable for maintaining the content and the look and feel of the online help as part of the overall product line. You should also discuss issues related to basing the online help on previous versions or on other documents. In addition, you should identify related online help and other documentation projects that are outside the specific scope of this documentation plan, such as CDs, marketing collateral, stand-alone help files that present background information, product inserts, and so on.

One of the most common related projects is a printed manual that also supports the product; however, many products (particularly web-based systems) rely primarily on the online help and provide only a small amount of documentation in a printed form (usually in the form of Getting Started manuals and quick reference guides).

As part of determining the relationships, consider to what uses the online help will be put in the future. For example, the online help that is being created initially for a general customer base may also see subsequent life in localized versions, as the foundation for customized OEM or VAR help, or edited for "lite" versions of the same product. It's not uncommon to create separate online help files for a family of products being developed simultaneously. While there may be no overlap of content between the various online help files, there will probably be cross-references and look-and-feel issues to coordinate between the individual files. (Knowing what is planned for each part of the online help is another excellent reason to plan your work before you begin.)

- **Who is the competition and what are their strengths and weaknesses?** While it's less than optimal to do something simply because your competitors are doing it, it's a good idea to know what the rest of the market is like so you can anticipate the expectations of your customers. If you're producing documentation for a product that is leading the competition, an understanding of the competition's strengths and weaknesses will show you what to do to maintain your lead.

- **What marketing strategies should you consider?** Although the Marketing department is primarily responsible for the marketing efforts for the product, the online help can support their efforts in this regard. For example, if the online help is going to be released as part of a 30-day trial, feature-reduced version, you may want to plan to modularize the online help to accommodate quick conversions of the online help. Similarly, if the online help is going to be made available on the company's web site as well as on the product CD, this may affect the choice of graphics and multimedia used in the file.

Production Information

The Production Information section describes what the online help will look like when it is completed. This section addresses standards, style, and formats that the online help will be available in as well as the art requirements for the online help.

The Production Information section typically provides answers to the following questions:

- **What writing and editing standards will be used for the online help?** State the writing and editing standards that will be used for the online help; for example, "The online help will follow the standards stated in the company style guide and the 14th edition of *The Chicago Manual of Style*."

- **Which formats will this online help be available in?** Identify the online help formats you will use. This will have a substantial effect on the choice of development environments; for example, if you are creating HTML Help only, you will want to develop in HTML Help, but developing online help that will be available in WinHelp and WebHelp Enterprise formats would probably be developed in WinHelp and then converted to WebHelp Enterprise.

 NOTE: *See "Which Type of Online Help Should You Use?" earlier in this chapter for information on the variety of formats available in RoboHelp Office and RoboHelp Enterprise and some suggestions for how to use each of them.*

■ **What are the stylistic and graphical standards for the online help?**
While general issues of look and feel may already be covered in your company's style guide, it is likely that there will be specific considerations for the way in which the online help should appear. Some of the elements you may want to consider for this section include things like general topic appearance (indents, leading, justification), colors and fonts for links, popups, headings, and body text, how secondary windows are used, and so on.

 TIP: *Like goatees and spiral staircases, it is frequently easier to show someone what you want than to describe it. It may be very helpful to create a sample online help file that demonstrates each of the design elements and features. This will be useful for obtaining buy-in on the look and feel from other managers as well as for providing an online style guide for the writers.*

■ **How will the online help be distributed?** It's most likely that the online help will be distributed with the program it documents. The most popular distribution methods currently are on CD or online. Depending on the way in which the online help will be distributed, there may be some limitations to the final size of the file (for example, if the online help is for a web-based system likely to be accessed by users using slower connections, it may be impractical to include large numbers of multimedia files).

■ **What are the art and multimedia requirements?** There are three broad classes of art and multimedia used in an online help:

   ◆ *Screen shots*—Graphics captured from the product, usually screens, dialog boxes, program buttons and toolbars, online versions of reports, and error messages.

 NOTE: *RoboHelp Office and RoboHelp Enterprise include tools for capturing and editing screen shots.*

   ◆ *Conceptual art*—Artwork to communicate conceptual information, such as block diagrams and process flows. Conceptual art usually requires more graphical ability than creating a screen shot; as a result, the size and quantity of conceptual art figures can have a significant effect on the schedule and resources.

   ◆ *Multimedia*—Audio and video files. As with conceptual art, multimedia can require a substantial effort to create and should be budgeted carefully.

■ **Are there other materials that will accompany the online help?** The answer to this question will be tied to the "Are there related documentation projects?" question in the Marketing Information section. Discuss related materials, such as packaging, marketing collateral, and so on.

Staffing

The Staffing section identifies who will be writing, editing, indexing, testing, reviewing, and approving.

The Staffing section typically provides answers to the following questions:

- **Who is the documentation project lead?** Identify the person on the project who is able to make decisions about the documentation and project. This may be a technical publications manager, a project lead, or a writer or editor who will have decision-making authority for the project.

- **Who is writing the online help?** List the writers who will be assigned to the project. If there is more than one writer on the project, identify the modules, sections, or tasks that each writer is responsible for.

- **Who is editing the online help?** List the editor who will be assigned to the project.

- **Who is indexing the online help?** Indexing (in the form of keywords) is frequently done by the writers, but you can delegate the task of indexing easily. (This may be a good task for a writing or editing intern.)

- **Who is reviewing the online help?** List the reviewers for the online help. Reviewers will come from inside and outside the group. Anyone who is involved with providing input and approval to the documentation plan will be a reviewer as well as anyone else you can draft for this purpose. If the online help is broken up into modules, such as tutorial versus technical reference information, you may have different sets of reviewers. You'll also likely have separate lists of reviewers for the technical accuracy, the overall content and style, and the compliance with standards and formatting.

 TIP: When you first create the documentation plan, you probably won't know all the reviewers. Update the documentation plan as necessary. And always state that reviewers' names will be listed alphabetically, and do so. This sidesteps any questions of political ranking in the organization.

- **Who is testing the online help?** The writers are responsible for basic testing, but you should coordinate with the testing group in your company to subject the online help to rigorous testing, particularly if it's context-sensitive help, to make sure that the links, jumps, and features work correctly.

- **Who is approving the online help?** While the online help should be reviewed by as many people as possible, only one person should be responsible for approving the content and style, technical accuracy, and standards and formatting of the online help. Never have a committee approve something.

Schedule

The Schedule shows the proposed schedule as well as the assumptions that went into creating the schedule. Budget for holidays, vacations and time off, a reasonable amount for sick time, and so on. A typical schedule will list the following benchmark dates:

- **Project start.** This is the date the project will begin, usually when you start working on the project documentation plan.

- **Handoff of the documentation plan for review.** This is the date the first draft of the documentation plan is distributed for review. The first draft should contain most of the information including the Detailed Outline (with the possible exception of staffing information). Include a copy of the sample online help style if you have managers who aren't used to the current look and feel of the online help or if you're making changes to the style.

- **Return of the documentation plan from review.** This is the date the review comments should be returned. Unless there is a substantial amount of political negotiation, you can probably handle the second draft comments and revisions one-on-one.

- **Approval of documentation plan.** After you have entered the review comments and resolved any disputes, distribute a physical copy of the documentation plan to the executives, managers, and leads who will be involved in the project. This should include people such as your boss, the product development manager, the marketing manager for the product, the technical support manager, and the testing manager. Depending on the size of the project, it may be advisable to get sign-offs from individual group leads as well. The choice of signatories is a political choice but it's likely to be obvious who should be involved. When you have the signed-off copy, save it in a secure location. The signed-off copy can provide valuable leverage for renegotiation if there are sudden changes to the scope and purpose of the project.

- **Handoff of online help for first draft review.** The first draft of the online help should contain at least 50% of the initial content and 60% of the topic headings. Basic navigational tools should be there so reviewers can navigate the online help, but browse sequences and many hyperlinks will not be present. Context-sensitive hooks to the program will probably not be implemented yet. There may be minimal formatting, although using style templates will make the formatting relatively automatic. The body text will be unedited. The reviewers should focus on the content and topics and skip all but the broadest formatting concerns.

■ **Return of first draft review comments.** Keep reminding your reviewers that their deadlines are approaching. Even so, you will probably have to pester some reviewers to get their review comments. If a reviewer is truly peripheral (for example, a courtesy copy to the VP of Marketing), it is acceptable to have no comments, but for important reviewers and source material experts, you must get active review comments.

■ **Handoff of online help for second draft review.** The second draft of the online help will contain at least 70% of the content and 90% of the topic headings. It will also contain the incorporated comments from the first review. The reviewers should be able to navigate all the sections and topics of the online help using all the methods of navigation that will be offered in the final version. Any incomplete topics or sections should have notes to that effect. The online help will have much of the final formatting, but some of the features (such as "See Also" links, which depend on keywords and indexing) may not be present. The majority of context-sensitive help should work. The reviewers should focus on reviewing the existing content and topics to make sure that it's complete and correct and also filling in any missing information.

 NOTE: Depending on where the online help is scheduled versus the product development, the second draft of the online help may ship with the first product beta release.

■ **Return of second draft review comments.** With any luck, the comments on this review will focus on revising and clarifying the existing content. It's not uncommon, however, to identify a section that needs to be covered that's not in the current outline. You may also get changes for formatting or presentation as well. This happens in part because reviewers who aren't visual thinkers or aren't familiar with the range of possibilities for online help may not be able to articulate what they want until they see it. It's also likely that seeing how a topic or section looks may inspire a new way of thinking about how to present the information. Always budget for the possibility that there will be some expansions and changes to the scope as a result of the second draft review comments.

■ **Handoff of online help for final draft.** The final draft of the online help will be nearly complete. All preceding review comments will be incorporated in the current version of the online help. At least 95% of the content, graphics, and multimedia and 99% of the topics will be complete. All context-sensitive links will be in place, and the formatting should comply with the final style. The indexing and ancillary links should be at least 80% complete. The content should have gone through most edits, but final proofreading will not yet be done. The reviewers should focus on the new or late-breaking material and the overall quality of the online help.

 NOTE: *Depending on where the online help is scheduled versus the product development, the final draft of the online help may ship with a second or third beta release. The final draft should also be used by Testing for use in their product builds.*

- **Return of final review comments.** The only review comments that should come back on the final review should be small, nit-picky details. For example, a reviewer might have spotted that you listed four options for a given field, but a late-breaking change had eliminated one. If there are significant changes to the online help at this review, there has been a breakdown of process or a scope change, either of which need to be addressed immediately.

- **Handoff of "gold master" candidate version.** With the incorporation of the final review comments and the continuing testing, the online help is ready for approval and final testing. It should be as complete as possible without external acceptance testing. The Testing group should use this candidate version for final acceptance tests with the gold master candidates of the software. If the online help and program pass final testing, they can be released for production.

- **Project wrap-up.** Once the online help has been released, all the online help source files must be archived. If your company uses a source control system, check the source files in as part of the source code for this product release. Archive copies of all emails, project documentation, memos, versions of the documentation plans, and all other materials in a secure location.

As part of the Schedule section, you should include another escape clause about the assumptions used in creating the schedule, such as this comment: "In general, the estimates in this schedule assume that the scope, purpose, and outline in this proposal are complete and correct, reviews will be returned on time, and no time will be lost due to sickness or other delays. Any changes to these assumptions will result in a comparable, day-for-day extension of the schedule."

By adding this boilerplate clause, you have another way to prevent assuming responsibility for delays upstream in the process flow, over which you have no control. It is safe to assume that there will be scope change and delays (invariably from Product Development), and this clause will give you some additional latitude for renegotiating the schedule.

Estimating Schedules

One of the most challenging parts of creating any documentation plan is estimating how much time you'll need. Many factors go into making a good project estimate, including the number of topics and the technical detail required, the number of screen shots, conceptual illustrations, and multimedia files, the number of words or topics the writers can generate in a given time, the degree of complexity obtaining information from the source material experts, and the probability of scope creep or scope changes. Making consistently good estimates—ones that correctly identify the time and resources you need for a project with at least 90% accuracy—is the mark of a true expert.

If you're new to estimating time, you should be aware that the basic metric for creating printed documentation requires four hours of writing time for each new page of documentation. This doesn't translate as smoothly to the creation of individual topics in an online help file, which can vary in length considerably. Because of this, you may want to estimate two hours/new topic for the initial estimate and then revise your estimate with respect to other factors. Keep track of your hours throughout the project and periodically review your actual versus estimated time to see how you're doing. (Also include hours spent in meetings, doing administrivia, and performing other tasks that may not be directly related to the writing. These are necessary—if possibly odious—parts of the writing process, and the time you spend on them should be part of your estimates.) As you gather data, you'll be able to come up with a metric that accurately reflects your writing style and throughput, which will help you make tighter estimates on future projects.

Detailed Outline

The Detailed Outline is the final section of the documentation plan. As with a printed document, the Detailed Outline is necessary to create good online help. Online help is less hierarchical than printed documentation, but you should still be able to create effective outlines for the modules, sections, and topics. Include topic headings to at least the third level. Include comments about the information under each heading. Again, as with printed documentation, you can use an existing online help file as the basis for the outline for a revision effort.

How to Use a Documentation Plan

The initial purpose of the documentation plan is to provide a clear understanding of what you're creating and how you want to create it. This information lets you make accurate estimates about the resources and time necessary to complete the project. In addition, the information in the documentation plan provides an objective picture (sometimes with sample online help files) that the other decision-makers can look at so they can make an informed decision about what they want. A well-written documentation plan at the start of a project can save you a great deal of wasted effort if there's subsequent disagreement about what was agreed to. (Voltaire said, "A good memory does not equal pale ink.")

After the initial documentation plan has been approved, give everyone who approved it a photocopy of the finished plan. This not only keeps everyone informed about your scope, purpose, resources, and schedule, but it will also enhance your standing as a competent professional. If other departments are not already using comparable planning tools, distributing the documentation plan might also encourage them to plan on their own.

As has been mentioned throughout this section, a documentation plan is a political document. It is a contract between you and your writers and the other departments (particularly Product Development) about everyone's responsibilities and commitments. When the inevitable changes to the scope occur, you can use the documentation plan to adjust the schedule, resources, or scope.

One use of the documentation plan that hasn't been discussed yet is as a roadmap for the writers. You can use the documentation plan as a touchstone for scope and purpose. Many questions of "Are we going to cover this?" can be answered unequivocally by referring to the scope statement and Detailed Outline in the documentation plan. You can also use the documentation plan for monitoring the progress of individual writers on their specific tasks within an online help project. By identifying the estimated number of hours for a given section or module and tracking the writer's progress for the task, you can spot schedule shortfalls and avoid getting jammed up as the project is in the final phases. The documentation plan can then be used for identifying individual sections of work that need to be delegated to other writers in the department or subcontractors.

Any documentation plan will evolve as the project continues. You'll want to add information about new reviewers, changes in the staffing, negotiated expansions to the scope and purpose, and (inevitably) the Detailed Outline. As part of the documentation plan, maintain a change log (showing the name of the person making the change, the date, and the nature of the change) at the front of the documentation plan. When you update the documentation plan significantly, route the revised copy to the signatories.

TIP: *A slick way to route updates without burying everyone in paper is to post a locked version of the documentation plan on a central location and then send everyone email that says what the changes to the plan are and tells the recipients where to find the revised documentation plan on the network.*

Finally, the documentation plan will be invaluable for the project wrap-up. You can use the information in the plan for your postmortem project analysis. The documentation plan will identify your original project assumptions for the scope and purpose and give you a benchmark against which to measure the finished online help. It's also very important to do final evaluations of estimated hours versus actual hours. Measure this with as much detail as possible against the number of topics and the number of words in the finished help. You can use this information for refining the metrics you use to estimate productivity when you create the schedule for the next project.

TIP: *Project estimating and project management are subtle, complex, and fascinating. If you're interested in finding out more about these topics, look for* Managing Your Documentation Projects *by JoAnn Hackos (Wiley & Sons, 1994) and* Standards for Online Communication *by JoAnn Hackos and Dawn Stevens (Wiley & Sons, 1997).*

Good online help can be created without a documentation plan in place, but the chances are overwhelming that you'd spend far more time and money doing so than you need to. Perhaps the best reason for creating a documentation plan can be summarized by a quote from Paul Magid of the Flying Karamazovs: "It doesn't matter how you get there if you don't know where you're going."

Summary

This chapter taught you about the various types of online help that can be created with RoboHelp Office and RoboHelp Enterprise. You also learned when to use online help (and when not to use it) and how to create a documentation plan.

The next chapter shows you how to create your first HTML Help file. You'll see how to start a new HTML Help project, add topics and information to it, compile it, and run it.

Chapter 3

Getting Started with RoboHelp HTML

This chapter shows you several ways to start the RoboHelp software. You'll learn about the components that make up a RoboHelp project and how to use the RoboHelp windows.

Starting RoboHelp HTML

If you've installed RoboHelp Enterprise using the standard installation method, there will be three RoboHelp icons on your desktop.

Table 3-1: The RoboHelp icons

Program	How to access
RoboHELP Classic	Double-click the RoboHelp Classic icon to start RoboHelp Classic. This is best for projects that will be viewed primarily on Microsoft Windows systems.
RoboHELP HTML	Double-click the RoboHelp HTML icon to start RoboHelp HTML. This is best for projects that may be viewed on a variety of operating systems.
RoboHelp Starter	Double-click the RoboHelp Starter icon to start the RoboHelp Starter Wizard and to set up the files needed for various types of projects. The following section describes how to use the RoboHelp Starter Wizard.

Using the RoboHelp Starter

The RoboHelp Starter is a convenient way to start new projects or open existing ones. The Starter program includes the New Project Wizard, which displays a series of windows that ask questions. The New Project Wizard then automatically sets up your initial files based on the choices you make. To use the RoboHelp Starter, follow these steps:

1. Double-click the RoboHelp Starter icon on your desktop to display the RoboHelp Starter. The New Project tab is already selected, displaying the types of help available, as shown in Figure 3-1.

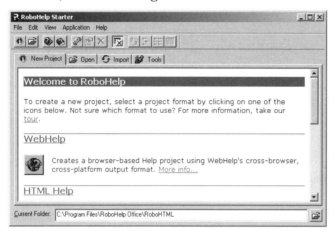

Figure 3-1: Available help formats in RoboHelp Starter

There are four tabs on the RoboHelp Starter window.

Table 3-2: The Starter tabs

Tab	Description
New Project	Click the New Project tab to display a list of help formats. The New Project tab allows you to start the New Project Wizard.
Open	Click the Open tab to display a list of existing RoboHelp HTML projects, including the sample project that comes with the software.
Import	Click the Import tab to display a list of software formats that can be imported directly into a RoboHelp HTML project.
Tools	Click the Tools tab to display other program icons. See Chapter 15 for more information about using the RoboHelp Tools.

2. With the New Project tab selected, move the scroll bar on the right side of the window to view additional help format options. For more information on any type of help, click on **More info...** for that type.

3. Click on the type of help you want to create. For example, to create Microsoft HTML Help, click on **HTML Help**. The New Project Wizard appears.

4. Enter the following information in the appropriate boxes:

   ■ **Project Title:** This will appear on the title bar of the finished help project.

   ■ **File Name:** This is the name that will appear in the list of available projects when you open a project. Notice that as you type, the filename appears as part of the project location as well as in the File Name box.

- **Project Location:** Enter the path name for the folder in which to store the project. In most cases, you won't need to change this, since the folder and file names are already filled in. If you need to change the location, you may either use the Browse button to change the folders or type the entire path and filename.

- **Title of the First Topic:** If you know what your first topic will be, enter the title here. This is the first topic you will create, not necessarily the first topic users will see. RoboHelp automatically assigns the filename and an extension of .htm to each topic.

- **Enable WebSearch:** Check this box to place a WebSearch button on the help system you are creating. WebSearch automatically creates an Internet search query and accesses the user's browser to conduct the search.

- **Language:** Choose an option from the drop-down menu to specify the language you want to use. This will define how the spell checker, the Smart Index Wizard, and the user interface of the finished help system will work. If you don't specify a language, the default is English.

- **Save as Default:** Click this box to use the specified language as the default for all subsequent help projects. If you don't specify a default language, RoboHelp will use English as the default.

Figure 3-2: The RoboHelp New Project Wizard

5. Click on **Finish** to create the project and display the RoboHelp window as shown in Figure 3-3.

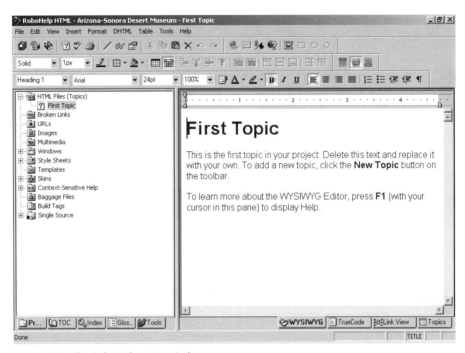

Figure 3-3: The RoboHelp main window

Using the RoboHelp Starter from within RoboHelp

You can access the RoboHelp Starter icon from your desktop at any time. If you have the RoboHelp window open, you can also start a project by following these steps:

1. From the RoboHelp window **File** menu, choose **New** to display a list of options. This list may vary, depending on where you are in the RoboHelp process.

2. From the list of options, choose **Project** to start the RoboHelp Starter Wizard, as shown in Figure 3-4.

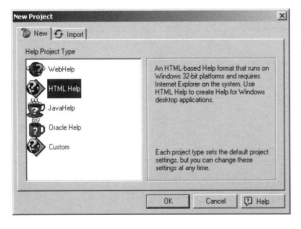

Figure 3-4: The New Project Wizard as selected from within RoboHelp

Notice that since RoboHelp is already open, the New Project Wizard does not display the Tools tab or the Open tab. These two functions are available from the RoboHelp toolbar menus.

3. Complete the Project Wizard in the same way as you would if using the RoboHelp Starter icon (see the previous section).

Understanding the RoboHelp HTML Window

The RoboHelp HTML main window consists of three main areas: the left pane, the right pane, and the menu bar/toolbars as shown in Figure 3-5.

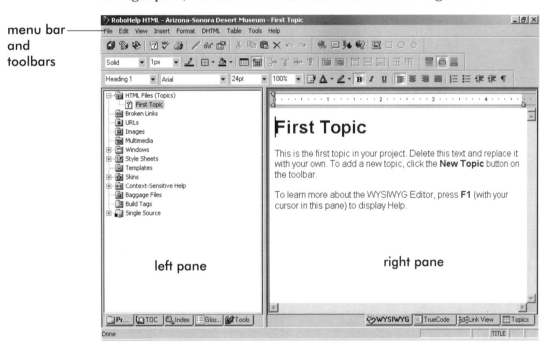

Figure 3-5: The RoboHelp main window

The left pane displays the tools with which you'll work. The right pane displays the help project you're working on in various ways. The menu bar and toolbars offer additional functionality and shortcuts.

Left Pane — Tools

The left pane displays the files, folders, and tools you'll use to create your RoboHelp project. There are five tabs across the bottom of the left pane. Click any of the tabs to access the tools for that tab.

Project tab The Project tab displays a list of the folders in which your project files are organized. RoboHelp automatically sets up default folders when you create the project as shown in Figure 3-6.

TOC tab The TOC tab displays table of contents entries as you create them. Before you create entries, this tab displays instructions for creating the table of contents as shown in Figure 3-7.

Index tab The Index tab displays index entries as you create them. Before you create entries, this tab displays instructions for creating the index. As you add entries, this window displays the actual entries as shown in Figure 3-8.

Figure 3-6: The Project tab

Figure 3-7: The TOC tab

Figure 3-8: The Index tab

Glossary tab The Glossary tab displays table of contents entries as you create them. Before you create entries, this tab displays instructions for creating the glossary. Use this tab to create and display the glossary entries as shown in Figure 3-9.

 TIP: *At startup, the definition portion of this tab may not be visible. To display it, click the line above the tabs and drag it upward.*

Tools tab The Tools tab displays other program icons. This is the same display available from the Starter wizard as shown in Figure 3-10. See Chapte 15 for more information about using the RoboHelp tools.

Figure 3-9: The Glossary tab

Figure 3-10: The Tools tab

Right Pane — Project

The right pane of the RoboHelp HTML window displays the project in various ways. There are four tabs across the bottom of the right pane:

WYSIWYG tab WYSIWYG stands for "what you see is what you get." This tab displays the project topics in the specified editor close to the way they will appear in the final help project. The sample in Figure 3-11 shows a topic displayed in Microsoft Word. Notice that the heading appears larger than the text.

TrueCode tab The TrueCode tab displays the selected topic and all of the codes that specify how the topic will work. Notice that the TrueCode view shown in Figure 3-12 displays HTML codes on either side of the heading text, rather than displaying the heading in larger type.

Link View tab The Link View tab displays multiple topics with lines indicating how they are connected to each other, as shown in Figure 3-13. This is particularly useful for identifying topics that are not linked to any others.

Topics tab The Topics tab displays a list of the topics you've created so far. In addition to the topic filenames, this tab also displays the title, status, and modification date for each topic, as well as displaying whether or not the topic has index and table of contents entries. Note that if the full display does not fit in the window, you may need to use the scroll bar across the bottom of the pane to display additional information, as shown in Figure 3-14.

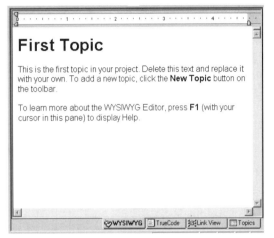

Figure 3-11: The WYSIWYG tab

Figure 3-12: The TrueCode tab

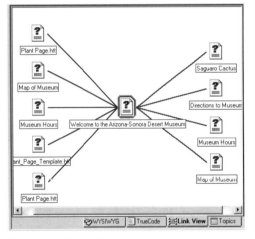

Figure 3-13: The Link View tab

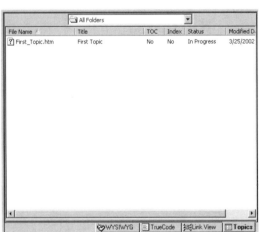

Figure 3-14: The Topics tab

Menu Bar and Toolbars

There are four bars at the top of the main menu. When you first start RoboHelp, many of the icons on the toolbars will be gray and unavailable for use as shown in Figure 3-15. These icons will become available as you move through the RoboHelp system.

The top of the RoboHelp main window displays the menus that list all of the RoboHelp functions. The options available will vary depending on which pane is active. For example, when in the Link View tab, you'll only see the File menu, Edit menu, View menu, Tools menu, and Help menu.

Figure 3-15: The RoboHelp menu bars and toolbars

File menu	This menu contains the functions that open, close, or create new project or topic files.
Edit menu	This menu lets you make changes to existing files.
View menu	This menu contains the functions that change the way the project appears on your screen.
Tools menu	This menu gives you access to the programs in the Tools tab (on the left pane) and also offers a variety of additional functions, such as generating reports and customizing the RoboHelp software.

The second row from the top of the RoboHelp main window contains icons that perform management functions, such as saving the project files or undoing an action you've just performed. There are also some editing functions on this toolbar.

The third and fourth rows contain icons that represent the functions you'll use while editing a topic file using the default RoboHelp internal HTML editor. These icons become active when you select the WYSIWYG tab on the right pane, as shown in Figure 3-16. When you're working in the WYSIWYG pane, the Insert menu, Format menu, DHTML menu, and Table menu will also be available.

Figure 3-16: The RoboHelp internal HTML editor icons

If you do not want to use the RoboHelp editor, you can specify any other HTML editing software on your system as the default.

Customizing the RoboHelp HTML Main Window Settings

Once you are familiar with the RoboHelp Main window, you may decide that you want to change some settings. You can specify which panes are displayed, how the icons look, and which buttons are available on the menu bars.

Adjusting the Panes

You can adjust the height and width of each pane and turn off the display of the left pane. To change the pane size, follow these steps:

1. Place the cursor over the edge of the pane that you want to adjust. The cursor turns into a line with arrows on each end.

2. Press the left mouse button and drag the edge of the pane to a new location. When you release the mouse button, the pane will adjust to the new size. The program maintains these settings until you adjust the panes again.

To turn the display of the left pane on or off, follow these steps:

1. Click the **View** menu to display the View options, as shown in Figure 3-17.

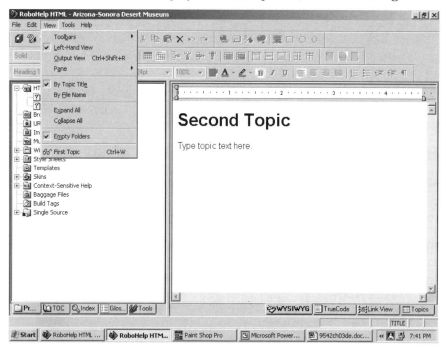

Figure 3-17: Changing the pane display with the View menu

2. Click the **Left-Hand View** box to clear it. The left pane is removed.

3. Click the **Left-Hand View** box again to select it and redisplay the left pane.

Changing the Toolbar Display

When you start RoboHelp HTML, the toolbars are displayed across the top of the window below the menu bar. You can change the position of the toolbars and turn them on or off.

To move a toolbar to a new location, follow these steps:

1. Place the cursor over an area of the toolbar that does not display a button or drop-down list, such as the title bar.

2. Press and hold the left mouse button, then drag the toolbar to a new location in your window.

3. Release the mouse button to place the toolbar in the new location.

To open or close a toolbar, follow these steps:

1. From the **View** menu, select **Toolbars** to display a list of available toolbars, as shown in Figure 3-18.

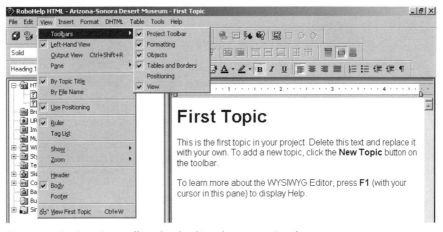

Figure 3-18: Opening toolbars by checking the appropriate box

2. Click the box next to the name of a toolbar you want to open. A check mark appears and the toolbar displays.

3. To clear the check mark from the box, click the box next to the name of the toolbar you want to close. The toolbar closes.

Displaying Topic Preview

RoboHelp lets you see what the topics will look like before you complete your help project. This is very useful for testing, particularly as you build more complex topics. You can view the topic previews in either the right-hand pane (beneath the topic list) or in a separate window. To choose a topic preview display option, follow these steps:

1. From the **Tools** menu, select **Options** to display the Options window.

2. Click the **General** tab to display the general options, as shown in Figure 3-19.

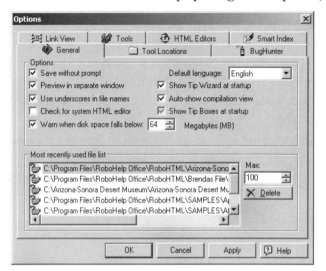

Figure 3-19: Displaying the Options window to set the preview display option

3. To preview topics in their own window, check **Preview in separate window**. To preview topics in the right-hand pane, clear the check mark from Preview in separate window. For example, Figure 3-20 shows a topic displayed in the right-hand pane.

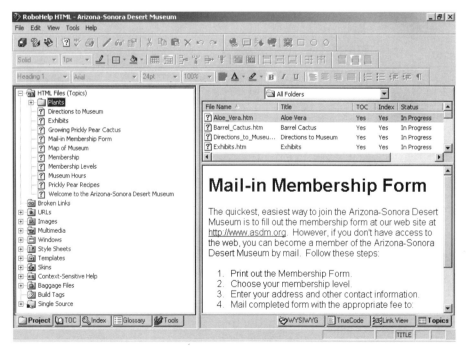

Figure 3-20: Previewing a topic in the right-hand pane

4. Click **OK** to close the Options window.

Specifying an HTML Editor

When you open a topic, RoboHelp automatically checks to see which editor created the file and uses that editor to make changes to it. For example, if you have a file created in FrameMaker, RoboHelp opens FrameMaker when you want to edit that file. If the system cannot determine which editor created the file, it will use the default editor (usually, this is the internal RoboHelp HTML editor).

You may specify that the system always use a single editor, regardless of what was used to create each topic, or you may change the default editor to any other editor on your system. The new default editor will be opened whenever you edit existing or new topics.

To change the default HTML editor, follow these steps:

1. From the **Tools** menu, select **Options**.

2. Click the **HTML Editors** tab. The available editors are displayed in a list, as shown in Figure 3-21. Note that your system may show other editors, depending on what is installed on your system.

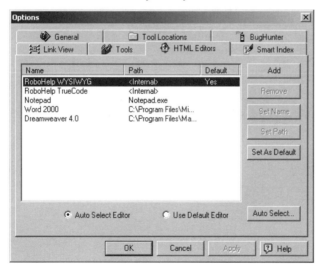

Figure 3-21: Options window showing that RoboHelp Editor is the default HTML editor

3. Click the name of the editor you want to use as the default, and then click **Set As Default**. The word Yes is displayed next to the chosen editor indicating that it is now the default HTML editor.

4. Click the **Use Default Editor** button to always use the specified default editor, or click the **Auto Select Editor** button to use whichever editor created each file.

5. Click **OK** to save your changes.

Summary

This chapter reviewed the components of the RoboHelp HTML window. You learned how to modify the window by changing pane size and other settings. You also saw how to change the default topic editor.

The following chapter describes how to create a basic help project from beginning to end.

Chapter 4

Creating Your First RoboHelp HTML Project

This chapter tells how to start a new help project in RoboHelp HTML. You'll create topics, insert keywords, and test the project to make sure it works.

Starting a RoboHelp HTML Project

The RoboHelp Starter program (described in Chapter 3) automatically sets up the files you'll need for any help file. As you follow the prompts in the New Project Wizard, you'll enter the name of the first topic. This is the topic that appears in the RoboHelp HTML main window at the beginning of your project, as shown in Figure 4-1.

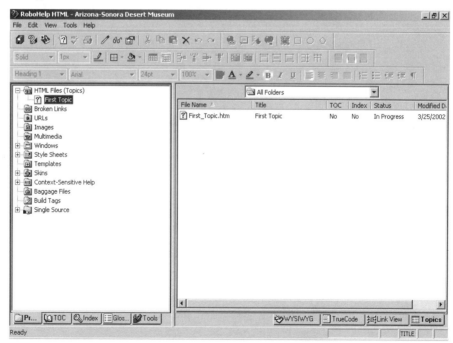

Figure 4-1: Displaying the first topic in the RoboHelp main window

Adding Content to a Topic Page

To add text or graphics to a topic page, you'll need to open the topic. RoboHelp will automatically open HTML topics in your specified HTML editor, depending on your system configuration (see "Customizing the RoboHelp HTML Main Window Settings" in Chapter 3).

 NOTE: *Examples in this book use the built-in RoboHelp HTML editor. If you've specified a different editor, your topics will appear in that editor.*

To open and edit a topic, follow these steps:

1. Specify the topic you want to edit in one of the following ways:
   - In the left-hand pane, open the **HTML Files (Topics)** folder and click the topic name.
   - In the right-hand pane, choose either the **Topics** or **Link View** tab, and then click the topic name.

2. Open the topic in one of the following ways:
   - Click the **Edit** icon (✎).
   - Click the **WYSIWYG** tab to display the topic in the HTML editor the way it will appear in the finished project.
   - Choose **Edit** *<topic name>* from the Edit menu.
   - Press **Ctrl+E**.

3. The editing controls are now active. Type your content in the right-hand pane. If you are using the built-in HTML editor, RoboHelp underlines words that may be misspelled as you are typing, as shown in Figure 4-2.

Figure 4-2: Misspellings as indicated in the RoboHelp HTML editor

Adding Topics

Your project will contain many topics. Each topic will appear in its own window or screen in the finished help system. Since this is an HTML project, each topic will be stored in its own file with an extension of .htm. All of your topics will be displayed in the HTML Files (Topics) list on the left-hand pane and in the Topics view on the right-hand pane.

The first topic in your RoboHelp project was created by the Starter program. For each of the other topics in your project, you'll have to create the topic file then insert or edit your topic text.

To create a second topic, follow these steps:

1. Open the New Topic window (shown in Figure 4-3) in one of the following ways:

   ■ Click the **New Topic** icon (⁑?]).

   ■ From the **File** menu, choose **New** and then **Topic**.

   ■ Press **Ctrl+T.**

   ■ With the cursor in the **HTML Files (Topics)** folder of the left-hand pane or the Topics tab of the right-hand pane, click the right mouse button, and then choose **New Topic** to create the topic in the default HTML editor.

   ■ With the cursor in the **HTML Files (Topics)** folder of the left-hand pane or the Topics tab of the right-hand pane, click the right mouse button, and then choose **New Topic With**. Choose one of the available HTML editors from the list to create a topic using that editor.

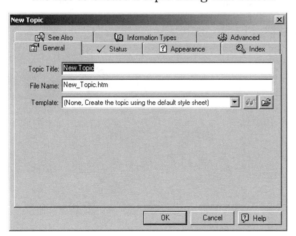

Figure 4-3: Entering a name for the topic in the New Topic window

2. Enter a title for the topic. The title will appear in the title bar of the finished help window and will be the default heading for the topic.

3. As you enter the title, RoboHelp enters the title as the filename (with underscores replacing spaces), as shown in Figure 4-4. While this is sometimes convenient, the filenames can get very long. If you want to use a shorter

filename, enter the new name in the File Name box. Remember, you cannot use spaces or special characters in a filename.

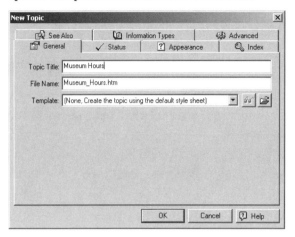

Figure 4-4: The renamed filename with underscores

 TIP: *Make sure the filename is descriptive enough to distinguish the topic from other similar topics. For example, this sample topic is called Museum Hours in order to distinguish it from later topics called Restaurant Hours or Demonstration Times.*

4. Click **OK** to create the topic. The topic opens in the specified editor (or the default editor) with the title you entered as the heading of the topic. The Topics folder on the left-hand pane displays the new topic along with previous topics in alphabetic order, as shown in Figure 4-5.

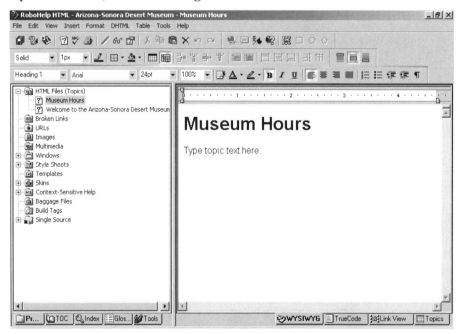

Figure 4-5: Displaying the new topic in the HTML Files folder

5. Like the first topic, each new topic uses the topic title as the heading and starts off with a block of text as a placeholder. Add and edit text in the new topic just as you did in the first topic.

6. When the topic looks the way you want it to, save your work in one of the following ways:

    ■   Click the **Save All** icon (🖫) to save all topics you've edited.

    ■   From the **File** menu, choose **Save** *<topic name>* to save the current topic.

    ■   Press **Ctrl+S** to save all topics you've edited.

7. Repeat steps 1 through 6 to add additional topics.

Connecting the Topics with Links

No matter how well-written your topics are, they won't be able to help anyone unless you give the users a way to find the information they need. In the finished HTML help system, there are several ways that your users can find information:

Table 4-1: Types of links

Tool	Description
Links	The user clicks on a word or phrase in one topic to display another topic or portion of a topic.
Index	List of keywords that you define in alphabetic order (see Chapter 9 for more information about RoboHelp indexing).
Table of Contents	Topic titles in a predefined order, usually by category (see Chapter 9 for more information about RoboHelp TOCs).
Search	List of topic titles based on keywords that the user enters. Search options are set when you run a project to create the final help system.

Adding a Link

To add simple links to a RoboHelp project, follow these steps:

1. Open the topic in which you want to insert a link. You may want to start with a main or top-level heading.

2. Highlight the word or phrase that will be the link to the second topic, as shown in Figure 4-6.

TIP: *Make sure that your link text provides enough information so that users get an idea of the topic that the link will display. For example, rather than use the word "map" for a link, use the phrase "directions to the museum."*

Hyperlink icon

Figure 4-6: Highlighting a phrase to activate the hyperlink icons

3. Once the phrase is highlighted, the Hyperlink icon becomes active. Insert a hyperlink any time you want the user to be able to link or jump to another topic. The Hyperlink window allows you to specify the type of link, the topic that will display, and the way that topic will display. Open the Hyperlink window (shown in Figure 4-7) in any one of the following ways:

    ■ Click the **Hyperlink** icon ( ).

    ■ From the **Insert** menu, choose **Hyperlink**.

    ■ Press **Ctrl+K**.

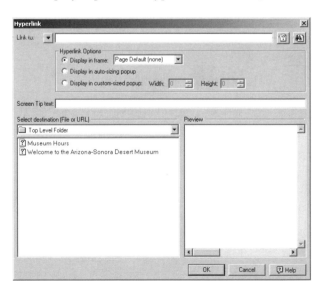

Figure 4-7: The Hyperlink window

4. A list of existing topics appears in the Hyperlink window. Click the title of the topic you want displayed when the user clicks the link. The topic filename appears in the Link to box at the top of the Hyperlink window, and the Preview pane displays the selected topic. You may need to use the scroll bar to view the entire topic, as shown in Figure 4-8.

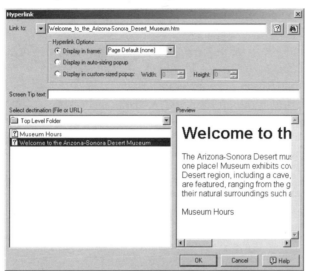

Figure 4-8: Selecting a topic for the hyperlink

5. Click **OK** to close the Hyperlink window and return to the RoboHelp main window. The phrase you selected will appear in the style set for hyperlinks. The default style for hyperlinks is in underlined blue text, as shown in Figure 4-9.

Figure 4-9: Completed link indicated by underlined blue text

> **TIP:** When creating links from one topic to another, think about what the user might want to do next. For example, after viewing the museum hours, the user may want to view directions to the museum or return to the Welcome topic. You could put links to both these topics in the Museum Hours topic.

Viewing Links

When you've put links into all of your topics, choose the Link View tab in the right-hand pane to check the links. The Link view displays the current topic in the center, topics that contain links to that topic on the left, and topics that are linked from the current topic on the right. For example, Figure 4-10 shows that the Welcome topic contains links to three topics: Museum Hours, Map of Museum, and Directions to Museum. The topics Museum Hours and Map of Museum contain links back to the Welcome screen, but Directions to Museum does not.

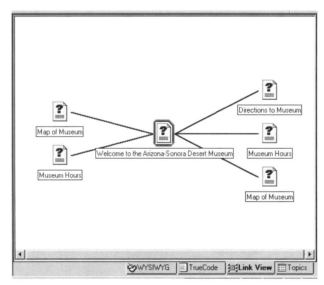

Figure 4-10: Checking the links in the Link View tab

Testing Your Help Project

The WYSIWYG tab displays each topic as it will be displayed in the final help window, but it doesn't show you what that window looks like. This is partly because you may have different windows for each topic (see Chapter 17 for more information about output formats). The Link View tab shows you one view of links but doesn't show the link text.

As you create each project, it's a good idea to check the output of each project as you go along, rather than waiting until the entire project is finished. There are several ways you can test a help project:

- Preview the individual topics
- Quick Generate the project using project defaults
- Generate output in the default or any other format

Preview the Individual Topic

You can preview the current topic in the final output window at any time during the editing process, as shown in Figure 4-11. If the displayed topic has links, you'll be able to click the links to test the display of other topics.

NOTE: *If you haven't yet generated the help project, the links may take longer to display topics than in the final project.*

You can preview the currently selected topic (the topic in the WYSIWYG window) in any of the following ways:

- Click the **View** icon (👓).
- From the **View** menu, choose **View** *<topic name>*.
- Press **Ctrl+W**.

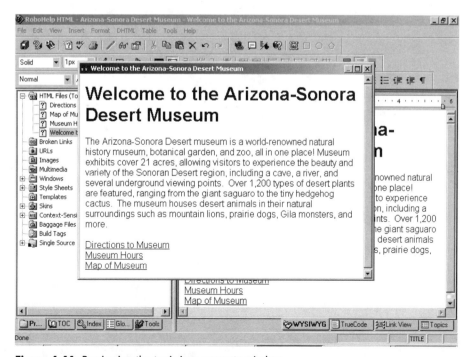

Figure 4-11: Previewing the topic in a separate window

Note that the title bar of the preview window contains the View icon. The final help system will not have this icon. To close the preview window, click the Close button in the upper-right corner of the window.

TIP: *If you leave the preview window open, you can easily view updates or edits as you make them in the other windows (WYSIWYG or TrueCode). Click anywhere in the preview window to update the display.*

You can also preview a topic that is not currently selected. This is useful if you want to display the contents of two topics at once, as shown in Figure 4-12. Select and preview topics in either of the following ways:

- From the **HTML Files (Topics)** list, move the cursor over the file you want to preview, click the right mouse button, and then choose **View.**

- From the **Topics** tab on the right-hand pane, move the cursor over the file you want to preview, click the right mouse button, and then choose **View.**

Figure 4-12: Displaying two topics at once with the preview window

TIP: *You can move or resize the preview window as needed. To move the preview window, click anywhere on the title bar and drag the window to a new location. To resize the window, click on the window border and drag the window to a new size.*

Quick Generate the Entire Project

When you started this project with the RoboHelp Starter Wizard, you specified an output format (in the sample, it was HTML Help). The Quick Generate function uses the specified output format and other defaults to generate the appropriate files and folders for that format. To generate and view a project, follow these steps:

1. Click the **Quick Generate** icon ( ) to generate a project using the defaults. An output pane opens across the bottom of the RoboHelp window, as shown in Figure 4-13.

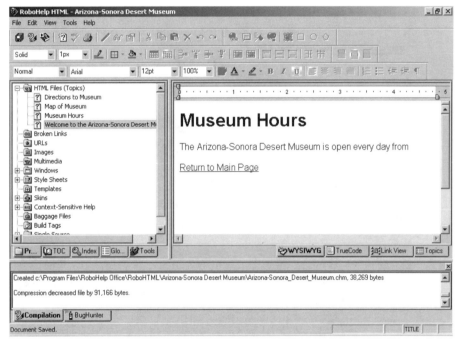

Figure 4-13: Using the Quick Generate icon to create a finished project

The output pane displays the status of the project as it generates. Note that this will vary depending on the output type. In most cases, the status includes information about the steps being taken and the length of time it takes for each step.

When the compilation is finished, the Wizard Result window will display buttons for each available option. This will vary with the output type. For example, if your primary target is WebHelp Enterprise, a Publish button will be available. If, as in our example, the primary target is HTML Help, the result window will be similar to that shown in Figure 4-14.

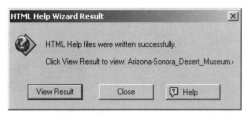

Figure 4-14: Viewing the result

2. To view the help file on your local machine, click **View Result**. Depending on the target output, RoboHelp will display a list of the client/server functionality, if any, that will be unavailable on your local machine. For many testing purposes, though, the local view will be enough.

3. Click **OK** to display the project as a finished help system in the default format and viewer, as shown in Figure 4-15.

Figure 4-15: Viewing the entire help system

4. If you've entered Table of Contents or Index entries, they'll appear in the left-hand pane of the viewer. You can test the help system by clicking all the links, entering search terms, and using the back and forward buttons.

5. Close the viewer to return to RoboHelp.

    You've just created a RoboHelp HTML project, connected topics with hyperlinks, and tested and previewed the final product. The rest of this book describes ways to use additional RoboHelp features to enhance your help system.

Summary

This chapter stepped through the basics of creating a topic, adding a simple link, and testing the project. The following chapter goes into more detail about the types of links you can use and other ways to let your user move from one topic to another.

Chapter 5

Linking Topics Together

This chapter shows you how to increase interactivity with different types of links. You'll add text and image links, learn about the two types of popups, work with controls, and make use of the Link view.

Linking in RoboHelp is a way to help your users find information by giving them pathways between different pieces of information. You can specify a single path by having just one link from one topic to the next, or you can give the user several options on each topic page. There are several types of links available in RoboHelp, and each link type can open different types of windows. Links can connect topics with external web pages or display popup windows that close when the user is finished with them.

 TIP: *Think carefully about the links you want to place on each page. Too many links can be distracting, and links that don't make sense to the user can be frustrating. For example, it might be appropriate to put a link from Museum Hours to Directions, but don't link from Museum Hours to cactus lifespans or coyote feeding habits. A good rule is to limit the links on each page to the four or five topics the user will most likely want to see next.*

Table 5-1: Types of links

Type of link	What it does	What it looks like
Text link	The most common type of link, this can open other topics, link to web pages, or display popup windows.	Text links appear as underlined words, usually a different color than the rest of the text.
Popup	When clicked, a secondary window displays a topic or web site. When the user clicks outside of the popup, the popup window closes automatically.	A popup link can appear as a text link, image link, or image map.
Text-only popup	When clicked, additional text appears in a small window.	This will appear as a text link, image link, or image map.
Image link	This links to another topic when the user clicks anywhere on an image.	The entire image is the link. When the cursor is over the image, a text box displays the description. This type of link is often used for navigation, such as a "next" icon.

Type of link	What it does	What it looks like
Image map	An image map is one image that is composed of several areas, each of which links to a different topic or web site.	When the user moves the cursor over each area of the image, a text box displays the description you've entered for that area.
Link control	These are objects that give users other options, such as a list of other related topics or keywords.	Link controls appear as buttons on the help window. You can specify the text for the button.
Expanding or drop-down link	When the user clicks either of these link types, additional text appears on the same topic page as the link.	Both expanding and drop-down links appear as underlined text.

Adding a Text, Image, or Popup Link

The steps for adding a text, image, or popup link are almost the same. To add any of these common links, you'll use the Hyperlink window. Follow these steps:

1. Open the topic in which you want to include the link. Make sure it is showing in the WYSIWYG tab in the left-hand pane.

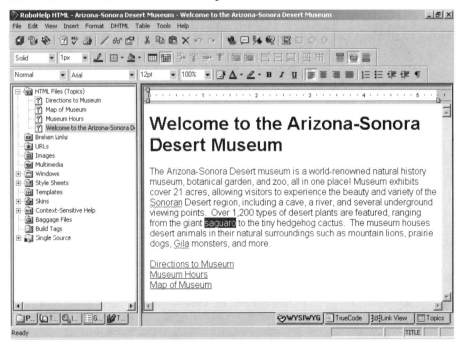

Figure 5-1: Highlighting text to activate hyperlink icons

2. Highlight the text or image you want to convert to a link. The hyperlink icons become active, as shown in Figure 5-1.

3. Click the **Insert Hyperlink** icon ( ) or the **Insert Popup** icon ( ) to open the Hyperlink window, as shown in Figure 5-2.

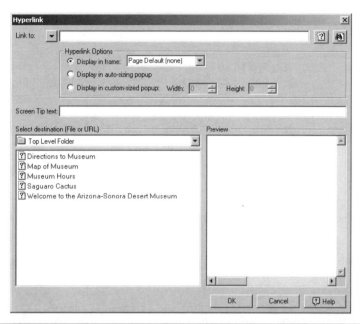

Figure 5-2: Displaying the Hyperlink window

 NOTE: *The Insert Hyperlink icon and the Insert Popup icon launch the same window—only the title is different. Everything described here applies to both windows.*

4. Specify the information that will appear when the user clicks the link in one of two ways:

■ From the Select destination box, double-click one of the displayed topics for this project. For example, if you've highlighted the word "Saguaro," you might choose the topic "Saguaro Cactus."

■ From the Link to drop-down menu, choose the type of information that will display when the link is clicked. Note that if you are linking to one of the topics displayed in the lower part of the Hyperlink window, you don't need to fill in this box. Available options are listed in Table 5-2.

Table 5-2: Link to options

Option	What it does	Enter this information
Web Address	Creates a link to a web site	Enter the URL in the text box.
E-mail	Creates a link that opens your user's default email program with a new message addressed to the address you provide	Enter the email address you want to appear in the user's email program.

Option	What it does	Enter this information
Multimedia	Creates a link to a multimedia file, such as a sound or movie file	Use the Select box to browse to the Multimedia file. Be sure to include the selected file in your project folder if it has not already been copied there.
UseNet News	Creates a link to a newsgroup	Enter the address of the newsgroup.
FTP	Creates a link to an FTP site where they can download files to their computer	Enter the Internet address, including the filename if you want your users to download a specific file when they click the link. Use only the mail folder for the FTP site if you want your users to be able to choose which file they are going to download.
File	Creates a link to a topic	Select topics in the current project by clicking the topic name in the lower portion of the Hyperlink window, or use the Select button to browse to other files not in the current topic.

CAUTION: *Do not alter any of the text with colons that RoboHelp HTML adds automatically to the text box, such as mailto:, ftp://, or news:. These prefixes are required to make the link work.*

5. Specify the frame, if any, in which the information should appear. The drop-down list shows all the default frames. If the file you are linking from does not already have a frameset designated, this setting is ignored. If the file you are linking from has a frameset designated, you must include this setting; otherwise, the link removes the frameset and opens as a standard window. See Chapter 14, "Using Frames and Framesets," for more information about frames.

6. (Optional) To create a link that causes information to appear in a popup window, select either of the two popup window options:

   ■ **Display in auto-sizing popup:** This option will automatically create a window large enough to fit your popup topic.

   ■ **Display in custom-sized popup:** This option allows you to specify the size of the popup window. Enter the width and height of the window in points. If the topic is taller or wider than the specified window size, scroll bars will be displayed on the popup window.

7. (Optional) Screen tips are the text that appears on the screen when a user pauses the cursor over the link. This gives the user a hint about what the link does. If you want to enter a screen tip, type the text into the Screen Tip text box just under the Hyperlink Options section in the Hyperlink window.

8. Click **OK** when you've finished defining the link. The Hyperlink window closes and the link appears on the topic in the WYSIWYG pane. Move the cursor over the link in the WYSIWYG pane to display the type of link and the topic to which it points, as shown in Figure 5-3.

Figure 5-3: Displaying link information in the WYSIWYG window

9. To preview your link, click the **View** icon ( ). As you move your cursor over the underlined text, you'll see the screen tip text you entered, if any, as shown in Figure 5-4. If you click on the underlined text, the specified topic appears in the Preview window.

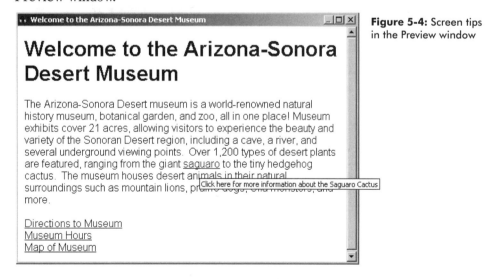

Figure 5-4: Screen tips in the Preview window

Adding a Text-only Popup

Like standard popups, text-only popups open when the user clicks on the link and close when the user clicks outside the text-only popup on the topic page. Unlike standard popups, text-only popups cannot include images or links of their own. Text-only popups are particularly useful when you have just a little information to give the reader, such as a definition. Popups open up over your HTML Help project topic page in a small, colored rectangle. You can specify the color and size of the rectangle and format the text to match your project style.

To create a text-only popup, follow these steps:

1. Open the topic in which you want to add the text popup. Make sure the topic is visible in the WYSIWYG tab in the right-hand pane.

2. Highlight the text or image for the link. If you want the link to include an image that is already on the topic page, select it.

3. From the **Insert** menu, choose **Text-Only Popup**. RoboHelp HTML places an empty text popup on the topic page, as shown in Figure 5-5. A cursor is in the text box.

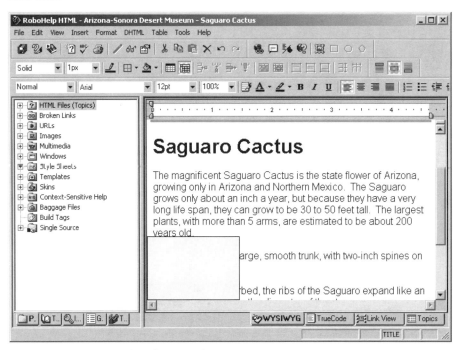

Figure 5-5: Entering text into the text-only popup

4. Enter the text you want to include on the text-only popup.

5. When you have finished adding text, click on the topic page outside the text-only popup. This closes the editing of the text-only popup.

6. Put your cursor over the new link and click the right mouse button.

7. Select **Text Popup Properties** from the list to open the Text Popup Properties window, as shown in Figure 5-6.

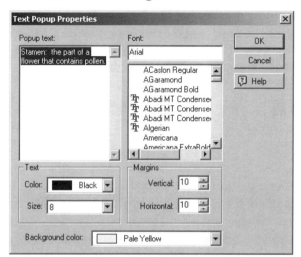

Figure 5-6: The Text Popup Properties window

8. Alter the text, choosing new formatting, colors, or size for the text and background of the popup.

9. When you have finished editing the text-only popup, click **OK**. RoboHelp HTML closes the window and reformats the text-only popup.

 The changes you make in the Text Popup Properties window become the default for all subsequent text-only popups.

10. To preview the popup, click the **View** icon. If you click on the underlined text, the specified text appears as on the screen. Click anywhere outside of the text box to close it.

Adding an Image Map

Image maps are a special type of link that lets you specify certain portions of an image for each linked topic. Each portion of the image becomes a link, also called a *hotspot*. For example, you might have a picture of a desert scene, with a hotspot over each animal to display a topic about that species. Or if you have a map, you can create hotspots over separate areas in the map to display information about each area.

To add an image map, you must have an image in your topic. (See Chapter 8, "Adding Images and Special Effects to RoboHelp HTML files," for information about adding images to topics.) Then follow these steps:

1. In the WYSIWYG Editor, right-click the image and select **Insert Image Map**.

2. To define the shape of the hotspot, select **Rectangle**, **Circle**, or **Polygon**. The method for specifying the location of the hotspot varies with the shape.

Table 5-3: Image map shapes

Shape	To specify the location
Rectangle	Click on one corner of the rectangle; then click on the corner diagonally opposite the first corner.
Circle	Click on the point at the center of the circle; then click on the outer edge of the circle.
Polygon	Click on each corner of the polygon except the last one. Double-click on the last corner or point to indicate that you have finished defining the polygon shape.

3. When you've finished defining the hotspot shape and location, the Image Map Properties window opens, as shown in Figure 5-7. This window is the same as the Text Link and Image Link windows, except that it has a different title. Specify the information that will display when the user clicks the hotspot by either double-clicking a topic name or entering information in the Link to box. You may also fill in the Screen Tip text box.

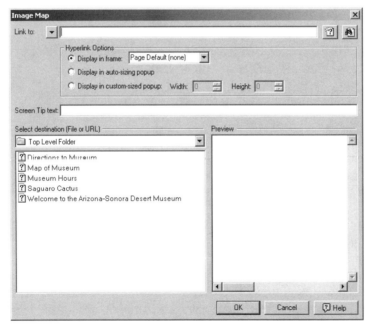

Figure 5-7: Editing hotspots with the Image Map window

4. Click **OK** to close the Image Map window and display the topic with the hotspot. The image map hotspot appears on the WYSIWYG pane as a red line. Figure 5-8 shows the three hotspot shapes.

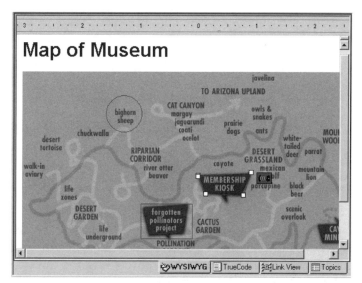

Figure 5-8: Image map hotspots

5. To edit an existing hotspot, click anywhere within the hotspot to select it. The corners of the hotspot become "active" by turning into handles that allow you reshape the spot if necessary. Click and drag any of the handles to a new location. Double-click the **Hotspot** icon ( ) to display the Image Map window to change the destination or other properties of the hotspot.

6. To preview the link, click the **View** icon. As you move your cursor over the image, you'll see the screen tip text you entered, if any. If you click on any hotspot, the specified topic appears in the preview window.

Adding Link Controls

Link controls appear on the finished topic page as buttons or icons that the user can click to display a list of additional topics. There are three types of link controls available in RoboHelp Enterprise. They all display lists of topics, but they vary in the way the list is built.

Table 5-4: Types of link controls

Link control	Function
Related Topics	Displays a list of topics that you specify for each control.
See Also	Generates and then displays a list of topics based on a code you place in each referenced topic. When the code is changed or removed, the controls are automatically updated.
Index	Displays a list of topics based on common keywords. Whenever you remove index keywords from topics, the controls are automatically updated.

For all types of link controls, you must first create the topics that will appear when the control is clicked. If you are creating a Related Topic control, you don't have to prepare the topics; you'll simply pick topics by their names. For the See Also and Index controls, you must first insert the See Also or Index keywords into the topics to which you want to link.

 NOTE: *See Also controls were called Alink controls in previous versions of RoboHelp. The functionality remains the same; only the name has changed.*

Preparing Topics for Link Controls

See Also and Index links are tools that cross-reference groups of topics. There are two components to these types of links. First, you must insert the See Also name or Index keyword into the properties of each topic that might be included in the link. This identifies the group or groups to which the topic belongs.

Then you can create the control on a topic page. When the user clicks the control, a list of topics associated with the See Also or Index keyword is displayed. You don't have to enter the whole list into each topic, as you do with Related Topics controls.

For example, you might have a See Also category for all types of cactus. You would put the See Also name "cactus" into the topics that describe the Saguaro, barrel, and ocotillo. Then you could add a See Also button titled "Cactus Types" to any topic in the project. When the user clicks on the button, the list of the names of all topics with the See Also name "cactus" will display. If you decide to add a topic to this list, simply insert the See Also name "cactus" in the new topic. When you generate the help file, all See Also controls that point to the cactus category will be updated.

Adding See Also Keywords to Topics

You'll need to insert a See Also keyword into each topic that you want included in the See Also list. You may have many See Also keywords for a single topic. For example, the topic Saguaro Cactus might be displayed in both a list of cactus types and a list of flowering plants. Each could be a See Also category keyword.

To add See Also keywords to a topic, follow these steps:

1. With the topic selected in the right-hand pane, click the **Properties** icon (📄) to display the Topic Properties window.

2. Click the **See Also** tab to display the list of existing See Also keywords for the topic, if any, as shown in Figure 5-9.

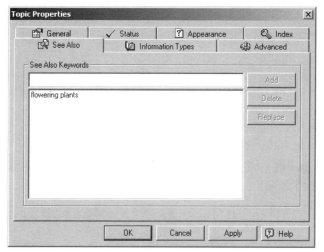

Figure 5-9: Displaying See Also names for the topic

3. Type the See Also name you want to add in the box at the top of the window. This will activate the Add button.

4. Click **Add** to add the new name. The name appears in the list, as shown in Figure 5-10.

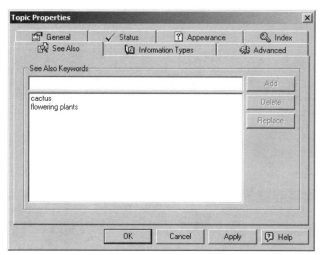

Figure 5-10: Adding each See Also name to the topic

 NOTE: *Make sure that you use exactly the same See Also name in topics that you want to group together. RoboHelp will consider "plant" and "plants" to be two separate groups.*

5. Click **OK** to save the See Also names and return to the topic display.

Adding Index Keywords to Topics

For the keyword links, you can use existing keywords generated by the Smart Index Wizard (see Chapter 9, "Getting Organized Using Folders, Tables of Contents, and Indexing Tools," for more information about indexing). Or you can add Index keywords to each topic as you go along. The Index keywords you enter will appear in the Index tab of the left-hand pane, as well as in the index you generate at the end of the project.

To manually add Index keywords to a topic, follow these steps:

1. With the topic selected in the right-hand pane, click the **Properties** icon ( ) to display the Properties window.

2. Click the **Index** tab to display the list of existing keywords for the topic, if any, as shown in Figure 5-11.

3. Type the keyword you want to add in the box at the top of the window or choose an existing keyword by clicking the **Add Existing** button.

4. If you choose to add an existing keyword, the list of existing keywords for the entire project is displayed in the Add Existing Index Keyword window, as shown in Figure 5-12.

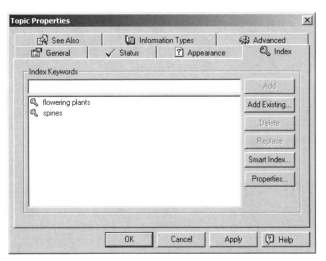

Figure 5-11: Displaying keywords for the topic on the Index tab

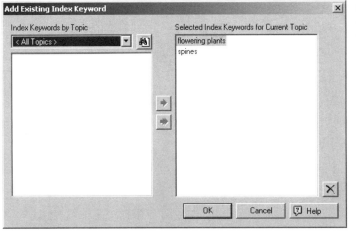

Figure 5-12: Adding existing keywords to the current topic

5. The left side of the window displays all of the keywords for the project. The right side of the window displays the keywords for the current topic. Click a keyword on the left side of the window, and then click the arrow to add it to the right side of the window and to the topic. Click **OK** when finished.

6. Click **Add** to add the new name. The name appears in the list.

7. Click **OK** to save the keywords and return to the topic display.

Creating Link Controls

To add link controls to a topic, use the Link Control Wizard. This will display a series of windows that prompt you to enter the information required for each type of link control. For each control, you simply choose from the list of existing topics. Depending on the type of control, you'll choose topics by topic name, See Also keyword, or Index keyword. The specified topics will be displayed when the user clicks the control. You may specify the text, font, and appearance of the control button, or you may use a graphic as an icon.

NOTE: *In the following example, the figures show the Related Topic Link Control Wizard windows. The windows for See Also and Keyword are the same, except for the window titles.*

To add a link control, follow these steps:

1. In the WYSIWYG Editor, click where you want to add the control in the topic.

2. Click the **Insert Link Control** icon ( ) to display the available link control types as shown in Figure 5-13.

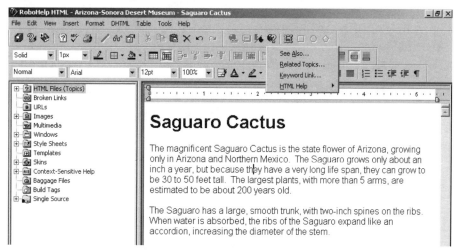

Figure 5-13: Choosing a link control type

3. Select the type of control you want to create to display the Button Options window, as shown in Figure 5-14.

Figure 5-14: Defining the control with the Buttons Options window

4. Define the appearance of the control by choosing one of the displayed options.

Table 5-5: Link control button options

Control appearance	How to display it
A standard gray button	Select Text (the default). Use the existing button label "Related Topics" or enter text that you want to display on the button.
A custom image (.BMP or .ICO)	Select Image, and then use the Graphics Locator to select and copy the file into your project.
An Invisible Control	This is an internal control that activates scripts. You'll need to specify the name of the script.

5. The box on the left of the window displays the available topics, See Also, or Index keywords for the current project. Select the first topic, See Also, or Index keyword, and then click **Add**. The topic is displayed in the box on the right, as shown in Figure 5-15. Repeat for each topic you want in the control.

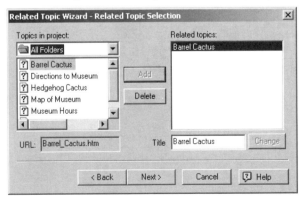

Figure 5-15: Choosing the related topics

TIP: *When creating a Related Topics control, try to limit the number of topics in each list to those most appropriate for the current topic. Too many related topics can be confusing. When creating a See Also or Index keyword control, remember that each See Also and Index keyword represents a number of topics. One or two See Also or Index keywords is usually enough for a link control.*

6. Click **Next** to display the Display Options window, as shown in Figure 5-16. This will vary depending on the primary target for your help system. For example, if you have specified HTML Help output, you'll be able to specify how the related topics will appear and choose the frame from any of the defined frames in the project (see Chapter 14, "Using Frames and Framesets," for more information about frames). For RoboHelp Enterprise output, the Choose topic from options will not be available.

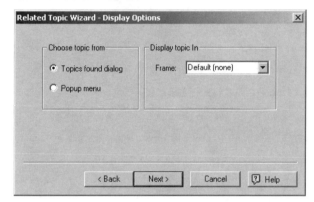

Figure 5-16: Specifying a frame for the topic list

7. For HTML Help output, choose one of the following options:

    Table 5-6: HTML Help output options

Option	How it displays topics
Topics found dialog	Displays the Related Topics, See Also topics, or Index topics in a new window. If you have a lot of topics, the window will have scroll bars. The user clicks a topic, and then clicks the Display button to display the specified topic.
Popup menu	Displays the Related Topics, See Also topics, or Index topics in a menu next to the button. The user chooses from the menu to display the specified topic.

8. If you chose to create a standard button in step 4, click **Next** to display the Font Options window, as shown in Figure 5-17. (This option does not apply to custom images or hidden controls.)

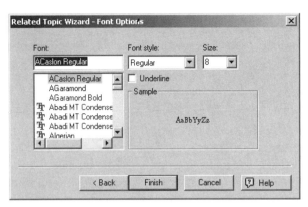

Figure 5-17: Defining the text font, style, and size

9. Click **Finish.** The control is added to your topic, as shown in Figure 5-18.

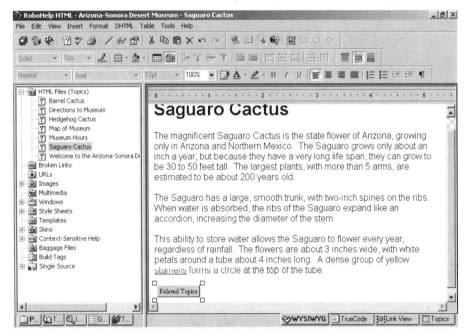

Figure 5-18: Finishing the wizard to display the link control

10. To preview thc link control, click the **View icon,** and then click the button you just created. The specified topics are displayed in either a popup menu list or a window, as shown in Figure 5-19. You'll be able to click the links to ensure that they work as you expect.

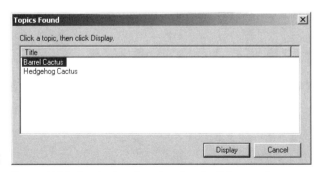

Figure 5-19: Previewing the related topics link control

CAUTION: *The Preview mode is a quick, easy way to see what your topic will look like, but it is not always exact. Depending on the output you choose, link controls may appear in a window when you preview but in a plain rectangular box in the final WebHelp Enterprise system. Always run the project to check for final appearance.*

11. To view the link control the way it will appear on the final system, choose **Run** from the **File** menu, and then choose a viewer option. For HTML output, you'll get a prompt that asks if you want to compile first (go ahead and click **OK**). The project will appear in the default HTML Help viewer, as shown in Figure 5-20. For WebHelp output, the prompt will ask if you want to generate the files. In either case, go ahead and click **OK**. Figure 5-21 shows the sample topic in Internet Explorer. Notice that the Related Topics button displays the same list that was displayed in the Preview mode, but the window varies based on the specific output and viewer.

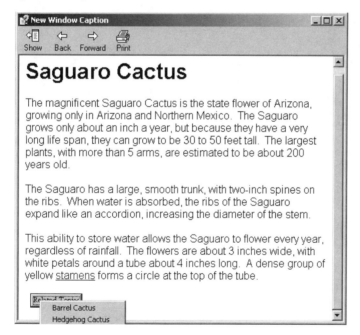

Figure 5-20: Final project appearance may vary from the preview

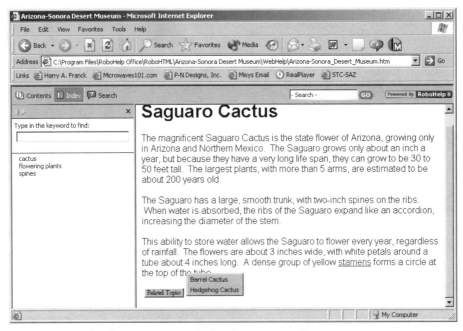

Figure 5-21: WebHelp output appears in the viewer you specify

Adding an Expanding or Drop-down Link

Expanding hotspots and drop-down hotspots are links that display additional information when the hotspot text is clicked. Expanding links display the new information immediately following the clickable hotspot, even if it is in the middle of a sentence. Drop-down links display information beginning on the line below the drop-down hotspot. For both types of links, the hotspot text appears as green italicized text so that users can identify the hotspots as clickable items. You can modify the font, style, or size of the hotspot text and include text and images in the expanding or drop-down information.

CAUTION: *When changing the appearance of these links, make sure they retain some uniqueness. If the hotspot text is the same size and font as the rest of the text on the page, the users may not recognize it as a link.*

To create an expanding or drop-down hotspot with new text, follow these steps:

1. In the WYSIWYG Editor, select the text that the users will click to display the additional information.

2. From the **DHTML** menu, select **Create Expanding Hotspot and Text** or **Create Drop-Down Hotspot and Text.** The selected text is formatted as the

hotspot, and the Hotspot Text Editor opens, as shown in Figure 5-22. Both types of hotspot links use the same editor; only the title of the editor box changes.

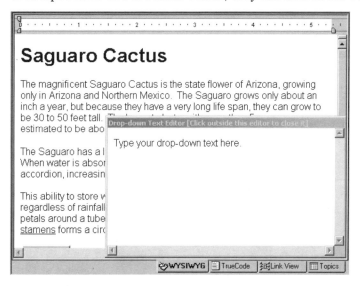

Figure 5-22: Entering drop-down text

3. Enter the text that will appear when the hotspot text is clicked. You can use any of the text formatting features or insert images. Click outside the window to close the editor and display the hotspot in the topic window, as shown in Figure 5-23.

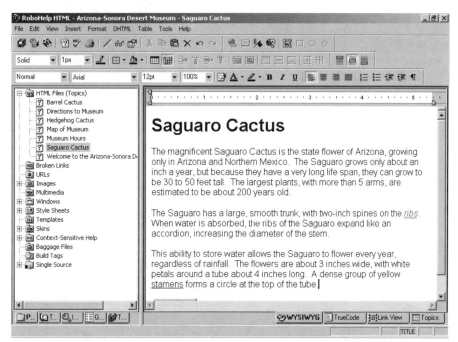

Figure 5-23: The drop-down and expanding hotspots use a green italic font

4. The default is to display the hotspot text as green and italic. If you want to change the font or style, use the editing tools as you would for normal text. For example, you may want to change the hotspot to blue underlined text to match other types of links.

5. Click **Preview** to test the special effect. When you click the hotspot, it expands to show the additional text.

6. To view the hotspot the way it will appear on the final system, choose **Run** from the **File** menu, and then choose a viewer option. Figure 5-24 shows the sample topic in the HTML Help viewer. When the link is clicked, the word "ribs" in this example, the text and a picture are displayed. If the link is clicked again, the text and accompanying picture are removed.

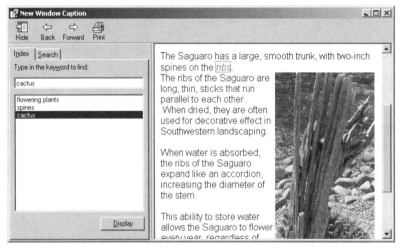

Figure 5-24: An expanding hotspot that includes text and images

Using the Link View

Once you have a number of links in your project, use the Link view to identify the way topics are linked together. The Link view can help identify broken links, "orphaned" topics (those with no links to or from them), and possibly missing links. For example, if you have six cactus pages, and the Link view only shows five of them, you know there is something missing. To display the Link view, click the Link View tab in the right-hand pane. The Link view always has one topic in the center, as shown in Figure 5-25 on the following page.

The topics to the left of the center topic contain links to the center topic. The topics to the right of the center icon represent topics for which the center topic contains links.

There are several ways to specify which topic should be the center topic in the Link view:

- Double-click any topic in Link view to move it to the center position.
- Select a topic icon in Link view, and then drag it on top of the one in the center.
- Right-click on a topic in Link view and select Make Center.
- Drag the topic name from the left pane of the window to the Link View pane.

The lines that connect the topics are color-coded.

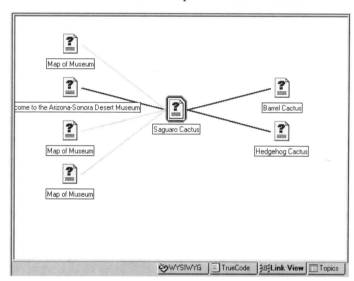

Figure 5-25: Displaying connections between topics in the Link view

Table 5-7: The Link view color codes

Line color	Type of link
Blue	Text or image hyperlink
Yellow	Image map
Green	Popup
Red	Link to an external web site URL

You can use the Link view at any time, but it is most helpful toward the end of a project.

Adding Links with ActiveX Controls

ActiveX is a Microsoft standard that allows many types of programs to use a single control, such as a close window button. There are two required components: the control, which is inserted into your topics, and the engine that processes the control (in either the HTML Help engine or Microsoft's Internet Explorer). This is useful when you need to perform a function in many help topics but don't want to write each one from scratch.

CAUTION: *If your users use a browser other than Microsoft Internet Explorer, you may be better off avoiding ActiveX controls.*

RoboHelp comes with a variety of predefined ActiveX controls for HTML Help output. You can insert these controls into your document much as you would insert any other type of link.

Table 5-8: ActiveX controls for HTML Help output

Control	Function
Shortcut	Starts a software program
WinHelp Topic	Displays an existing WinHelp Help project
Close button	Closes the browser window
HHCTRL	Displays the version number of Microsoft HTML Help that is on the user's system

 NOTE: *These controls only work in HTML Help output, not WebHelp or WebHelp Enterprise output.*

Inserting a Shortcut Link

The Shortcut control allows you to start another program from within your help system.

 TIP: *This control simply sends the command. You must ensure that the program you are trying to start exists on the user's system. One way to do this would be to include the executable in your help system folder.*

To insert a shortcut button into a topic, follow these steps:

1. In the WYSIWYG Editor, click where you want to add the control in the topic.
2. From the **Insert** menu, choose **HTML Help** and then **Shortcut** to start the Shortcut Wizard, as shown in Figure 5-26.

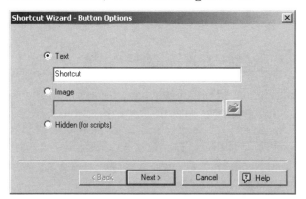

Figure 5-26: Using the Shortcut Wizard to insert a shortcut button

3. Define the appearance of the control by choosing one of the displayed options.

Table 5-9: ActiveX control button options

Control appearance	How to display it
A standard gray button	Select Text (the default); then replace the existing button label "Shortcut" with something descriptive.
A custom image (.BMP or .ICO)	Select Image, and then use the Graphics Locator to select and copy the file into your project.
An invisible control	This is an internal control that activates scripts. You'll need to specify the name of the script.

4. Click **Next** to display the Shortcut Properties, as shown in Figure 5-27.

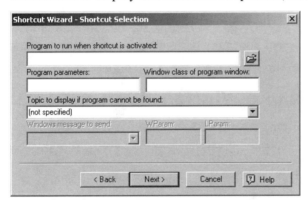

Figure 5-27: Specifying the program you want to run

5. Enter the command that executes the program in the top text box. You may use the browse function to find the program on your system. You may also enter program parameters or a window class if necessary.

CAUTION: *If you include a path name in this text box, the help topic will look for the program in that path on the user's system. Make sure you know where the program will be on the user's system.*

6. Use the pull-down menu to display a list of topics in the project. Then select a topic to display if the program cannot be found on the user's system. You may make a unique topic with an error message and perhaps contact information, or you may display the referring topic again.

7. Click **Next** to display the final window in the Shortcut Wizard, as shown in Figure 5-28.

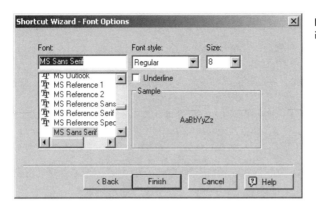

Figure 5-28: Entering font information

8. Specify a font, style, and size for the text on the button. Remember, the buttons can be quite small, so try not to use a complicated or hard-to-read font style.

9. Click **Finish** to close the wizard and insert the button.

Inserting a Link to a WinHelp Topic

The WinHelp Topic control allows you to display a topic from a compiled WinHelp project. The project must exist on the user's system in order for this control to work.

To insert a WinHelp button into a topic, follow these steps:

1. In the WYSIWYG Editor, click where you want to add the control in the topic.

2. From the **Insert** menu, choose **HTML Help** and then **WinHelp Topic** to start the WinHelp Topic Wizard, as shown in Figure 5-29.

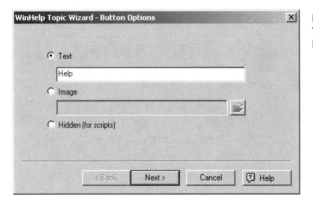

Figure 5-29: Using the WinHelp Topic Wizard to insert a WinHelp button

3. Define the appearance of the control by choosing one of the displayed options.

Table 5-10: WinHelp button options

Control appearance	How to display it
A standard gray button	Select Text (the default); then replace the existing button label "Help" with something descriptive.
A custom image (.BMP or .ICO)	Select Image, and then use the Graphics Locator to select and copy the file into your project.
An invisible control	This is an internal control that activates scripts. You'll need to specify the name of the script.

4. Click **Next** to display the Shortcut properties, as shown in Figure 5-30.

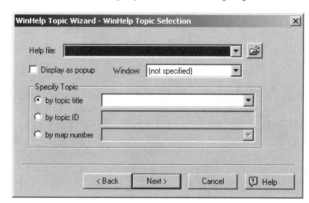

Figure 5-30: Specifying the name of the help file you want to display

5. Enter the name of the help file that you want to display. This help file must also exist on the user's system.

6. (Optional) You may specify that the WinHelp topic appear in a popup window by clicking the **Display as popup** check box, or you may specify a custom window by choosing from the window drop-down menu.

7. Specify the topic to display in one of the following ways:

   ■ Use the pull-down menu to display a list of topics in the specified help file. Then choose the topic.

   ■ Enter a topic ID.

   ■ Choose a map number from the pull-down menu.

8. Click **Next** to display the font options for the control.

9. Specify a font, style, and size for the text on the button. Remember, the buttons can be quite small, so try not to use a complicated or hard-to-read font style.

10. Click **Finish** to close the wizard and insert the new control.

Closing a Window or Displaying Version Information with ActiveX Controls

RoboHelp comes with two buttons that use ActiveX for common functions. The Close Window button closes whatever window the topic is displayed in. The HHCTRL button displays the version number of the HTML Help that exists on the user's system. Both of these buttons are inserted the same way—only the title bars change.

To insert either a Close button or an HHCTRL button into a topic, follow these steps:

1. In the WYSIWYG Editor, click where you want to add the control in the topic.

2. From the **Insert** menu, choose **HTML Help**, and then either **HHCTRL** or **Close Window** to start the wizard, as shown in Figure 5-31.

Figure 5-31: Using the wizard to insert a Close Window or HHCTRL button

3. Define the appearance of the control by choosing one of the displayed options.

Table 5-11: ActiveX control button options

Control appearance	How to display it
A standard gray button	Select Text (the default); then replace the existing button label with something descriptive.
A custom image (.BMP or .ICO)	Select Image, and then use the Graphics Locator to select and copy the file into your project.
An invisible control	This is an internal control that activates scripts. You'll need to specify the name of the script.

4. Click **Next** to display the font options window.

5. Specify a font, style, and size for the text on the button. Remember, the buttons can be quite small, so try not to use a complicated or hard-to-read font style.

6. Click **Finish** to close the wizard and insert the new control.

Summary

This chapter reviewed the various types of links and describe how to insert each one into your topics. It also described how to use the preview feature, as well as preview limitations. Finally, it discussed how to use the Link View tab to check your links.

Chapter 6

Formatting Text, Paragraphs, and Topic Pages

This chapter describes several ways to enhance the appearance of the RoboHelp HTML files using the formatting controls. You'll learn how to make text larger and smaller and use different fonts for different purposes. You'll see the different ways to arrange text into paragraphs and position them on the screen. You'll also learn about the different ways to format entire topic pages.

Planning Your Formats

Most of your formatting decisions should be made before you begin creating your help topics. You'll want to give all of your topics a similar "look and feel" so that users know what to expect from each screen. It's much easier to create them all the same way than it is to go back later and change them to match. See "Planning Your Online Help System" in Chapter 2 for more details on planning.

When you planned your help project, you had to make decisions about stylistic and graphical standards. These issues include:

- Formatting fonts — What will the text look like?
- Formatting topic pages — What will the overall page look like?

Formatting Text

When text appears on your computer screen, each character appears in a specific font, size, shape, and color. Together, these elements make up the character format of the text. The letters and words also appear with specific spacing, alignment, and positioning on the screen. These are the elements of paragraph formatting.

Table 6-1: Text formatting methods

Method	Function
Character formatting	Changes the way individual letters or characters look.
Paragraph formatting	Changes the way words are positioned within a paragraph or on the screen.

There are four ways you can change the text formatting.

Table 6-2: Formatting character options

Level of format	Function
Formatting menu bar	Changes just a few letters, words, or paragraphs. Although quick and easy, this can be unwieldy for large blocks of text or across many topics.
Format windows	Changes just a few letters, words, or paragraphs. Like the menu bar icons, this applies only to the selected text and must be set for each individual block of text.
Embedded styles	Changes the defaults for the topic. The changes you make will apply to all similarly tagged blocks of text in the topic but not to similar text in other topics.
Style sheets	Changes the defaults for the entire project. If you use style sheets, you can easily make changes in all topics at once. Changes you make with the Formatting menu bar or the Format windows will override any style sheet settings.

Specifying Character Formats

Character formatting includes the specific font, or shape of each letter, as well as the size, color, and special. When you first create a topic, RoboHelp HTML uses a set of default character formats.

Table 6-3: Some RoboHelp default character formats

Text	Default font	Default size	Default style	Default color
Plain text	Arial	12 point	regular	black
Heading 1	Arial	24 point	bold	black
Heading 2	Arial	18 point	bold	black
Heading 3	Arial	14 point	bold	black
Heading 4	Arial	12 point	bold	black
Expanding hotspot	Arial	12 point	italic	green
Expanding text	Arial	12 point	italic	red
Drop-down hotspot	Arial	12 point	italic	green
Glossary term	Arial	12 point	italic	maroon
Glossary text	Arial	12 point	italic	blue
Links	Arial	12 point	underlined	blue

CAUTION: *As you choose text formats, remember that your users may not have the same fonts on their system that you have on yours. Your carefully chosen font may appear in unexpected ways on their systems. One way to work around this is to use font sets, described later in this chapter.*

Using the Formatting Menu Bar to Specify Character Formats

The quickest and easiest way to specify text formatting is to use the elements on the Formatting menu bar. You can use these icons and menus to change the font, size, color, and style of text.

 NOTE: *Text style is not the same thing as style sheets. Text style refers to the special characteristics of the individual letters, such as bold, italic, or underlined. Style sheets allow you to specify page, paragraph, and text formatting for an entire project.*

1. Open the topic in the WYSIWYG tab in the right pane.
2. Select the text you'd like to format.
3. To change the text style of the selected text, click any of the following icons.

Table 6-4: The text style icons

Icon	Effect
B	bold
I	*italic*
<u>U</u>	underlined

You may use more than one text style on the same text. The text in Figure 6-1 shows the text "Arizona-Sonora Desert Museum" in both bold and italic.

Figure 6-1: Using text styles to emphasize certain words

4. To change the size of the selected text, click the down arrow next to the current text size to display a list of size options, as shown in Figure 6-2. Then click the size you want. There are two ways to specify text size. One method is to specify a numeric size, such as 12 or 18 points. The text will always appear in that size, regardless of the user's monitor settings. Or you may specify a font size in relation to the user's normal settings. The heading "Welcome to the Arizona-Sonora Desert Museum" in Figure 6-2 is at 24 points, or extra-large on standard settings.

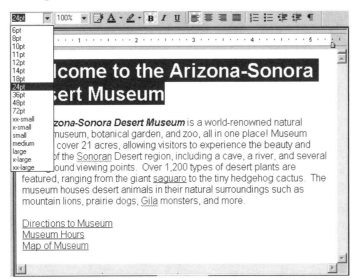

Figure 6-2: Using a larger font for the heading

5. To change the font, click the down arrow next to the current font, as shown in Figure 6-3, and then click the font you want. If you are using the built-in RoboHelp editor, the font names will appear in the corresponding fonts, so you can see what each one looks like. The list of available fonts will vary based on the fonts you have installed on your system.

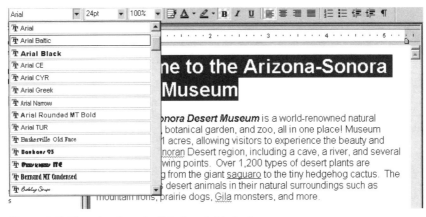

Figure 6-3: Choosing from the list of available fonts

6. To change the text color, click the **Text Color** icon (**A**) to display a palette of colors. The default colors are the ones most likely to be displayable on most systems. As you move the cursor over the color palette, the names of each color will appear in screen tip text, as shown in Figure 6-4. Also in Figure 6-4, notice that the name "Arizona-Sonora Desert Museum" has been changed to red.

Figure 6-4: Selecting from the palette of available colors

TIP: *Once you've selected a text color, the small horizontal line under the letter A on the Text Color icon changes to that text color. The next time you want to change color, you may click the text icon to quickly change selected text to the color on the icon.*

To change the highlight color of the selected text, click the **Highlight** icon (✎) to display the color palette, then choose the color for the highlight. Highlighting is the color that appears behind the selected text, as shown in Figure 6-5.

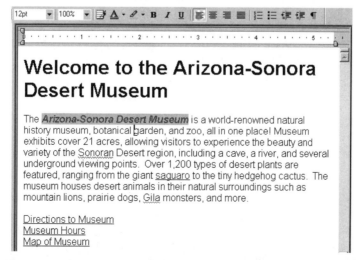

Figure 6-5: Placing color behind the selected text with highlighting

CAUTION: *RoboHelp allows you to add many types of formatting to the text. However, too much formatting can be distracting to the user, as you can see in Figure 6-5. Too much character formatting can also lead the user to think there are links when there aren't any. Remember, in addition to your regular and heading text formats, there are special formats for different types of links.*

Using the Font Window to Specify Character Formats

Like the Formatting menu bar, the Font window allows you to modify text style, font, size, and color. In addition, the Font window lets you specify special text effects, such as superscript, subscript, and strike-through.

1. Open the topic in the WYSIWYG tab in the right pane.
2. Select the text you'd like to format.
3. From the Format window, select **Font** to display the Font window, as shown in Figure 6-6. Many of the options are the same as those available through the Formatting menu bar but are displayed in a different way. For example, the color options display the color names instead of the color palette, and the underline option is separate from the other text styles. The Font window also includes some text effects. Like the other formatting options, you may apply multiple effects to the selected text, but too many effects will make the text difficult to read.

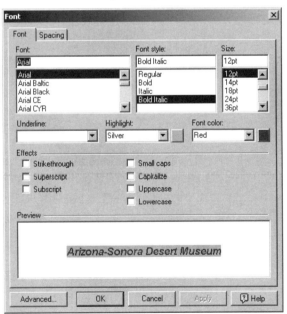

4. Select the formatting you want for the selected text. As you choose options from the list, the Preview pane displays the changes
5. Once you are satisfied with the changes, click **OK** to close the Font window and display the new formats.

Figure 6-6: Specifying text effects with the Font window

Creating Font Sets

RoboHelp HTML lets you specify fonts, but it can't guarantee that the user will have those fonts installed. If the specified font does not exist on a user's system, the default system font is substituted instead, which may change the look of your topics.

There are two ways out of this common HTML dilemma:

- Use a font you know is installed on the user's system.
- Specify alternative fonts using font sets.

Limiting yourself to known fonts only works if you are certain about the type of system and platform the user will have. This is very difficult when you're publishing to the web.

A *font set* is a defined group of fonts in a specific order. When the HTML viewer sees a font set, it attempts to display the text in the first font of the set. If that font is not available, the viewer will attempt to use the second font in the set, and so on. The default system font is only used if all of the specified fonts in the font set are unavailable.

Font sets give you a much greater chance of finding and using a font your user has than a single font name does.

Once you've created a font set, RoboHelp HTML displays the set on the formatting toolbar, the same as any other named font on your system. The font set will be stored with the project and available to any topic in the project. However, if you want to use the same font set in several projects, you'll have to define it separately for each project.

1. Display the Font Sets window in one of two ways:

    - From the Format menu, choose **Font Sets**.
    - From the Font window, click **Advanced**, then click **Font Sets**.

    All of the fonts for your system are listed in the Font Sets window, as shown in Figure 6-7, with each listed font appearing as the font set name as well as the only font in each set.

2. To create a new font set, click **New**. A new, blank font set will be created and displayed in the list with the temporary name of "Untitled."

3. Type a new name for the font set, and then press **Enter**. The new font set name is displayed in the list of fonts, with the Fonts Included box empty.

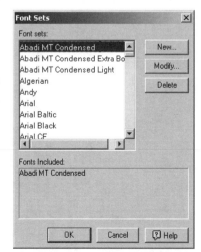

Figure 6-7: The Font Sets window

> **TIP:** *Use the word "set" or some other identifying feature in the font set name. This will help you distinguish between the font sets and the single fonts when you are creating your topics.*

4. To add fonts to your new font set, highlight the font set name, and then click **Modify** to display the Modify Font Set window, as shown in Figure 6-8.

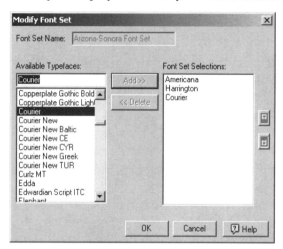

Figure 6-8: The Edit Font Sets window

5. Select a font you want in the font set from the list of Available Typefaces box at the left of the window, and then click **Add** to display the selected font in the Font Set Selections box at the right. Repeat for each font you want to include in the set.

6. Since the HTML viewers will start with the first font, you want to ensure that the first font on the list is the one you really want to display, if it exists on the user's system. To move a font within the Font Set Selections list, click the font name to activate the positioning icons on the far right of the window. Click these icons to move the selected font up or down one position in the list, until you have all the fonts in the order you want them.

> **TIP:** *Remember that the user's system will start at the top of your list. Place the font you really want to use at the top, and then include more common fonts toward the bottom.*

7. Once all the fonts are included and in the correct order, click **OK** to save the font set, and close the Modify Font Set window.

8. The new font set will be available in the standard list of fonts on the Format Font window and in the Formatting menu bar font list. You can treat the font set exactly like a single font when creating your topics. If you look at the code created on the TrueCode tab, you'll see each of the fonts listed instead of the font set name.

Specifying Paragraph Formats

Paragraph formatting includes the alignment of the paragraph on the topic page, the spacing of the lines in a paragraph, and paragraph borders and background shading. When you first create a topic, RoboHelp HTML uses a set of default paragraph formats.

Table 6-5: Some RoboHelp default paragraph formats

Type of text	Alignment	Spacing	Background	Borders
Body text	Flush left	12 point	white	none
Heading 1	Flush left	24 point	white	none
Heading 2	Flush left	18 point	white	none
Heading 3	Flush left	14 point	white	none
Heading 4	Flush left	12 point	white	none

Using the Formatting Menu Bar to Specify Paragraph Formats

The quickest and easiest way to specify paragraph formatting is to use the elements on the Formatting menu bar. You can use Formatting menu bar options to change alignment of the text, the lines around each paragraph (borders), and the color behind the paragraph text (the paragraph shading). Borders can be just on the top or bottom of the paragraph (or either side) or any combination.

1. Open the topic in the WYSIWYG tab in the right pane.
2. Place the cursor anywhere in the paragraph you'd like to format.
3. To change the alignment of the selected paragraph, click any of the following icons.

Table 6-6: The paragraph alignment icons

Icon	Effect
≣	Aligns text to the left
≣	Aligns text in the center
≣	Aligns text to the right
≣	Fully justifies the text (aligns to both sides)

4. To add a border around a paragraph, first set the border parameters using the Formatting menu bar.

 CAUTION: *Some border styles are created by combining the specified border color with black to create effects such as a ridge or groove. If your border color is set to black, these border styles will appear as solid black lines. To see the special effects, choose a color other than black for the border line color.*

Table 6-7: The border style icons

Icon	Parameter
Solid ▼	Choose the border style. Available styles are: Solid, Inset, Ridge, Groove, Double, Outset
✎ (line color icon)	Choose the color for the border line. Click the Line Color icon to display the color palette.
1px ▼	Choose the width, in pixels, for the border line. If you've chosen a border style other than solid, you must specify a line width that is wide enough for the effect (at least 3 pixels).

5. To add a border around the paragraph, click the pull-down menu next to the Border icon (⊞) to display the border options, as shown in Figure 6-9.

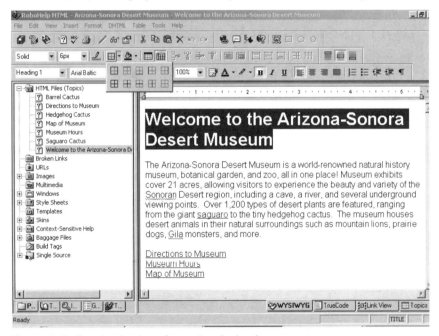

Figure 6-9: Choosing borders after setting the border parameters

6. Click the box that corresponds to the areas where you want to place a border line. The darker lines on the icon indicate where the borders will be placed relative to the current paragraph. Since this example only places borders around a paragraph (not a table), the inside and outside border placement icons in the second row will not work. The borders will appear as you specify around your paragraph. The bottom right icon, with no dark lines, can be used to erase any paragraph borders you may have entered.

> **TIP:** *Once you've selected all border parameters, including placement, the border icon changes to reflect your current choices. To quickly place the current border choices around a paragraph, click the Border icon (not the drop-down menu arrow).*

7. To change the shading (the color behind the text of the paragraph), click the **Shading** icon ( ) to display the color palette, and then choose the color for the paragraph background. This will override any character highlighting you may have entered. The example in Figure 6-10 shows the topic heading text with a black, double line at 6 pixels, with silver shading.

Figure 6-10: Placing color behind the selected paragraph

Using Format Windows to Specify Paragraph Formats

RoboHelp format windows let you perform the same functions as the paragraph format menu bar options, plus offer additional controls. The Paragraph format window lets you set the paragraph alignment and specify indentation and spacing between lines. The Borders and Shading window lets you set the padding or space between text and the border.

Using the Paragraph Format Window

Like the Alignment icon, the Paragraph format window lets you specify how the lines of a paragraph are placed. In addition, you can set the indentation and space for the paragraph. Indentation is the amount of space between the paragraph and the edge of the topic page. Spacing refers to the amount of space between lines in a paragraph as well as the amount of space between paragraphs. For all three types of paragraph formatting, a preview window displays a sample paragraph that reflects the formatting as you choose it.

To set the paragraph indents and spacing, follow these steps:

1. Open the topic in the WYSIWYG tab in the right pane.

2. Place the cursor in the paragraph you'd like to format.

3. From the Format window, select **Paragraph** to display the Paragraph format window, as shown in Figure 6-11.

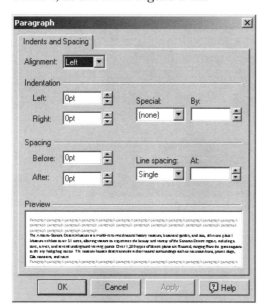

Figure 6-11: Specifying alignment, indentation, and spacing with the Paragraph format window

4. Select the formatting you want for the selected paragraph. As you enter values in each of the boxes, the Preview pane displays sample paragraphs in the new format.

5. Once you are satisfied with the changes, click **OK** to close the Paragraph format window and display the new formats.

Using the Borders and Shading Window

Like the Borders and Shading icons, the Borders and Shading window lets you specify the style, color, and width of lines around each paragraph, as well as the color behind the text. In addition, you can set a padding value for the paragraph. Padding is the amount of space between the text and the borders. For all border and shading formatting, a preview window displays a sample paragraph that reflects the formatting as you choose it.

To set the borders using the Borders and Shading window, follow these steps:

1. Open the topic in the WYSIWYG tab in the right pane.

2. Place the cursor in the paragraph you'd like to format.

3. From the Format window, select **Borders and Shading** to display the Borders and Shading window.

4. Click the **Borders** tab to display border options, as shown in Figure 6-12.

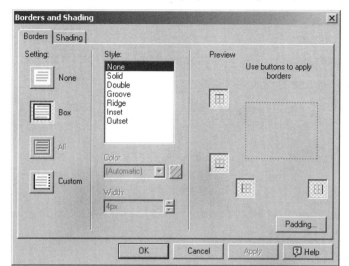

Figure 6-12: Specifying border options with the Borders and Shading window

5. Select the formatting you want for the selected paragraph. As you enter values in each of the boxes, the Preview pane displays sample paragraphs in the new format.

6. Click the **Padding** button to display the Padding window, as shown in Figure 6-13. The gray box in the Preview area represents the table contents; the blue area represents the specified padding space.

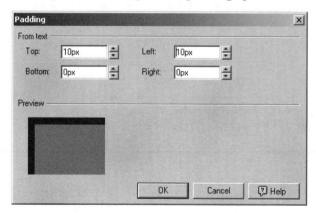

Figure 6-13: Specifying the distance between text and borders with padding

7. Once you are satisfied with the changes, click **OK** to close the Paragraph format window and display the new formats.

To set the shading using the Borders and Shading window, follow these steps:

1. Open the topic in the WYSIWYG tab in the right pane.

2. Place the cursor in the paragraph you'd like to format.

3. From the Format window, select **Borders and Shading** to display the Borders and Shading window.

4. Click the **Shading** tab to display shading options, as shown in Figure 6-14.

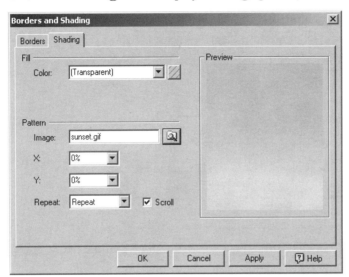

Figure 6-14: Putting color or pattern behind a paragraph with the Shading tab

5. Choose a Fill color from the Color palette, or specify an image that you want to place behind the paragraph. Make sure that the image you choose is fairly plain and light. Dark or busy images make it difficult to read the paragraph text.

6. When finished, click **OK** to close the Borders and Shading window and display your changes in the WYSIWYG pane, as shown in Figure 6-15.

Figure 6-15: Placing a pattern or image behind one paragraph

Using Embedded Styles and Style Sheets

Embedded styles and style sheets allow you to specify formatting once and have it apply across many paragraphs or many topics. A *style* is a combination of format instructions that make it easy to change several formats at once. You can create styles that contain only character formatting or styles that contain both character and paragraph instructions. All styles will be available in the Styles menu on the Formatting menu bar, and all styles can be created or modified using the Styles window.

Styles can be stored in either of two ways. Embedded styles are created and stored for use in one topic at a time. Style sheets store many styles in a central project folder and can be used by any topic in the project. If you need to make changes as your project progresses, you can change one style sheet, and every topic will automatically reflect that change. Both embedded styles and style sheet styles will be available in the Styles menu on the Formatting menu bar, and both types can be created or modified using the Styles window.

Choosing Formats from the Style Sheet

To apply an existing embedded style or style sheet style to text in your topic, follow these steps:

1. Open the topic in the WYSIWYG tab in the right pane.
2. Select the text you'd like to format.
3. To change the style of the selected text, click the down arrow next to the style drop-down menu to display the available styles. Each style name is displayed in its font, size, and text style. Icons on the right of the drop-down menu display the paragraph formatting, if any, and symbol indicating whether the style is paragraph formatting (¶) or character formatting (∂), as shown in Figure 6-16.

Figure 6-16: Displaying available formatting options with the Style menu

4. Click the format you want to use for the selected text. The text appears in the new format on the WYSIWYG tab.

NOTE: *If you change one of the embedded styles or a format on the style sheet, as described in the next section, all text of that style will reflect the changes you make. However, style sheet changes will not take effect on text that you manually changed with menu bar icons or formatting windows.*

Changing Defaults in an Embedded Style or Style Sheet

RoboHelp starts every project with the default style sheet that specifies the character and paragraph formatting for the project. You can change these defaults for current styles or add new styles with the Styles window. The Styles window lets you change or create both embedded styles and style sheets.

To create or change a default format, follow these steps:

1. If you are planning to change an embedded style that will only be available in one topic, display that topic in the WYSIWYG Editor.

2. Display the Styles window, as shown in Figure 6-17, in one of two ways:

    ■ From the **Format** menu, choose **Styles**.

    ■ From the list of folders on the left-hand pane, click the **Styles** folder. All style sheets associated with the project appear in the Styles folder with an extension of .css. Double-click the name of the style sheet.

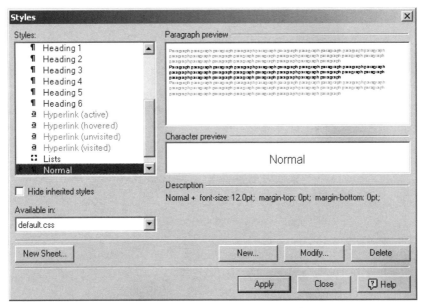

Figure 6-17: Displaying the Styles window to change default formats

3. The Styles window lists all of the styles available to the current topic, both from the style sheet and the embedded styles, if any. Next to each style name is a symbol indicating whether the style is paragraph formatting (¶), character formatting (ª), or system defaults (⁚⁚). The system defaults also start out in a lighter color gray than the rest of the styles in the list to indicate that they are system defaults not set by the current style sheet. RoboHelp calls these *inherited* styles. You can't create new system default styles, but you can modify them. When you modify them, they'll change to the same dark color as the others to indicate that they are now customized for your topic or project.

    To see what any of the existing styles look like, click the style name. The two preview boxes will display sample text in the selected style.

4. Click either the **New** or the **Modify** button. Since creating a new style and modifying existing styles require almost the same steps, the New Style and Modify Style windows are almost the same. The title indicates which window you're displaying, and the Modify Style window does not allow you to change the style name or type. The example in Figure 6-18 shows the New Style window.

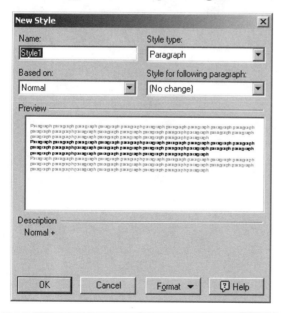

Figure 6-18: Using the New Style and Modify Style windows to change style defaults

5. If you're creating a new style, complete the following information. If you're modifying an existing style, these boxes will display the current style's information, and you won't be able to change it.

    ■   **Style Name:** Use something descriptive, so you'll be able to identify it easily later. For example, you might need a style called "Boxed Text."

NOTE: *The style name cannot have any spaces and cannot begin with a number. In addition, as of publication, Internet Explorer is the only web browser that will properly display styles with numbers or special characters like an underline. If you aren't sure which viewer your users will have, it's best to stick to all letters for style names.*

- **Based On:** If your style is exactly like an existing style, with just one or two changes, you don't have to respecify all the elements of the existing style. Simply choose the style from the list, and the style you're creating or modifying will automatically use all of the "based on" style's formatting. For example, the style "Boxed Text" may use the same character formatting as normal text, but add a border around it.

- **Style Type:** Choose either Paragraph or Character from the drop-down menu.

6. Click the **Modify** button to display the Format options menu, as shown in Figure 6-19. For example, to place a box around the text for the "Boxed Text" style, choose **Borders and Shading** from the Format options menu.

7. Enter the new formatting parameters in the Format window for the option you chose. These windows are the same windows you used when specifying format options from the menu bar. For example, see "Using the Borders and Shading Window" section earlier in this chapter to place a box around the text for the Boxed Text style. When finished, click **OK** to close the Format window and return to the Styles window.

8. The Preview pane in the Styles window displays the changes you've made to the style.

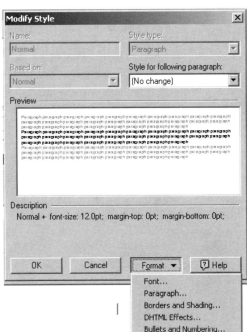

Figure 6-19: Choosing the formatting you want to modify

The changes are also displayed in text format in the Description pane of the Styles window. Once the style looks the way you want it to, specify the location where you want this new style stored in one of two ways:

- To create an embedded style, choose the topic name from the Available in drop-down menu.

■ To create a new style in the current style sheet, choose the style sheet name from the Available in drop-down menu.

9. Click **Apply** to apply your changes to the new style, and save the information to the topic or style sheet.

Formatting Topic Pages

In addition to formatting the text and paragraphs, you can also specify formatting for an entire topic. Topic formatting includes borders around the edge of the topic window, shading behind the topic, and headers and footers.

Specifying Topic Borders and Shading

Like the Borders and Shading window for paragraphs, the Borders and Shading window for topics lets you specify the style, color, and width of lines around the entire topic page, as well as the color behind the text and images on the page. In addition, you can set a padding value for the page to specify the amount of space between the topic content and the edge of the topic screen. For all border and shading formatting, a preview window displays a sample that reflects the formatting as you choose it.

To set the borders using the Borders and Shading window, follow these steps:

1. Open the topic in the WYSIWYG tab in the right pane.

2. From the Format window, select **Topic Borders and Shading** to display the Borders and Shading window. This Borders and Shading window is the same as the Borders and Shading window you used to define paragraph formatting. However, when you set parameters in the Topic Borders and Shading window, they'll apply to the whole topic, not just one paragraph.

3. Click the **Borders** tab to display border options or **Shading** to display the shading options, as shown in Figure 6-20.

4. Choose a Fill color from the Color palette, or specify an image that you want to place behind the paragraph. Make sure that the image you choose is fairly plain and light. Dark or busy images make it difficult to read the text.

5. When finished, click **OK** to close the Borders and Shading window and display your changes in the WYSIWYG pane.

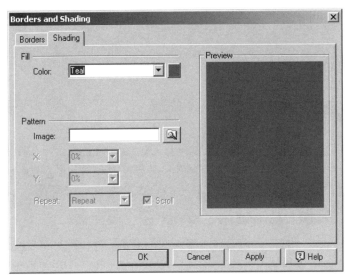

Figure 6-20: Using the Shading tab to put color or pattern behind the topic text and images

6. Click the **View** icon to display the topic as it will appear in the final help project. Figure 6-21 shows a topic with a pattern called sunset.gif as the topic shading. This is the same image used in the paragraph formatting example back in Figure 6-15. Notice that with topic shading, the image fills the whole page, not just the space behind a single paragraph. Topic shading does not cover paragraph shading, shown here as silver behind the heading paragraph, but it does appear behind text that has "transparent" shading (the default).

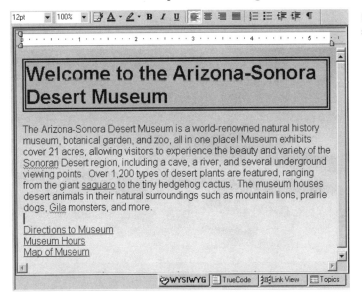

Figure 6-21: Paragraph shading

Using Headers and Footers

Headers contain the text, images, and other elements that appear at the top of each topic. Footers appear at the bottom. Headers and footers can include all of the formatting and elements that the rest of the topic has (such as colors, borders, images, or dynamic HTML). You cannot include text popups in headers or footers.

Headers and footers are usually part of a topic template, described in Chapter 10, "Maintaining Consistency with Templates and Skins." However, you may have a topic that requires a unique header or footer. You can either create a new header or footer from scratch for any topic or you can start with information from a template and customize it for the topic.

Creating and Editing Headers and Footers

To create a new header or footer for a single topic, follow these steps:

1. Open the topic in the WYSIWYG tab in the right pane.
2. On the toolbar, click either the **Header** icon (▤) or the **Footer** icon (▤) to change the focus of the display to the header or footer. The header or footer appears as a text box surrounded by dashed, gray lines. The rest of the topic will be temporarily grayed out.
3. Enter the information you want to include into the header or footer box. Figure 6-22 shows a sample header that includes text and an image. While the header is active, the text in the body of the topic is gray.

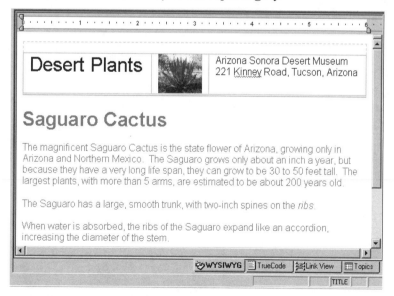

Figure 6-22: Clicking the Header icon to display header images

4. Click outside the header/footer to return focus to the body of the topic (or click the **Body** icon (▤) on the toolbar). This returns the focus of the screen to the main topic. The header and footer text is grayed out, and any images you may have in the header or footer will be displayed as boxes with the word [image] in them.

5. Click **Save** to save your changes. If the displayed header or footer was created and stored in a template, a window will be displayed, as shown in Figure 6-23.

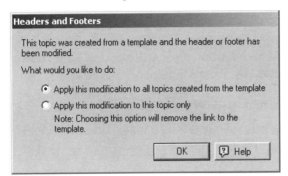

Figure 6-23: Saving template changes

6. Choose the first option to change all other topics that use the current template. Choose the second option to disassociate the current topic from the template. Template changes will no longer affect this topic. Click **OK** to close the Headers and Footers window and save the topic.

Summary

This chapter covered the basics of formatting text to make it look the way you want it to. It discussed using the formatting icons and the formatting windows to modify characters and formats and described how to create font sets. This chapter also discussed using style sheets to automate formatting. The last section described how to format topics by adding borders, shading, and headers and footers.

In the next chapter, you'll learn how to format information into bulleted and numbered lists and how to create and format tables.

Chapter 7

Using Lists and Tables

This chapter describes several ways to display text information other than paragraphs. You'll learn how to use bulleted and numbered lists, and how (and when) to create indented lists. You'll learn ways to format your lists including how to create your own custom bullets. Then you'll see how to create and modify tables to organize information.

Bulleted and Numbered Lists

Lists provide very useful ways to organize information so it clearly stands out from other text on the page. RoboHelp lets you create two types of lists, bulleted and numbered. A bulleted list is a list where each item is preceded by a bullet or other small icon. There is usually no particular order to a bulleted list. A numbered list implies that the order of the items is important. Each item in the list is numbered, as in step-by-step procedures.

For either type of list, you can specify nesting, which is a way to build a list within a list. For example, if step 3 in a numbered list has three components, you could create a bulleted list within list item number three, as follows:

1. Decide what kind of list you want to create.
2. Type your list items.
3. Format your list. There are several ways to do this:
   - Use the icons.
   - Use the Format window.
   - Create and apply styles.
4. To undo a list, click the list icon to remove bullets or numbering.

When nesting lists within lists, you can use either the indenting icons or the Paragraph Format window.

Creating Bulleted Lists

There are three ways to create bulleted lists. Choose the method that best
applies to each situation.

Table 7-1: Methods for creating bulleted lists

Method	Type of bullet
Bulleted List icon	Quick, simple, round, filled bullets
Bulleted List Format window	A different type of bullet, such as a square, an unfilled circle, or custom bullet icons
Bullets and Numbering styles	Customized bullets that you want to use throughout your project or that have special character or paragraph formatting. See "Creating a Reusable List Style" later in this chapter.

Creating Bulleted Lists with the Menu Bar Icons

If you use the menu bar icons to create a bulleted list, the bullets will default to
the solid round bullet. If you're adding a new list item to an existing bulleted list,
the default bullet will be the same as the existing ones around it. The bullet type
can be changed at any time using the Bullets and Numbering Format window, as
described in the following section.

To create a bulleted list using the menu bar icons, follow these steps:

1. Highlight the text you want to format. Each paragraph will be considered one
    bullet point.

2. Click the **Bulleted List** icon (:≡). The selected paragraph is indented and pre-
    ceded by a round, filled circle as shown in Figure 7-1.

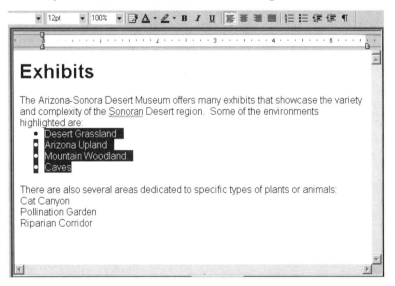

Figure 7-1:
Using the
Bulleted List icon
for round, filled
circles

3. The Bulleted List icon automatically indents the selected paragraphs by one indent level (approximately ½ inch). To move the selected text back flush with the rest of the text, click the **Decrease Indent** icon ( ). If you want to move some or all of the bullets to the next indent level (farther away from the left margin) click the **Increase Indent** icon ( ).

4. To remove the bullets and take away the indentation, click the **Bulleted List** icon again.

Creating or Modifying Bulleted Lists with the Bulleted List Format Window

You can format an existing bulleted list or create a new bulleted list with the Bulleted List Format window. In addition to the round filled circle, you can choose from several other types of bullets or specify any graphic image you want to use for a bullet.

NOTE: *Be careful when using images for bullets. Remember that the result will be quite small, and complex graphics may not display in all the detail you want. It's best to stick with something very simple.*

To format a bulleted list, follow these steps:

1. Highlight the text you want to format.

2. From the **Format** menu, select **Bullets and Numbering**. The Bullets and Numbering dialog opens.

3. Click the **Bulleted** tab to display the bullets format pane, as shown in Figure 7-2.

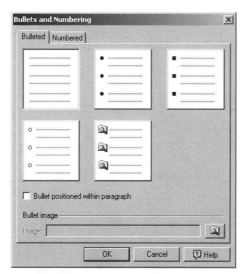

Figure 7-2: Choosing a bullet type

4. Click the thumbnail image that represents the type of bullet symbol you want to use. The upper-left thumbnail has no bullets and can be used to remove bullets from text. Click **OK** after selecting the desired bullet image or click the lower-middle image to specify a graphic file to use for custom bullets.

5. If you are specifying a custom bullet image, type the name of the graphic file in the **Image** box or use the Browse button to point to the filename. Images for bullets must be in .gif format and small enough to fit on the text line. This will vary with the size of text you want to use. Click **OK** to add the specified image to your bullet formats. The image will also be copied to your Baggage Files folder in Project Manager.

 TIP: *You may use any of the images that come with RoboHelp HTML for bullets by browsing to the RoboHelp HTML folder and then to \gallery\images\bullets.*

6. Click **View** to see what the bullets will look like in the finished project. The two bulleted lists shown in Figure 7-3 use 12-point text with bullet images that are approximately 16x16 pixels.

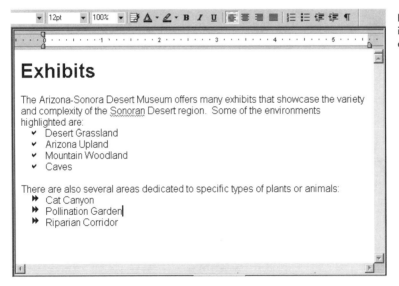

Figure 7-3: Using image files for custom bullets

Creating Numbered Lists

There are three ways to create numbered lists. Choose the method that best applies to each situation.

Table 7-2: Methods for creating numbered lists

Method	Type of numbered list
Numbered List icon	Quick, simple, numbered list starting with number 1 in the default font of the selected paragraphs
Numbered List Format window	A different type of numbering, such as Roman numerals or letters instead of numbers
Bullets and Numbering styles	Customized lists that you want to use throughout your project or that have special character or paragraph formatting. See "Creating a Reusable List Style" later in this chapter.

Creating Numbered Lists with the Menu Bar Icons

If you use the menu bar icons to create a numbered list, the numbers will default to regular Arabic numbers (1, 2, 3, etc.) in the same font as the paragraph text. Each list will start with the number 1. The numbering format can be changed at any time using the Bullets and Numbering Format window, as described in the following section.

To create a numbered list using the menu bar icons, follow these steps:

1. Highlight the text you want to format. Each paragraph will be considered one list item and will get its own number.

2. Click the **Numbered List** icon (⅓☰). The selected paragraph is indented and numbered, as shown in Figure 7-4.

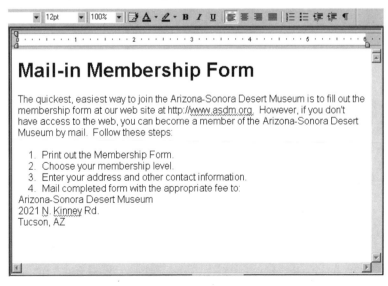

Figure 7-4: Using the Numbered List icon for Arabic numerals starting with 1

3. The Numbered List icon automatically indents the selected paragraphs by one indent level (approximately ½ inch). To move the selected text back flush with the rest of the text, click the **Decrease Indent** icon ( ). If you want to move some or all of the list items to the next indent level (farther away from the left margin) click the **Increase Indent** icon ( ).

4. To remove the numbers and take away the indentation, click the **Numbered List** icon again.

Creating or Modifying Numbered Lists with the Numbered List Format Window

You can format an existing numbered list or create a new numbered list with the Numbered List Format window. In addition to Arabic numerals, you can choose from several other types of numbering. You can also specify a starting number for lists that don't start with 1.

To format a numbered list, follow these steps:

1. Highlight the text you want to format.

2. From the **Format** menu, select **Bullets and Numbering**. The Bullets and Numbering dialog opens.

3. Click the **Numbered** tab to display the numbered format pane, as shown in Figure 7-5.

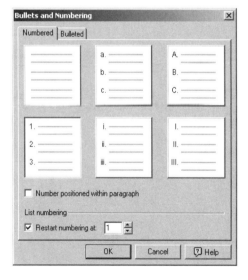

Figure 7-5: Choosing a numbering type

4. Click the thumbnail image that represents the type of numbering you want to use. The upper-left thumbnail has no numbers and can be used to remove numbering from text.

5. If you want the list to start with a number other than 1 (or A or I or i), click the **Restart numbering at** box to activate the text box next to it. Enter the number

for the first bullet. For example, if you have a procedure that spans several topics, you may want to put steps 1 through 5 in one topic and steps 6 through 10 in another. The list on the second topic would begin with number 6. If you are using letters instead of numbers, enter the numerical equivalent for the start letter. For example, entering 6 would start the list with the letter F.

6. Click **OK** to close the Bullets and Numbering window and return to the WYSIWYG pane. Click **View** to see what the numbering will look like in the finished project.

Creating a Reusable List Style

You can use the menu bar icons or the Format window to specify bulleted and numbered lists. However, if you are going to use the same formatting for many lists throughout your project, you'll want to create a style for the list and store it in the style sheet. That way, you only have to set the formatting once.

To create a list style, use the Styles window as follows:

1. Display the Styles window, as shown in Figure 7-6, in one of two ways:

   ■ From the **Format** menu, choose **Styles**.

   ■ From the list of folders on the left-hand pane, click the **Styles** folder, and then double-click the name of the style sheet. All style sheets associated with the project appear in the Styles folder with an extension of .css.

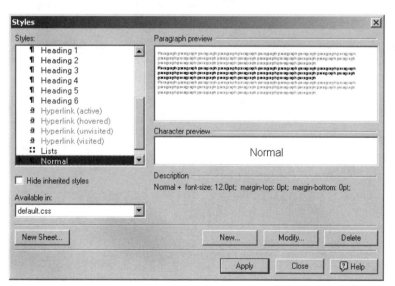

Figure 7-6:
Displaying the Styles window to change list formats

2. Click the **New** button to display the New Style window, as shown in Figure 7-7.

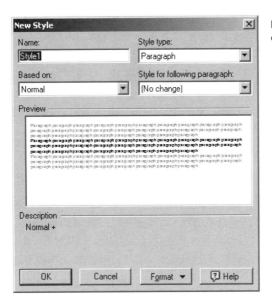

Figure 7-7: Using the New Style window to create a list style

3. Enter a name for the style. Make it a descriptive name that will clearly identify the style later. A name like "checkmarks" is more descriptive and easier to use than a name like "bullets2."

NOTE: *The style name cannot have any spaces or begin with a number. In addition, as of publication, Internet Explorer is the only web browser that will properly display styles with numbers or special characters like an underline. If you aren't sure which viewer your users will have, it's best to stick to all letters for style names.*

4. Make sure that the style type is Paragraph. Font formatting will not allow you to specify bullets or numbering.

5. Click the **Format** button and choose **Bullets and Numbering** to display the Bullets and Numbering window. This is the same window described in earlier sections of this chapter.

6. Choose the list formatting you want for the style. For example, to create the list style "checkmarks," you would enter the image name in the Bulleted tab, as shown in Figure 7-8.

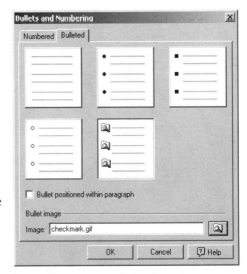

Figure 7-8: Defining the list formatting

7. Click **OK** to close the Bullets and Numbering window. The specified formatting appears in the New Style window's Preview and Description areas.

8. Click **OK** to close the New Style window. The new style will now be displayed in the Styles drop-down menu.

Tables

Tables are used throughout HTML projects to format, organize, and display information. In addition to classic table information, such as in tables in this book, topic pages can use tables as a layout tool. Because each user may have a different browser that displays using different sized windows, you cannot always be certain how your HTML project will appear. Tables give you more control over the placement of various elements. You can place anything into a table—text, links, graphics, and even other tables.

Each table is made up of cells arranged in rows and columns. You can control the size of each cell or let RoboHelp HTML determine the size for you based on the information in the cell. You can also control how the borders of each cell display and how the text will be aligned, as well as specify colors or shading.

Creating Tables

In RoboHelp HTML, you must create an empty table first and then fill it with text or images. The Insert Table menu bar icon lets you quickly insert a basic table up to four rows by five columns. You can use the other table icons to add rows or columns, change cell size, or format the table borders. You can also create and format the table with the Table menu, which gives you more options and a variety of predefined table formats from which to choose.

Creating Tables with the Menu Bar Icon

To insert a table using the menu bar icon, follow these steps:

1. Place the cursor in the topic where you want to add the table.

2. Click the **Insert Table** icon (▦) to display the table grid, as shown in Figure 7-9 on the following page.

3. Drag the cursor to highlight the number of rows (horizontally) and columns (vertically) you want in the finished table. The example in Figure 7-9 will create a table that has three rows and four columns. The maximum table size you can create with the Insert Table icon has four rows and five columns. If you need a larger table, you can add rows or columns later with either the menu bar icons or the Table menu.

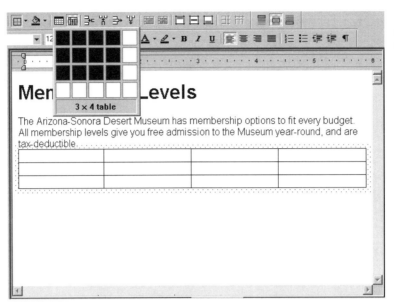

Figure 7-9: Using the Insert Table icon to create a table

4. When you have the correct number of rows and columns selected, click in the highlighted table grid. An empty table of the size you specified will display in the WYSIWYG pane, as shown in Figure 7-10. The default table makes all the rows the same height and all the columns the same width. The default border will be a one-pixel solid line around each cell. You can change the table formatting at any time, as described in the "Working with Rows and Columns"and "Adding Table Borders" sections later in this chapter.

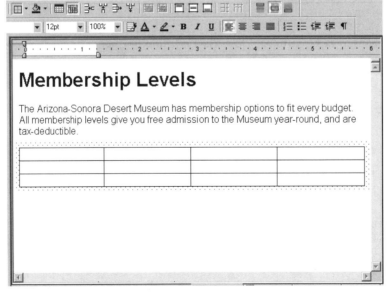

Figure 7-10: The default table

5. Enter content (such as text, images, or links) into each cell in the table. You can use the Tab key to move from one cell to the next, or you can click in a cell and then type. Either way, the cell widths will remain the same, wrapping the text as necessary to fit in the cell. The row heights will expand to accommodate the text you enter, as shown in Figure 7-11.

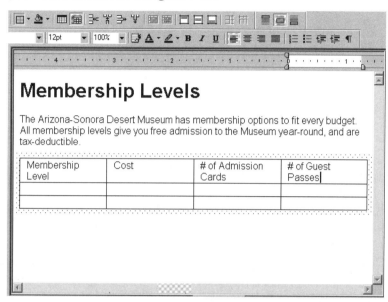

Figure 7-11:
Entering text in the table cells

 TIP: *To quickly add another row while entering text into a table, place the cursor in the bottom right-hand cell, and then press the Tab key. A row identical to the last row will be added at the end of the table.*

6. Click anywhere outside of the table to continue editing the rest of the topic.

Creating Tables with the Table Menu

To insert a table using the Table menu, follow these steps:

1. Place the cursor in the topic where you want to add the table.

2. From the **Table** menu, select **Insert** and then **Table**. The Insert Table window opens, as shown in Figure 7-12.

3. The box on the left displays the available predefined table formats. Click a format name to display the format in the Preview window. There are formats that have simple underlines and ones that use shading to highlight heading rows. Use the scroll bar to the right of the format list to display additional formats. If none of the predefined formats fit your needs, you can change the table formatting at any time, as described in the "Working with Rows and Columns" and "Adding Table Borders" sections later in this chapter.

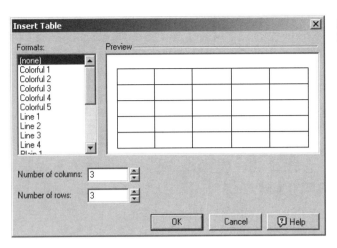

Figure 7-12: Displaying the Insert Table window

4. Specify the number of columns and rows you want in the table using the **Number of columns** and **Number of rows** boxes. You can specify up to ten columns and 100 rows in the Insert Table window. If you need more rows or columns, you can add them later with the Add Rows or Add Columns icons.

TIP: *Keep your user's screen size limitations in mind. Many users may not be able to display large tables on their screens.*

5. Click **OK** to close the Insert Table window and display the table in the WYSIWYG pane.

6. Enter content (such as text, images, or links) into each cell in the table. You can use the Tab key to move from one cell to the next, or you can click in a cell and then type. Either way, the cell widths will remain the same, wrapping the text as necessary to fit in the cell. The row heights will expand to accommodate the text you enter, as shown in Figure 7-13.

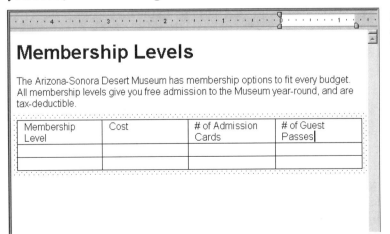

Figure 7-13: Adding text to the new table

TIP: *To quickly add another row while entering text into a table, place the cursor in the bottom right-hand cell and then press the Tab key. A row identical to the last row will be added at the end of the table.*

7. Click anywhere outside of the table to continue editing the rest of the topic.

Formatting Tables

Once you've created a table, you can make changes to the table rows, columns, borders, shading, and alignment. You can also adjust the position of text within each cell and the position of table captions.

Working with Rows and Columns

As with other types of formatting, most table functions can be accessed either through the menu bar icons or the Table menu options. In addition, many of the table functions are also available in the right-click menu. No matter which method you use to access a function, it works the same way.

Inserting Rows and Columns

To insert columns, use any of the following methods:

Table 7-3: Adding columns

Column location	Method	Result
Click in any cell, or highlight any cell or set of cells.	From the Table menu, choose Insert and then Column	The new column will be inserted to the left of the selected cell, moving existing columns to the right. If you highlighted cells in more than one column, that number of columns will be added.
Click in any cell, or highlight any cell or set of cells.	Click the Insert Column icon ( ).	The new column will be inserted to the left of the selected cell, moving existing columns to the right. If you highlighted cells in more than one column, that number of columns will be added.
Highlight one or more entire columns.	Click the right mouse button and choose Insert Column.	The new column will be inserted to the left of the selected column, moving existing columns to the right. If you highlighted more than one column, that number of columns will be added.

To add rows, use any of the following methods:

Table 7-4: Adding rows

Row location	Method	Result
Click in any cell, or highlight any cell or set of cells.	From the Table menu, choose Insert and then Row.	The new row will be inserted above the selected cell, moving existing rows down. If you highlighted cells in more than one row, that number of rows will be added.
Click in any cell, or highlight any cell or set of cells.	Click the Insert Row icon (⊒+ᴄ).	The new row will be inserted above the selected cell, moving existing rows down. If you highlighted cells in more than one row, that number of rows will be added.
Highlight one or more entire rows.	Click the right mouse button and then choose Insert Row.	The new row will be inserted above the selected row, moving existing rows down. If you highlighted more than one row, that number of rows will be added.

Deleting Rows and Columns

If you need to remove or delete rows or columns from the table, you can use either the right mouse button menu or the Table menu.

 NOTE: *If you highlight a column and press the Delete key, you will delete only the contents of the highlighted cells. The empty rows or columns will remain in the table. You must use one of the methods in Table 7-5 to delete rows or columns.*

 CAUTION: *When you delete table cells, you also delete the content in the cells, if any. If you have text or links you want to save, copy and paste them outside of the table or into other cells before deleting table rows or columns.*

To delete rows or columns from a table or an entire table, use any of the following methods:

Table 7-5: Deleting tables, rows, and columns

Delete	Specify the location	Methods
One or more columns	Click anywhere in the column.	From the Table menu, choose Delete then Column OR Click the Delete Column icon (⟂).
One or more columns	Highlight the entire column or set of columns.	Click the right mouse button and then choose Delete Column.
One or more rows	Click anywhere in the row.	From the Table menu, choose Delete and then Row.

To delete this	Specify the location	Use one of these methods
		OR Click the Delete Row icon (⮞).
One or more rows	Highlight the entire row or set of rows.	Click the right mouse button and choose Delete Row.
The whole table	Click anywhere in the table.	From the Table menu, choose Delete and then Table.
The whole table	Click anywhere on the perimeter of the table to select the whole table.	From the Table menu, choose Delete and then Table. OR Click the right mouse button and choose Delete Table.

Merging Rows and Columns

Sometimes simply adding or deleting entire rows or columns won't give you the table you want. For example, you may want to have one header cell with two separate columns beneath it. To create this effect in RoboHelp HTML, create two columns, and then merge the top row cells together. The cell contents will be combined as if it was entered into a single cell.

To merge cells together, follow these steps:

1. Select the cells by clicking in the first cell and dragging the mouse across the other cells you want to work with. The cells must be adjacent to each other in order to merge them. The selected cells will be highlighted, as shown in Figure 7-14.

2. Choose the Merge command using one of the following methods:

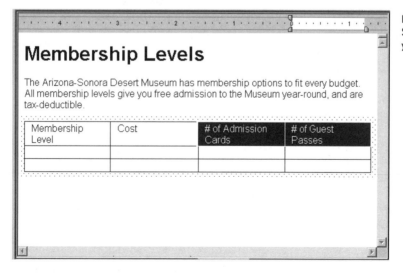

Figure 7-14: Selecting the cells you want to merge

- Click the **Merge Cells** icon (▦).
- From the **Table** menu, choose **Merge Cells**.
- Click the right mouse button and choose **Merge Cells**.

The content of the cells will be treated like a single cell, as shown in Figure 7-15.

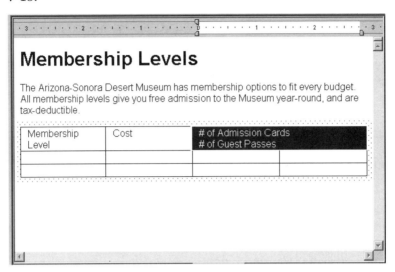

Figure 7-15:
Merging two cells together for complex tables

3. If you decide you don't like the merged cells, you can undo the merge with the Split Cells command. Click anywhere in a merged cell, and then use one of the following methods:

- Click the **Split Cells** icon (▦).
- From the **Table** menu, choose **Split Cells**.
- Click the right mouse button and choose **Split Cells**.

NOTE: *When you split merged cells, the contents of the merged cells will be stored in the first cell, not redistributed among the split cells. You'll have to cut and paste to move the text, images, or links to where you want them.*

Changing Row and Column Size

When you first create a table, RoboHelp HTML automatically makes all of the columns the same width and sets the row heights to adjust for the content you add to them. You can change these defaults using the click and drag feature, the cell distribution feature, or the Autofit feature, or by specifying exact measurements.

Using Click and Drag

The easiest way to change column width or cell height is to click on the line you want to move and drag it to a new location. You'll know when you've clicked on the right place because the cursor will change to a line movement shape (either ╬ or ╪).

Using Evenly Distributed Spacing

RoboHelp HTML can automatically adjust the cells so that they are all the same height or width. This feature is only available through the right-click menu or the menu bar icons.

To make rows the same height, follow these steps:

1. Highlight cells in the rows you want to distribute. You don't have to select the whole row or a whole column, but you must select cells in at least two rows.

2. To adjust the rows to equal widths, do one of the following:

   ▪ Click the right mouse button and choose **Distribute Rows Evenly.**

   ▪ Click the **Distribute Rows** icon (⊟).

To make columns the same width, follow these steps:

1. Highlight cells in the columns you want to distribute. You don't have to select the whole column or a whole row, but you must select cells in at least two columns.

2. To adjust the columns to equal widths, do one of the following:

   ▪ Click the right mouse button and choose **Distribute Columns Evenly.**

   ▪ Click the **Distribute Columns** icon (⊞).

Using Autofit

The Autofit feature changes the size of the table and adjusts the row height or column width.

Table 7-6: Autofit options

Option	Effects
Autofit to Contents	Eliminates extra space within cells to make the columns and rows as small as possible given the current contents
Autofit to Window	Changes the height and width of the table to fill the display window
Fixed Column Width	Stores the current column widths, and then always displays the table with those dimensions regardless of the table contents or window size

To resize a table using the Autofit feature, follow these steps:

1. Click anywhere in the table to select it.

2. Display the Autofit options in one of the following ways:

   ▪ Click the right mouse button and choose **Autofit.**

   ▪ From the **Table** menu and choose **Autofit.**

3. Choose one of the Autofit options (Autofit to Contents, Autofit to Window, or Fixed Column Width).

Specifying Exact Measurements

If you need to specify exact measurements for table cells, use the Table Properties windows. These will allow you to set the row height and column width in any of the following units:

Table 7-7: Units of measurement

Type of measurement	Unit
pixels	px
percentages of window width	%
points	pt
picas	pc
centimeters	cm
millimeters	mm
inches	in
em spaces	em

To set the exact row height or column width, follow these steps:

1. Click anywhere in the table to select it.

2. Display the Table Properties window using either of the following methods:

    ■ Click the right mouse button and choose **Table Properties**.

    ■ From the **Table** menu, choose **Table Properties**.

3. Click the **Row** or **Column** tab to display the appropriate window. Both of these windows are the same except for the word Row or Column in the title bar and on the buttons, and both work the same way. Figure 7-16 shows the Row tab of the Table Properties window.

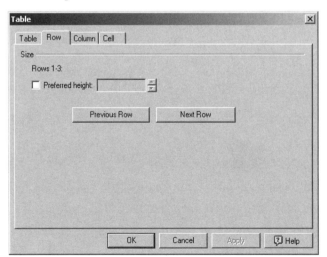

Figure 7-16: Entering a dimension for row height

4. At the top of the window is a text label that indicates which row or column you are working with. This may show a range of rows or columns if you selected more than one before opening the Table Properties window. Enter a number and the units for the measurement you want to specify. In this example, the row height will be 1 inch. If you don't specify a unit, RoboHelp HTML will assume the unit of pixels, which may not give you the results you want.

5. Click the **Previous** or **Next** button to enter measurements for other rows or columns.

6. Click **Apply** when you are done and **OK** to close the Table Properties window.

Adding Table Borders

Like the Borders commands for paragraphs and topics, you can use either the menu bar icons or the Borders and Shading window to specify the style, color, and width of lines around each cell and the entire table. The menu bar icons are quick and easy; the Borders and Shading window lets you preview a sample of the borders before you apply them.

Using the Menu Bar Icons to Specify Table Borders

You can use the same menu bar icons to place borders around table cells or entire tables as you used to place borders around paragraphs. Follow these steps:

1. Select the cells around which you want to place the border.

2. Set the border parameters using the menu bar icons.

CAUTION: *Some border styles are created by combining the specified border color with black to create effects such as a ridge or groove. If your border color is set to black, these border styles will appear as solid black lines. To see the special effects, choose a color other than black for the border line color.*

Table 7-8: The Border Style icons

Border icon	Sets this parameter
Solid ▾	Chooses the border style. Available styles are: Solid, Inset, Ridge, Groove, Double, Outset
	Chooses the color for the border line. Click the line color icon to display the color palette.
1px ▾	Chooses the width, in pixels, for the border line. If you've chosen a border style other than solid, you must specify a line width that is wide enough for the effect (at least 3 pixels).

3. To add a border around the cell or cells, click the pull-down menu next to the Border icon (▦) to display the border options, as shown in Figure 7-17.

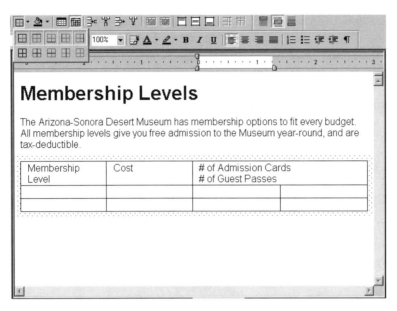

Figure 7-17:
Choosing borders
after setting the
border parameters

4. Click the box that corresponds to the areas where you want to place a border. The darker lines on the icon indicate where the borders will be placed relative to the current selection. The borders will appear as you specify around the cells. The bottom-right icon, with no dark lines, can be used to erase any borders you may have entered.

TIP: *Once you've selected all border parameters, including placement, the Border icon changes to reflect your current choices. To quickly place the current border choices around a paragraph, click the Bicon (not the drop-down menu arrow).*

Using the Borders Window to Specify Table Borders

Like the Border and Shading icons, the Borders and Shading window lets you specify the style, color, and width of lines around each cell, as well as the color behind the text. In addition, you can set a padding value. Padding is the amount of space between the cell content and the borders. For all border and shading formatting, a preview window displays a sample table that reflects the formatting as you choose it.

To set the borders using the Borders and Shading window, follow these steps:

1. Highlight the cells for which you are creating borders. This can be one cell, a row or column, or an entire table.

2. Display the Borders and Shading window in one of the following ways:

   ■ From the **Format** menu, choose **Borders and Shading**.

■ From the **Table** menu, choose **Table Properties**, then click either the **Cell Borders** or **Table Borders** button. Both buttons display the same window.

■ Click the right mouse button and choose **Borders and Shading**.

3. Click the **Borders** tab to display border options, as shown in Figure 7-18.

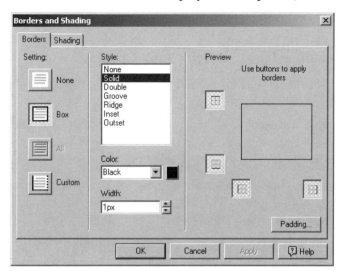

Figure 7-18: Specifying border options with the Borders and Shading window

4. Select the formatting you want for the selected cells. As you enter values in each of the boxes, the Preview pane displays a sample table in the new format.

5. Click the **Padding** button to display the Padding window, as shown in Figure 7-19. The gray box in the Preview area represents the table contents; the blue area (the dark area to the left and top) represents the specified padding space.

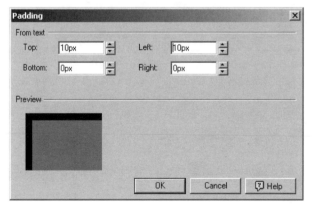

Figure 7-19: Specifying the distance between cell content and borders with padding

6. Enter measurements for the padding. The default unit is pixels, but you can specify whatever units you want. Click **OK** to close the Padding window.

7. Once you are satisfied with the changes, click **OK** to close the Borders and Shading window and display the new formats.

Adding Table Shading

Shading is the color that fills each cell behind the text or images. It is sometimes called the fill color. This is particularly useful to distinguish between heading rows and the rest of the table or to highlight a specific area of a table. To set the shading, you can use either the menu bar icon or the Borders and Shading window.

Using the Menu Bar Icon to Specify Table Shading

To change the shading (the color behind the content of the cell), follow these steps:

1. Highlight the cells you want to shade. You can click and drag to select any set of adjacent cells.
2. Click the **Fill Color** icon (🖫) to display the Color palette.
3. Choose the color for the cell background. This will override any character highlighting you may have entered. The example in Figure 7-20 shows a table where the top row has silver shading.

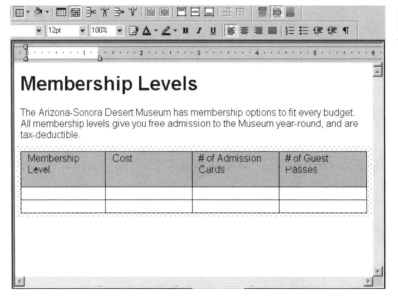

Figure 7-20: Placing color behind the selected cells

Using the Borders and Shading Window to Set Table Shading

To set the shading using the Borders and Shading window, follow these steps:

1. Highlight the cells you want to shade. You can click and drag to select any set of adjacent cells.

2. Display the Borders and Shading window in one of the following ways:

   ▪ From the **Format** window, select **Borders and Shading**.

   ▪ Click the right mouse button and choose **Borders and Shading**.

   ▪ From the **Table** menu, choose **Table Properties**, and then click the **Shading** button.

3. Click the **Shading** tab to display shading options, as shown in Figure 7-21.

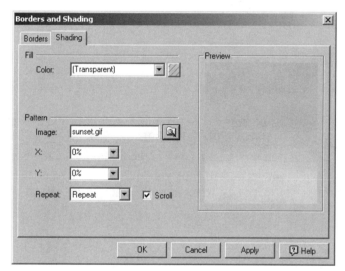

Figure 7-21: Putting color or pattern behind a cell

4. Choose a fill color from the Color palette, or specify an image that you want to place behind the paragraph. Make sure that the image you choose is fairly plain and light. Dark or busy images make it difficult to read the paragraph text.

NOTE: *When specifying an image for table cells, remember that the image will be repeated in each cell (not spread across multiple cells). This may give you an unexpected repeating pattern, depending on the size of the cells.*

5. When finished, click **OK** to close the Borders and Shading window and display your changes in the WYSIWYG pane. You can also use the preview mode to see the table shading. Figure 7-22 on the following page shows a preview window of a table that has an image behind each of the four cells in the top row.

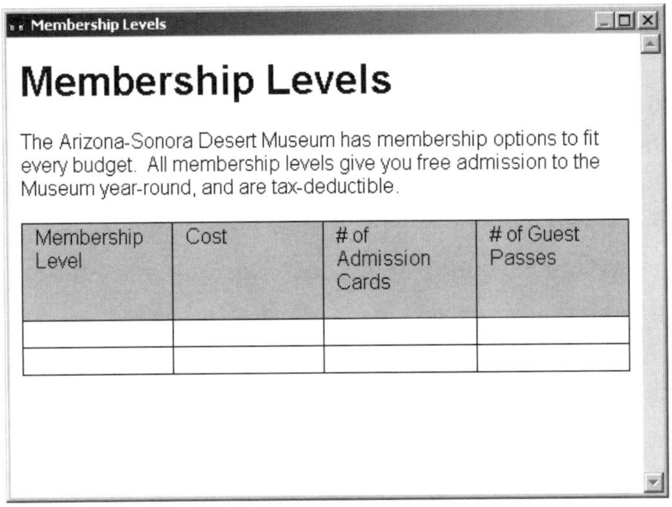

Figure 7-22: The image appears behind each cell

Summary

In this chapter, you learned how to create and format lists and the differences between bulleted and numbered lists. This chapter also discussed many ways to create tables, add, delete, and merge rows and columns, and use borders and shading. You also learned how to use images for shading or bullets.

The following chapter goes into more detail about images and graphic formatting.

Chapter 8

Adding Images and Special Effects to RoboHelp HTML Files

This chapter describes how to add images and special effects to your project and manipulate them using the RoboHelp HTML tools. You'll learn to find, import, and resize images, add special effects with Dynamic HTML, and use the Image Report. You'll also see how to add other types of effects, such as a splash screen and multimedia files.

Working with Images

Preparing Images

Before you can insert an image into a RoboHelp HTML project, the image must exist somewhere on your system. You'll also need to consider size, colors, and format before importing an image into RoboHelp HTML.

Size

Larger pictures have more detail but will take longer to display. You'll have to evaluate the trade-off between size and resolution to determine what is best for your project. When creating any form of WebHelp, remember that some users may have slower connections (and thus longer download times) than your test setup.

Colors

In general, the more colors you use, the larger your image file will be. Some formats, such as JPG, allow up to 16 million colors. However, this many colors may not be supported by every user's display configuration. If a user cannot display all of the colors in your image, his system will attempt to display the image in available colors, which may cause the image to display differently than you intended. To avoid this, it is best to limit your total number of colors to 256 or less.

Format

RoboHelp HTML allows you to insert graphics in any of the following formats:

Table 8-1: Image formats

Format	Description
GIF (Graphics Interchange Format)	Small, concise graphics with limited colors
JPEG, JPG (Joint Photographic Experts Group)	Larger than GIF, more colors, and greater resolution capability
PNG (Portable Network Graphics)	A relatively new format, similar to GIF, but may not display at all on older browsers
BMP (Windows bitmap format)	A standard in Microsoft Windows, this format may not display correctly on Macintosh-based browsers.

RoboHelp HTML comes with the ReSize tool that lets you change the size, format, and number of colors for any image. See "Changing Image Size and Format with the ReSize Tool" later in this chapter for more information. RoboHelp HTML also comes with a variety of graphics, such as lines, buttons, and bullets, stored in the Image Gallery. The Gallery includes both GIF and JPG images.

Inserting Images into Your Project

To insert an image into your project, follow these steps:

1. Place the cursor in a topic where you want the image to be.
2. Open the Image window, shown in Figure 8-1, in one of the following ways:
    - Click the **Image** icon (![icon]).
    - From the **Insert** menu, choose **Image**.

Figure 8-1: Inserting an image with the Image window

3. The Image window displays a list of the images currently used in the project. Specify the image you want to use in one of the following ways:

   ■ Click one of the displayed image names.

   ■ Use the **Browse** button (⊞) to specify an image that has not yet been used in the project. The image browser defaults to display only GIF, JPG, PNG, and BMP files.

   ■ Click the **Gallery** tab to preview and choose one of the images that comes with RoboHelp HTML. The gallery contains buttons, lines, backgrounds, and other commonly used HTML elements.

Once you've chosen an image filename, the Preview pane displays the image, as shown in Figure 8-2. If it is a large image, you may see only part of the image in the Preview pane.

4. You can edit any of the image parameters now, as you are inserting the image or at a later time. See "Editing an Image in the Image Window" later in this chapter for more information about image parameters. Or you can insert the image using the system defaults. When you've set any of the image parameters that you want to change, click **OK**.

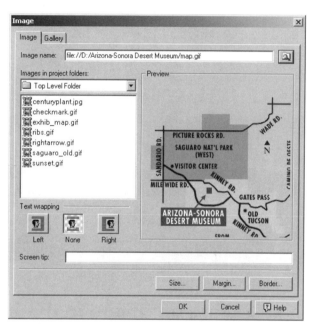

Figure 8-2: Previewing the image before inserting

5. If you chose a file from a location other than the project folder, a prompt appears asking if you want to copy the file to the project. If you choose not to copy the image, RoboHelp HTML will display the image anyway but may not be able to properly run the file, and the image may not appear in the final help project. Click OK to copy the file to the project folder. You'll see the image in the WYSIWYG window, as well as the image name in the Images folder as shown in Figure 8-3.

NOTE: *Although RoboHelp HTML will copy and display BMP and PNG format images correctly, they will not appear in the Images folder until you save the topic file.*

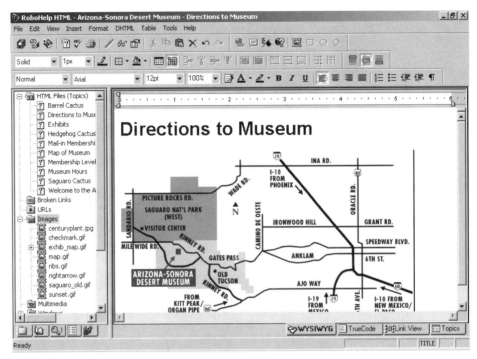

Figure 8-3: Displaying the image in WYSIWYG and the Images folder

TIP: *Once the image has been copied to the project Images folder, you can drag the image name onto the WYSIWYG pane to quickly insert the image into other topics.*

Editing an Image in the Image WIndow

RoboHelp HTML inserts images into your project topics using the original file size. However, you can use the features of the Image window to change the size that each image displays without changing the actual image. The image window also lets you specify other properties, such as the distance between an image, the text around an image, and borders around an image.

To edit image properties, follow these steps:

1. Select the image you want to work on by clicking anywhere on the image.

2. Open the Image window, as shown in Figure 8-4 on the following page, in one of the following ways:

   ■ Click the **Image** icon (🖼).

   ■ Double-click anywhere on the image.

   ■ Click the right mouse button and choose **Image Properties**.

   ■ From the **Insert** menu, choose **Image**.

3. In the Image window, set the text wrapping property by clicking on one of the three Text Wrapping icons just below the list of images. Each icon displays a sample of how the text will be placed around the image. The default is to place the image on its own line, with no text on either side (None).

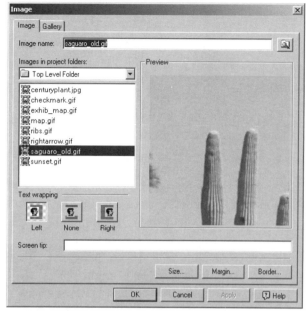

Figure 8-4: Displaying the Image window to set image properties

4. Enter an optional screen tip. The screen tip will appear when the user holds the cursor over the image. It will also display if the user has graphics turned off, which is very useful for Section 508 compliance.

5. To change the size of the displayed image, click the **Size** button to display the Size window, as shown in Figure 8-5.

Figure 8-5: Setting the image display size

6. The Size window displays the current image width and height in pixels. You can change either or both of these settings by using the up or down arrows or by typing a new dimension. If you leave the Maintain aspect ratio check box selected, any width change you make will automatically change the height to keep the same relative dimensions. Similarly, height changes will change the width dimension. If you want to change the aspect ratio, click the check box to remove the check mark. Click **OK** when you have finished setting the image display size to return to the Image properties window.

NOTE: *The Size window changes only the display of the current image, not the image size itself. A large image will still take up the same amount of disk space and download time whether you set it to display full size or use smaller dimensions. See "Changing Image Size and Format with the ReSize Tool" to change the size of the image file.*

7. To set the space between the image and the surrounding text, click the **Margin** button to display the Margins window, as shown in Figure 8-6.

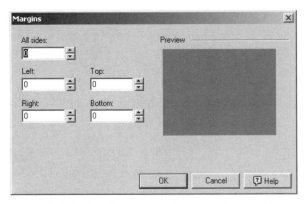

Figure 8-6: Setting the margin between the image and surrounding text

8. The Preview box on the Margins window shows a gray box representing the image, surrounded by a blue outline representing the space between the image and the surrounding text. Change the margins by either changing the All sides box to automatically set the four sides to the same dimension or by changing the Left, Right, Top, and Bottom margins individually. Click **OK** when the margins are set to return to the Image properties window.

9. To add a border around the image, click the **Border** button to display the Borders window, as shown in Figure 8-7.

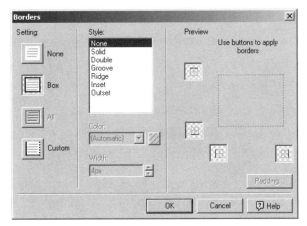

Figure 8-7: Adding borders to an image

10. The Borders window lets you specify the style, color, and width of lines around the selected image. This is the same window used for paragraph and topic borders, except the Padding button is not active. For images, the Margins window takes care of the padding function. A Preview area displays a sample of the border options as you choose them. When you've specified the border you want, click **OK** to return to the Image properties window.

11. Click **OK** to display the WYSIWYG pane with the new image parameters. You'll see the effects of the wrapping, size, margin, and border properties in the WYSIWYG window. You'll have to preview the topic to see the screen tip. The example in Figure 8-8 shows a preview of an image with left text wrapping, a double line border, margins set to 0, and a screen tip.

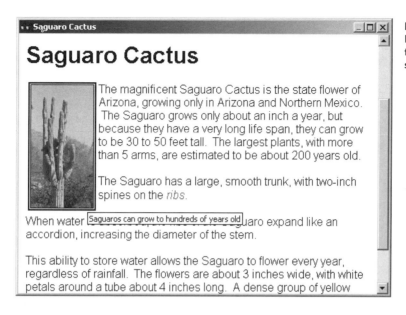

Figure 8-8:
Previewing the topic to view the screen tip

Images Report

The Images Report gives you an easy way to see which images are used by each topic. You can display the report either in order by topic or in order by image.

To view the Images Report, follow these steps:

1. From the **Tools** menu, choose **Reports** and then **Images** to display the Images Report. The report shown in Figure 8-9 displays a list of topics that use each image.

Figure 8-9:
Displaying the images in order by image name in the Images Report

2. To see a report that displays the images for each topic, choose **Topic** from the **Sort By** pull-down menu, as shown in Figure 8-10.

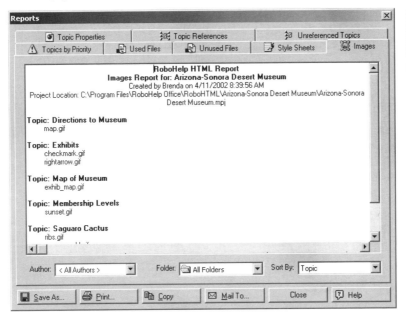

Figure 8-10: Displaying the images in order by topic in the Images Report

3. Click **Print** to send the displayed report to the default printer, or click **Copy** to copy the report to the clipboard. This is useful if you need to include an Images Report in a memo or other type of report.

4. Click **Close** to close the Reports window.

Using the RoboHelp Office Image Tools

When you are working within RoboHelp, you can modify the way that images are displayed but not the original image files themselves. RoboHelp Office comes with two tools that help you work with graphic images, as well as a gallery of image files. The Graphics Locator lets you preview images anywhere on your system and easily copy them into project files. The ReSize tool lets you change image size, format, and color depth. Although you can access these tools from within RoboHelp HTML, they run separately from the RoboHelp program.

Finding Images on Your System with the Graphics Locator Tool

When you insert images, you can use the Browse function to point to the image wherever it may be on your system. If you aren't sure where an image is or which image you want, you can use the RoboHelp HTML Graphics Locator tool to identify and copy the image. This tool will list and then let you preview images anywhere on your system. All images will be listed in order by filename, regardless of which folders they are in. For example, the list would display c:/ProgramFiles/Samples/arrow.gif next to c:/windows/desktop/arrow.gif. The preview feature allows you to see what the two files look like.

To use the Graphics Locator tool, follow these steps:

1. Select the **Tools** tab (🐾) on the left-hand pane of the RoboHelp HTML window.

2. Double-click the **Graphics Locator** icon (🖼️) to display the Graphics Locator window, as shown in Figure 8-11.

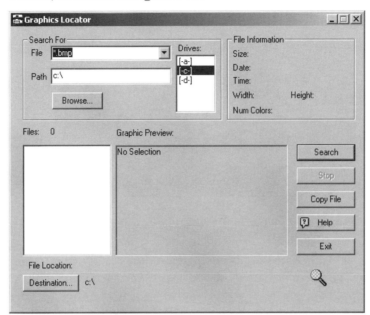

Figure 8-11: Using the Graphics Locator tool to find image files

3. Specify the type of file you are seeking by choosing from the drop-down menu on the **File** text box. You can search for single file types, such as .GIF or .JPG, or for all graphic file types. If you know the filename but not the location, you can also type the filename in the File text box.

4. Enter the name of a folder you'd like to search in, or use the **Browse** button to point to a folder.

NOTE: *While you could choose to search an entire drive, this may give you more results than you expect. The Graphics Locator is a powerful tool that will display all graphics in all specified folders, and if you search an entire drive, you may find thousands of results.*

5. Click the **Search** button. The Graphics Locator displays a list of all files that meet the search criteria in alphabetic order by filename, regardless of folder location. For example, note that the sample in Figure 8-12 shows several files named "contents.gif." There is one entry listed for each of the several files called contents.gif throughout the RoboHelp Office folders.

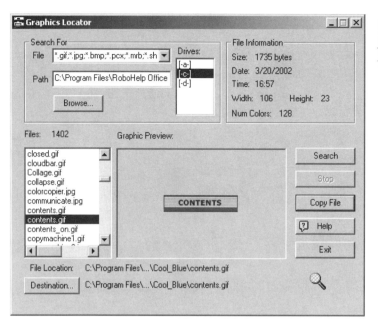

Figure 8-12:
Displaying graphic files from many folders in the Graphics Locator

6. Click the filename to display a preview of any file.

7. When the file you want to use is displayed in the Graphics Preview pane, the path name for that file is displayed beneath the preview next to the label File Location. The file information (size, dimensions, saved date, and color depth) is displayed in the upper-right corner of the Graphics Locator window. To copy the file to a new location, such as a project folder, click the **Destination** button to display a browse window.

8. Point to the folder where you'd like to copy the previewed file. The new location appears next to the File Location display.

9. Click the **Copy** button to copy the selected file to the specified destination.

10. You can repeat steps 3 through 9 to locate and copy the graphic files you need. Click the **Exit** button when you are finished using the Graphics Locator.

Changing Image Size and Format with the ReSize Tool

ReSize lets you change the size and color depth of any image. This tool is very useful for reducing images so that they display more efficiently with a variety of web browsers. It will also convert BMP, SHG, or PCX files to JPG or GIF format for use with WebHelp projects.

TIP: *Although ReSize can resize graphics and retain hotspots used in WinHelp and other output format (SHED Format), WebHelp stores image maps differently, and ReSize will not retain the image map links for GIF or JPG files. Use the ReSize tool to make sure the image is the size you want it to be before setting map links.*

To use the ReSize tool, follow these steps:

1. Select the **Tools** tab (👋) on the left-hand pane of the RoboHelp HTML window.

2. Double-click the **ReSize** icon (🖼) to display the ReSize window.

3. Open the image you want to change by either clicking the **Open File** icon or choosing **Open** from the **File** menu. ReSize displays the image in the main part of the ReSize window with the Image Properties window open, as shown in Figure 8-13.

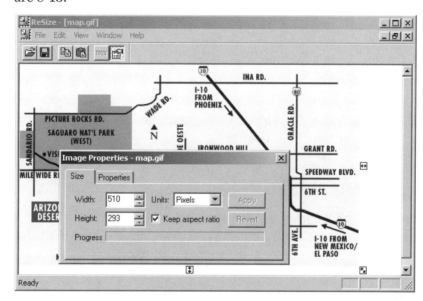

Figure 8-13: Opening the ReSize tool

4. To change the image size, use one of the following methods:
   - Enter new dimensions in the Properties window Size tab.
   - Click and drag the image handles (↔).

5. To change the image color depth, click the **Properties** tab on the **Properties** window, as shown in Figure 8-14.

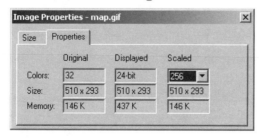

Figure 8-14: Viewing image size on the Properties tab

6. The Properties tab displays the original image dimensions and file size, the dimensions and file size of the image as displayed, and a third column ("Scaled") that displays the file size required for each of the color depths. Choose a color depth from the drop-down menu. Remember, as you decrease the number of

colors, you may also be decreasing the quality of the image. The ReSize tool displays the image as you make changes to either tab in the Properties window.

7. At any point while working with an image, you can easily undo all your changes since the last time you saved the file. Use either of the following ways:

   - Click the **Revert** icon (100%).
   - From the **Edit** menu, choose **Revert to Original**.

8. When the image looks the way you want it to, you can either save the image to the same file type or choose a different file type:

   - From the **File** menu, choose **Save**, or click the **Save** icon to save the image in the original file type.
   - From the **File** menu, choose **Save As**, and then choose the new file type from the drop-down list.

9. To close the image file, choose **Close** from the **File** menu. To exit ReSize, choose **Exit** from the **File** menu.

Inserting Special Effects

RoboHelp HTML lets you add special effects to your help system, such as sounds that play when the topic opens, text that scrolls across the screen, images that fly in or out of topic windows, or pages that fade in or out. These effects fall into three categories:

- Multimedia, which plays sound or movie files

> **CAUTION:** Multimedia requires that the user have the appropriate player software in order to hear or see the files. Also, multimedia files often work on only one type of system (UNIX files may not play on Windows systems, or Windows files may not play on Macintosh systems). Make sure you test multimedia files on the system configuration your users are likely to have.

- Marquee, which scrolls text across the topic window
- DHTML, which moves portions of the topic (text or images) in various ways

> **CAUTION:** DHTML, while offering a lot of cool effects, requires the user to have Internet Explorer version 5.0 or higher. If your users may have other browsers or older versions of IE, it is best to avoid DHTML effects.

Adding Multimedia

RoboHelp HTML can import video or sound files into your help project and play them when you specify. It cannot, however, create multimedia files. You must create the files using another tool and then import it into the RoboHelp project. For example, you can play sound files when topics open or play video when certain links are clicked.

TIP: *Sometimes too much multimedia in a single topic can be confusing to your end user, so it is best to limit these elements for the most impact. Also, different browsers will often handle multimedia files in different ways, and many multimedia files will not play at all on certain types of systems. For example, a UNIX format such as AU may not play on a Macintosh system. Always be sure to test your final output with the system configuration your users are likely to have.*

RoboHelp HTML can import the following types of sound and video:

- Sound: .au, .mid, .mp3, .wav
- Video: .asf, .asx, .avi, .mpe, .mpeg, .mov, .mpg, .qt, .ra, .rm, .rpm, .swf, .wax, .wma, .wmv, .wvx

You can add multimedia to topics in any of the following ways:

- Specify a background sound that will play whenever the topic is opened but will not appear on the screen.
- Insert an icon representing the sound or movie into the topic. This will play when the topic is opened and whenever the icon is clicked.
- Create a link to the multimedia file. The link will open the user's default player for that type of file. This method is useful when you want to let the user control the file with buttons such as play, pause, and stop.

CAUTION: *If you want to include more than one sound file in a single topic, create links to the sound files. Otherwise, you may end up playing multiple sound files at the same time.*

Adding Background Sounds

Background sounds play automatically when a topic is displayed. You can set background sounds to play once, play a set number of times, or play for as long as the topic is displayed. To add background sound to a topic, follow these steps:

1. Open the topic in the WYSIWYG pane.
2. Display the Topic Properties window in one of the following ways:
   - Click the **Properties** icon ( ).
   - From the **Edit** menu, choose **Properties**.

- Click the right mouse button and choose **Topic Properties**.

- Right-click on the topic name in the left-hand pane and choose **Properties**.

3. Click the **Appearance** tab to display the Appearance options, as shown in Figure 8-15.

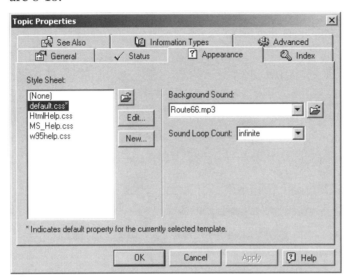

Figure 8-15: Setting background sounds in the Topic Properties window

4. Enter the name of the sound file in the Background Sound text box. You may use the Browse feature to point to the filename.

TIP: *The Browse feature will only display file types .au, .wav, .mid, and .rmi. To display other file types, enter the file type with a wildcard in the File name box. For example, enter *.mp3 to display a list of .mp3 files. As always, test any files you use to make sure they'll work with your user's system configuration.*

5. Choose the number of times you want the sound file to play from the drop-down box next to Sound Loop Count. Choose **infinite** to play the sound repeatedly as long as the topic window is open.

6. Click **Apply** to save your changes to the topic

7. Test the sound file by clicking the **View** button (👓) to open the topic. There will be no visual indication on the topic that there is a sound file associated with it, but the sound file will play.

Inserting a Sound or Movie File into a Topic

You can add any sound or movie file to a topic. It will appear as an image of the system default player for that file type. For example, on a Windows system, a sound file may appear on a topic as the "flying windows" icon. The file will automatically play as soon as the topic is opened, and the user can click on the icon to play the file again or stop the sound or movie from playing.

To insert a multimedia sound or movie file, follow these steps:

1. Open the topic in the WYSIWYG pane.

2. Place the cursor where you want the multimedia icon to display.

3. From the **Insert** menu, choose **Multimedia**. The Multimedia window opens, displaying a list of multimedia files that are already in the current project.

4. Specify the file that you want to use in one of the following ways:

   ■ Click one of the displayed image names.

   ■ Use the Browse button to specify an image that has not yet been used in the project. The image browser defaults to display all multimedia file types.

5. The Preview pane displays the icon for the selected file based on your own system defaults and a set of controls for the default multimedia player. For example, when inserting a sound on a Windows system, the controls might look like the sample shown in Figure 8-16. Depending on your system configuration and the size of your multimedia file, the preview may take a few seconds to load. The controls allow you to play the multimedia file while in the Multimedia window, but they will not appear in the finished help project. When you've selected the file, click **OK**.

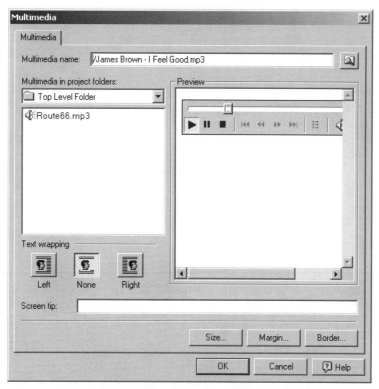

Figure 8-16: Previewing the multimedia file before inserting

6. You can set any of the parameters (borders, screen tip, etc.) for the icon as if it were any other type of image. See "Editing an Image in the Image Window"

earlier in this chapter for more information about setting parameters for the icon. When you've set any of the parameters that you want to change, click **OK**.

 TIP: *If you are using Internet Explorer 5.0 for your preview window, sound files may not play correctly in the Preview window. To work around this, place a border around sound files. They should then play correctly.*

7. If you chose a file from a location other than the project folder, a prompt appears asking if you want to copy the file to the project. If you choose not to copy the file, RoboHelp HTML will display it anyway, but it may not be able to properly play it and may not properly include the file in the finished, delivered help file. Click **OK** to copy the file to the project folder. You'll see a text description of the file in the WYSIWYG window surrounded by a green box (or whatever borders you specified). The filename will be displayed in the Multimedia folder, as shown in Figure 8-17.

 NOTE: *For some file types, the file name may not appear in the Multimedia folder until you save the output file.*

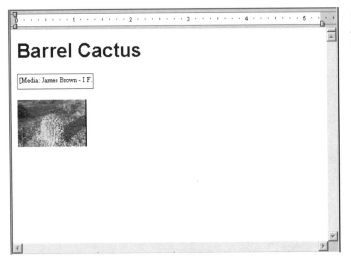

Figure 8-17:
Multimedia files display as text in WYSIWYG

 TIP: *If the sound file already exists in the project, you simply click and drag the sound file icon to the displayed topic. The sound file will be inserted at the cursor location.*

8. Test the multimedia output by clicking the **View** button to open the topic. Movie files will play through once automatically. Sound files will appear as the icon associated with the system player, as shown in Figure 8-18, and play through

once. If the user clicks the icon, the music will stop. When the user clicks the icon again, the music will continue.

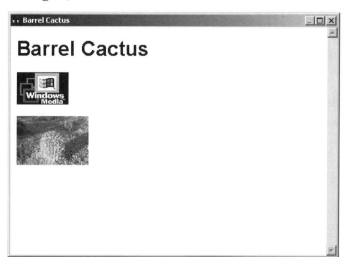

Figure 8-18: A sound file displayed as an icon

Inserting a Link to a Sound or Movie File

The most versatile way to add multimedia to your HTML files is to create a link to the sound or movie file. This will automatically open the user's default player for the specific type of multimedia, allowing the user to control the way the file is played. This method also gives you more control over the appearance of the topic. You can insert links into text paragraphs, images, popups, or image maps. See Chapter 5, "Linking Topics Together" for more information about specific types of links.

To insert a link to a sound or movie file, follow these steps:

1. Open the topic in which you want to include the link. Make sure it is showing in the WYSIWYG tab in the left hand pane.
2. Highlight the text or image you want to convert to a link
3. Click the **Insert Hyperlink** icon ( ) or the **Insert Popup** icon ( ) to open the Hyperlink window.

NOTE: *The Insert Hyperlink icon and the Insert Popup icon launch the same window—only the title is different. Everything described here applies to both windows.*

4. From the **Link to** drop-down menu, choose **Multimedia** to display a browse window.
5. Point to the name of the sound or movie file, and then click **Open**. The selected filename appears in the Link to box, as shown in Figure 8-19. Since hyperlink options don't apply to multimedia links, they'll be grayed out.

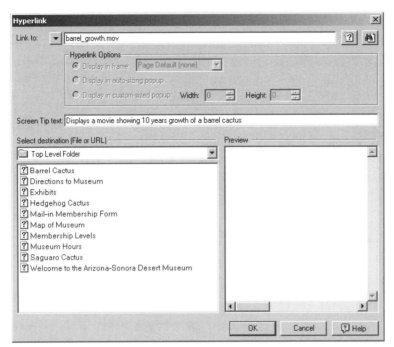

Figure 8-19:
Selecting a multimedia file in the Hyperlink window

6. (Optional) Screen tips are the text that appears on the screen when a user pauses the cursor over the link. This gives the user a hint about what the link does. The screen tip will also appear if the user has multimedia turned off. This can also be useful if you are trying to comply with the U.S. federal regulation section 508, which requires text substitutes for all graphic elements. If you want to enter a screen tip, type the text into the **Screen Tip** text box.

7. Click **OK** when you've finished defining the link. The Hyperlink window closes and the link appears on the topic in the WYSIWYG pane. Move the cursor over the link in the WYSIWYG pane to display the type of link and the name of the multimedia file to which it points.

8. To test the link, click the **Preview** icon, and then click the link. The sound or movie you entered will play in your system's default player for that multimedia file type.

Adding a Marquee

A *marquee* is text or images that scroll across your topic page, either horizontally like a stock ticker or vertically like movie credits. You can specify the location, speed, and direction of scroll for the contents of a marquee. You can also specify other marquee properties, such as the number of times the marquee repeats and the type of movement.

To add a marquee effect, follow these steps:

1. Specify where you want the scrolling text to appear, either by clicking in a topic or highlighting existing text.

2. From the **Insert** menu, choose **Marquee**. A box with a green outline will be displayed on the topic at the location of the cursor, as shown in Figure 8-20. If you highlighted text, the text will be in the green box.

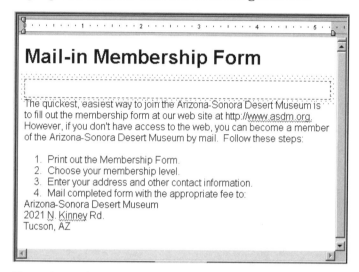

Figure 8-20: The marquee

3. If you haven't already specified the text, type it into the box at the cursor. You can also add images to the scroll box, and they'll move right along with the text. There is no limit to the amount of text you can enter. You can use any of the format icons or other formatting tools described in Chapter 6.

TIP: *Remember, marquee text will be moving across the user's screen and may be difficult for some users to read. It is best to keep to short sentences, large type, and simple graphics.*

4. To set or change the scrolling properties, display the Marquee properties window in one of the following ways:

   ■ Double-click on the marquee outline.

   ■ Click the right mouse button and choose **Marquee Properties**.

5. You can specify margins, borders, shading, and size of the marquee box with the tabs in the Marquee properties window. These all work exactly the same way as the margins, borders, shading, and size options for images (see "Editing an Image with the Image Window" earlier in this chapter) and for text (see "Formatting Text" in Chapter 6).

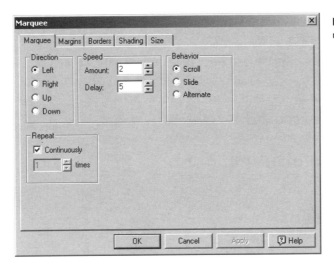

Figure 8-21: Setting the marquee properties

6. Click the **Marquee** tab in the Marquee properties window to display the properties unique to marquee movement.

7. Specify the direction you want the marquee contents to move. Choose one of the following:

Table 8-2: Marquee directions

Direction	Effect
Left	The content moves toward the left from the right side of the green marquee box (like a stock ticker).
Right	The content moves toward the right from the left side of the green marquee box. **TIP:** This may be difficult to read at first, since the first character that is displayed will be the last character in the sentence.
Up	The content moves from the bottom toward the top of the green marquee box, like movie credits.
Down	The content moves from the top toward the bottom of the green marquee box.

8. Specify the speed at which the text will move by entering a combination of Amount and Delay. Amount is the number of pixels the scroll will move. Delay is the length of time in milliseconds that the text (or the visible portion of it) will stay still on the screen before moving the number of pixels specified in Amount. Larger Delay values mean faster text movement.

TIP: *Large numbers in the Amount field can make the marquee look choppy and uneven. For smooth scrolling, leave the Amount at 1 and use the Delay setting to slow down or speed up the text. Don't make the delay too great, though, or the marquee will move too fast to read. A good setting to start at is a Delay of 20 milliseconds.*

9. Specify how you want the text to move in the Behavior box. Choose one of the following:

Table 8-3: Marquee behaviors

Behavior	Effect
Scroll	The marquee content moves continuously from one edge of the green marquee box to the other in the specified direction, continuing until it is off the screen. If you have specified a number of repetitions or set the repetitions to Continuously, the next repetition will then start from the same direction as the first.
Slide	The marquee content moves from one edge of the green marquee box to the other in the specified direction until it has all been displayed the specified number of times. It then stops and remains on the screen. If there is too much content in the marquee box, only the last portion of the content will remain on the screen.
Alternate	The marquee content moves from one edge of the screen to the other in the specified direction until all of the contents have been displayed. It then moves back in the opposite direction, like a ball bouncing off a wall.

10. Specify the number of times you want the marquee contents to display by entering a number in the **Repeat** box. If you want the marquee to scroll as long as the topic is displayed, check the **Continuously** box.

11. You can specify borders, shading, or marquee box size the same way you would for other types of text or images. You can use the formatting icons or the formatting tabs in the Marquee properties box.

12. To test the marquee, click the **Preview** icon. The marquee will scroll on the preview window.

Adding DHTML Effects

RoboHelp HTML includes a number of Dynamic HTML (DHTML) elements that add special graphics and animation to your topics.

 NOTE: *DHTML is not yet supported by Netscape Navigator, and many of the effects only work in Internet Explorer 5.0 or later. If you aren't sure which browsers your users have, you may want to stay away from DHTML effects.*

Most DHTML effects can be applied to either text or images. When adding basic DHTML effects, you must complete three steps:

1. Specify the text or image you want to change or animate (the *target*).

2. Specify the action that will cause an effect to occur, such as a page loading or mouse click.

3. Specify the effect you want to use. Each effect will have property options that you may set or leave as is.

If you want to animate one element when a different element is clicked, you'll need two additional steps:

4. Identify the text or image that will be clicked to initiate your effect (the *trigger*).

5. Connect the trigger to your target text or images.

The DHTML effects that come with RoboHelp HTML are:

Table 8-4: Available DHTML effects

Effect	Description
Blur	Makes the edges look fuzzy
Drop Shadow	Adds a shadow to text or images
Elastic	The target moves from the outside edge toward the center of the window, and then back a little bit.
Fade In	The target starts out invisible, grows very dim, and then becomes more solid.
Fade Out	The target starts solid and then becomes dimmer and dimmer until it disappears.
Flip Horizontally	The target is turned upside down.
Flip Vertically	The target is turned into a mirror image of itself.
Fly In	The target moves from any edge or corner of the screen into the center of the window.
Fly Out	The target moves from the center of the window to any point on the edge until it disappears.
Font Change	The target text changes font formatting. This is only available when the user moves the mouse over the target.
Glow	The target has a fuzzy, colored border around every contour (for text, this means individual letters).
Gray	The target changes to shades of gray.
Hide	The target is removed from the window. Use in conjunction with Show.
Invert	Changes the colors of the target to make a negative image. Black will turn to white, yellow will turn to blue, green will turn to purple, etc.
Rock 'n Roll	Causes the center of the image or text to move in one direction while the top and bottom of the target move in the opposite direction. This looks sort of like the image is waving or dancing.
Show	Displays the target. Use in conjunction with Hide.
Spiral In	The target moves into the center of the window with a circular motion.
Spiral Out	The target moves out from the center of the window with a circular motion until it has disappeared.
Transition	The target moves into or off of the window in a specified manner. There are 24 different transition effects to choose from, such as vertical blinds, checkerboard, or wipe.
Zoom In	The target starts out very small and then grows until it is the original target size.
Zoom Out	The target starts out very large and then shrinks until it is the original target size.

Adding a Basic DHTML Effect

To insert DHTML effects, follow these steps:

1. Specify the target text or image in one of the following ways:

   - To specify text, highlight the text.

   - To specify an entire paragraph, click anywhere inside the paragraph.

   - To specify an image, click the image. The image **Cable Drum** icon ( ) appears next to the image.

   - To specify text that will display on Internet Explorer 4.0, select text, then choose **Text Box** from the **Insert** menu to prepare the text for DHTML.

2. Ensure that the target is on the topic page in the correct location. This will vary by effect. For some effects, the location in the topic identifies the final position of the target contents (such as Elastic, Fly In, Spiral In, and Zoom In). For others, the location of the target in the topic is the starting position, and the text will move off the window when the effect is initiated (such as Fly Out or Spiral Out). Other effects do not move the target at all; they just change the target appearance (such as Drop Shadow, Flip, or Transition).

> **TIP:** It is a good idea to include some sort of text near the DHTML effect that tells the users what you expect them to do, particularly if you are basing your effects on user clicks. For example, if a page click causes a picture of a bird to fly into the page, you may want to include text elsewhere on the page that says "click on this page to view a Desert Sparrow."

3. To specify the DHTML action, select **Insert/Edit Dynamic HTML Effects** from the **DHTML** menu to display the DHTML Effects window, as shown in Figure 8-22. The DHTML action identifies the activity that initiates the DHTML effects. Each option has its own available list of effects that appears in the What box as you highlight each action in the When box.

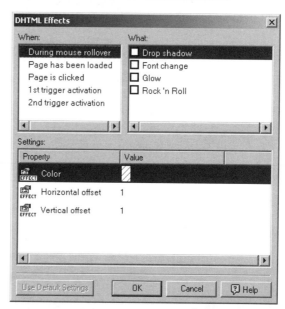

Figure 8-22: Choosing effects from the DHTML Effects window

Table 8-5: DHTML actions

Action	Description
During mouse rollover	Initiates the effect when the mouse is dragged over the target text or image. This action only works for four DHTML effects (Drop Shadow, Font Change, Glow, and Rock 'n Roll).
Page has been loaded	Initiates the effect as soon as the page is opened in the browser. The user does not have to click anything or move the mouse at all.
Page is clicked	Initiates the effect when the user clicks anywhere on the page
1st trigger activation	Initiates the effect only when the user clicks on the trigger for the effect. See "Using Triggers with DHTML Effects" later in this chapter to complete this type of effect action.
2nd trigger activation	Initiates the effect the second time the user clicks on the trigger for the effect. See "Using Triggers with DHTML Effects" later in this chapter to complete this type of effect action.

4. Click an action in the **When** box. The available effects for that action are displayed in the What box.

5. Click an effect in the **What** box. The properties for that effect appear in the Settings box. This will vary with the type of effect you've chosen. For example, the Rock 'n Roll effect has four properties, as shown in Figure 8-23.

6. Change any of the properties by clicking on the value to display either a drop-down box or text box, depending on the type of property. For example, in the Rock 'n Roll settings, you can specify effect Frequency, Light strength, and Strength in text boxes. Choose a value from the **Duration** box to specify how long the effect will last (Forever, Long, Medium, or Short).

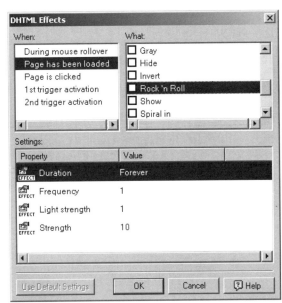

Figure 8-23: Entering the Rock 'n Roll effect settings

7. Repeat steps 4 through 6 to add multiple effects to the selected target text or image. Click **OK** when you are done.

TIP: *While RoboHelp HTML will allow you to add many effects to a single target, it is best to select just one or two at a time. Otherwise, the result can overwhelm your users and hide the message you are trying to convey.*

8. Click **OK** to display the target in the WYSIWYG pane. The specified text or image will have hash marks over it to indicate there is at least one DHTML effect, as shown in Figure 8-24. In addition, if you've specified a trigger action, the target will also have a Cable Outlet icon (■).

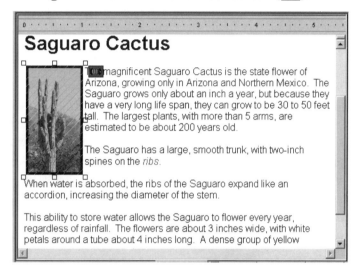

Figure 8-24: Hash marks indicate a DHTML effect

9. To view the effect, click the **View** icon to display the topic in preview mode, and then perform the specified action (mouse over or click). The RoboHelp HTML help files include a variety of samples that show you what the effects are supposed to look like. Figure 8-25 illustrates the above example of a Rock 'n Roll effect.

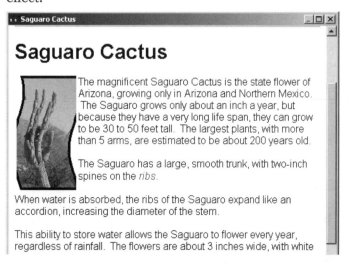

Figure 8-25: A cactus that rocks and rolls

10. To remove DHTML effects, click the target, and then choose **Remove Dynamic HTML Effect** from the **DHTML** menu.

Using Triggers with DHTML Effects

Basic DHTML effects occur when the user opens a window, rolls the mouse over the target, or clicks anywhere on the page. You can also set up triggers, which allow you to click in one place to activate an effect somewhere else. This is particularly handy when you want to show hidden objects or start effects that begin off of the page.

To use a trigger to start a DHTML effect, follow these steps:

1. Set up the effect as described in the previous section, "Adding a Basic DHTML Effect." Make sure you select either **1st trigger activation** or **2nd trigger activation** in the When box.

2. On the same topic as the target, define a trigger by highlighting some text or an image that you want the user to click. The image might be a button, like the button images that come in the RoboHelp HTML Gallery, or an image of your own. The text can be a whole paragraph or just a few words. Whichever you choose, make sure that it is clear where the user is supposed to click to initiate the DHTML effect.

3. From the **DHTML** menu, click **Make Trigger**. A Cable Drum icon (▩) is displayed next to the selected element, and hash marks are displayed over the new trigger, as shown in Figure 8-26.

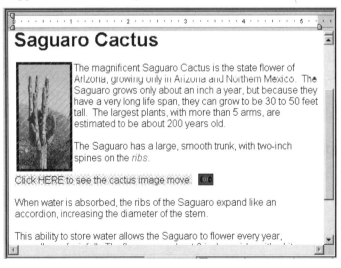

Figure 8-26: Indicating the trigger with hash marks and a Cable Drum icon

4. Click on the **Cable Drum** for the trigger, then, holding the mouse button down, drag the cursor to the target. You'll see a green line connecting the cursor to the Cable Drum. As you move the cursor over the target, in this case an image, the green line will extend around the target, as shown in Figure 8-27.

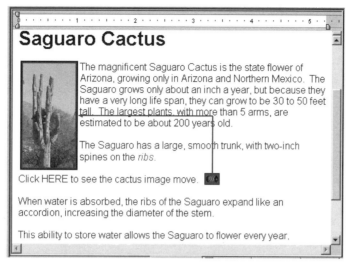

Figure 8-27: A green line connects the trigger to the target

5. Release the mouse when the target is selected. When you next click the image, it will display a Cable Outlet icon ( ), as well as the Cable Drum. The outlet icon indicates that this target has an associated trigger.

6. To test the DHTML effect, click the **View** icon, and then click the trigger. The image will display the specified effect.

NOTE: *If you've specified both 1st trigger activation and 2nd trigger activation for the same target, you'll get the first effect the first time you click the trigger and the second effect the second time you click the trigger. This is very useful when using effect pairs, such as Hide and Show or Zoom In and Zoom Out.*

Adding a Splash Screen

A *splash screen* is an image that appears when a help topic is first opened and then automatically disappears to reveal the selected topic. RoboHelp comes with an ActiveX control that lets you automatically insert a splash screen into an HTML help project.

You can specify either .bmp or .gif images for splash screens. Although typically used when opening the help file for the first time, you could insert a splash screen into any topic.

To specify a splash screen, follow these steps:

1. In the WYSIWYG Editor, click where you want to add the control in the topic.

2. From the **Insert** menu, choose **HTML Help** and then **Splash Screen** to start the Splash Screen Wizard, as shown in Figure 8-28.

Figure 8-28: Specifying an image for the splash screen

3. Enter the name of the image you want to use, or use the **Browse** button to point to the image. You may specify either .bmp or .gif images.

4. Specify the length of time, in seconds, that the image should be displayed before it appears.

5. Click **Finish** to close the wizard. An icon ( ) appears in the topic to indicate that a splash screen has been configured. This icon will not appear in the final topic.

6. To test the splash screen, click the **View** icon. The specified image will be displayed for the specified length of time.

Summary

This chapter discussed many ways to add graphics and special effects to your topics. You learned how to insert and format images, add borders, and change colors. You also saw how to insert sound and movies and make text move across the window with the Marquee function. Finally, this chapter described how to work with Dynamic HTML effects that come with RoboHelp HTML and how to add a splash screen.

The next chapter will describe how to organize your project with tools and folders and how to make it easier for your users to find information using tables of contents and the Index feature.

Chapter 9

Getting Organized Using Folders, Tables of Contents, and Indexing Tools

As your project grows, the number of files that make up the project also grows. This is particularly true in HTML projects, where every topic is a separate file and all images are stored separately from the topics. RoboHelp HTML has tools that help you keep track of files while you are working on projects. It also has features that help you organize your final output, making it easy for your users to find the information they are seeking.

Working with Project Folders

When you first create a project, RoboHelp HTML creates a series of folders that are displayed in the left-hand pane of the RoboHelp HTML window. The RoboHelp HTML folders for each project fall into two categories: file folders and system folders.

File folders are not actual folders on your hard drive. Rather, they are more like filters that only display certain file types. For example, the RoboHelp HTML folder called Style Sheets displays names of the files in the project directory that have the extension .css. The Images folder displays files with extensions like .jpg, .gif, and .bmp.

RoboHelp HTML system folders do not display filenames. Rather, they display lists of information generated by the RoboHelp system as you are working, creating, compiling, and generating help output. For example, the URL folder lists the web addresses of Internet files to which you've linked. The files themselves do not exist on your system. The Broken Links folder lists the names of files to which your project points but that RoboHelp HTML can't find.

The default folders are on the left-hand side of the RoboHelp HTML window, as shown in Figure 9-1.

The plus signs ( ) indicate folders that have some-thing in them that is not currently displayed on the window. Click the plus sign (or double-click the folder icon) to open the folder, display its contents, and turn the plus sign to a minus sign. Click the minus sign to close the folder and display the plus sign again.

Figure 9-1: Default folders in RoboHelp HTML

NOTE: *Empty folders will not have a plus or a minus sign next to them. You can turn the display of empty folders on or off by selecting or unselecting the Empty Folders check box in the View menu.*

To see the options available for working with each type of file, click the right mouse button to display a menu. This menu will vary with the type of file. The following table lists the default folders and where you can find more information about the types of files in each folder.

Table 9-1: RoboHelp HTML

HTML folder	Contents	Covered in
HTML Files (Topics)	This file folder lists the names of the topics in the project. Each topic is stored as a unique file with the extension .htm. The HTML Files (Topics) folder can also be used for auto-generating a TOC and creating browse sequences.	Discussed throughout book
Broken Links	This system folder lists the names of the files that the project links to but can't find.	Chapter 5
URLs	This system folder lists the names of web addresses, FTP sites, newsgroups, email addresses, or external HTML topics that are refer-enced by topics in the project.	Chapter 5
Images	This file folder lists the names of images and image maps used in your project.	Chapters 5 and 8
Multimedia	This file folder lists the names of all sound and video files used in your project.	Chapter 8
Windows	This system folder lists the windows defined by your project for displaying the final output.	Chapter 11
Style Sheets	This file folder lists the names of style sheets used in the project, including RoboHelp HTML's default default.css.	Chapter 6
Templates	This system folder lists the names of templates used by the project.	Chapter 10
Skins	This system folder lists the names of skins used in your project, including RoboHelp HTML's default default.zkn.	Chapter 10

HTML folder	Contents	Covered in
Context-Sensitive Help	This system folder contains a number of subfolders that organize the information you'll need to work with map files, aliases, and text-only topic files.	Chapter 12
Baggage Files	This file folder lists the files that are required by RoboHelp HTML for display of finished projects. The files are automatically copied to this folder so that they'll be available to the users when you deliver the final help. For example, bullet icons are stored in the Baggage Files folder, not the Images folder. This folder also lists the support files, such as ehlpdhtm.js (for DHTML effects) and ehelp.xml (for skins and WebHelp output).	Appendix A
Build Tags	This system folder lists the tags that let you control which topics to include in the RoboHelp HTML output.	Chapter 17
Single Source	This system folder lists the formats for different types of output. Although you may have specified a primary output of WebHelp Enterprise, you can still create any of the other formats from the same project files.	Chapter 16

Creating a New File Folder

By default, RoboHelp HTML stores all the project files in the root project folder. Although the file folders in the Project tab sort these files and display them by type (such as images or style sheets), the actual files are all stored in one large directory. For large projects, you may want to create subfolders to help organize your project.

Each subfolder will be displayed in all of the RoboHelp HTML file folders. You can add as many subfolders as you need and nest folders within other folders to help organize information. For example, for a large project, you may want to add subfolders for cateorgies such as plants, animals, and administration. Within the plants folder, you might have folders for cacti, trees, and flowers. As long as you create, modify, and move folders within the RoboHelp window, the links between the folder contents and the topics, keywords, images, and other RoboHelp elements remain intact.

CAUTION: *When adding or editing RoboHelp HTML folders, always make your changes from within the RoboHelp HTML window. This ensures that all links and references to all topics, keywords, images, and other tools are automatically updated. If you use your operating system to add or change folders, RoboHelp HTML will not be able to recognize your changes correctly.*

To add a folder to your project, follow these steps:

1. Click the **Project** tab (P..) on the left-hand side of the program window to display the list of folders, as shown in Figure 9-2.

2. Click on any of the RoboHelp HTML file folders (HTML Files, Images, Multimedia, Style Sheets, or Baggage Files).

3. Click the right mouse button and choose **New Folder**. RoboHelp HTML adds a new folder with the default name "New Folder," as shown in Figure 9-3.

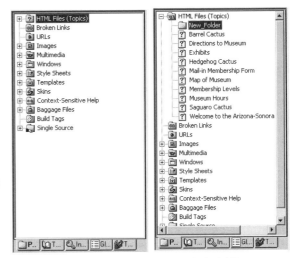

Figure 9-2: Displaying the project folders

Figure 9-3: Adding a new folder

4. Type a new name for the folder. Make it something descriptive, so you'll know what types of information it contains. As you type the folder name, RoboHelp HTML automatically converts spaces to underscores.

5. Once you've created a folder, it is automatically available in all of the other file folders. To move files into a new folder, simply click the name of the file you want to move, and then drag it to the new folder. The new folder will behave exactly like the other folders, displaying a plus sign when there are files in it and a minus sign when it is open, as shown in Figure 9-4. Notice that the other RoboHelp file folders, such as the Multimedia folder, display the new folder name, even if there are no files in the folder.

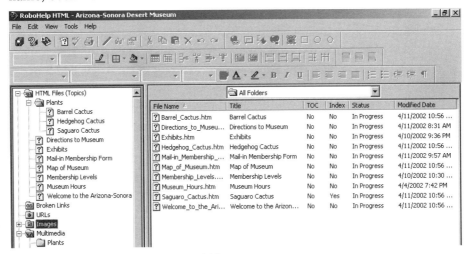

Figure 9-4: Dragging files into the new folder

Removing Folders

Occasionally, you'll want to remove a folder from a project. When you do this, make sure you remove or rename the folder from within RoboHelp; otherwise, you may lose some links or references to topics, keywords, or other RoboHelp elements.

To remove a folder, follow these steps:

1. Make sure the folder is empty. Because the RoboHelp HTML folders filter for specific file types, you'll have to check all of the file folders (HTML Files, Images, Multimedia, Style Sheets, and Baggage Files) to ensure there are no files of any type in the folder. Remember, a plus sign indicates there is something in the folder, and a minus sign indicates the files are displayed. Empty folders will have neither a plus nor a minus sign.

2. Highlight the folder name in the HTML Files (Topics) folder. You will not be able to delete folders from any of the other folders.

3. Click the right mouse button and choose **Delete**. The subfolder will be removed from all file folders.

Using the RoboHelp HTML Multi-File Find and Replace Tool

As you create topics, RoboHelp HTML stores each topic in a separate file with the extension .htm. Although this will make the final help file flexible and portable, working with a large number of files can be time-consuming. If, for example, your product name changes mid-project, you'll need to edit the name in every file. RoboHelp HTML comes with a tool that makes this chore fast and easy. Multi-File Find and Replace works like the find and replace features in most word processors, except that you can automatically change or delete any text string in many files at once.

This is particularly useful when working with HTML files, which use text strings to code formatting, styles, links, and other elements. Multi-File Find and Replace can recognize and search HTML strings or omit them from the search. It can also make backups of all your HTML files at once.

Multi-File Find and Replace can create backups of your files before replacing text. If you make a mistake, you can revert to the backup file. Backup files are saved in the same folder as the original files.

To use Multi-File Find and Replace, follow these steps:

1. From the left-hand menu, click the **Tools** tab (🖋️) to display system tools.

2. Click the **Multi-File Find and Replace** icon (🖳) to display the Multi-File Find and Replace window, as shown in Figure 9-5.

Figure 9-5: Using the Multi-File Find and Replace tool to change or delete text

3. Enter text you are looking for in the **Find** box. You can search for strings with embedded spaces or use the special wildcard characters (* for any set of characters; ? for any single character).

TIP: *It is best to be as specific as possible so that you'll change the least number of files and still make the changes you need. For example, don't search for a whole sentence if you only need to replace a few words.*

4. Enter the new, replacement text in the **Replace** box.

5. In the **Named** box, specify the types of files to include in the search. You can enter the type or select from the available list. Criteria can include wildcards (* and ?), filenames, or extensions. For example, enter *.htm to only search for HTML topic files. You can also specify the extension of the files you want to change. You can choose .htm (HTML files), .txt (text files), or *.* from the drop-down box or type in a unique extension.

6. Specify the folder in which the files you want to change are stored. You can either type in a folder location or use the Browse button to point to a folder.

7. Click any of the optional check boxes you want to use.

Table 9-2: Find and Replace options

Option	Effect
Case Sensitive	The find function will make a distinction between capital and lower-case letters.
Whole Word	The find function will only search for the find string if it is a word by itself. For example, if Whole Word is checked and the Find box contains "plant," the find function will not identify "planted" or "planting" as matches.
Ignore HTML Tags	The find function will not search inside of HTML tags (identified by angle brackets, such as <name>).
Make Backups	Find and Replace will automatically make a backup copy of each file before it makes the specified change. The first backup file will have the same filename as the original but with the extension .bak. Subsequent backups will have numbered extensions starting with .b00. For example, the first backup you make of the saguaro.htm file will be called saguaro.bak; the second time you back up the file, it will be called saguaro.b00; the third time will create saguaro.b01, etc.
Overwrite Backups	This option is only available when the Make Backups check box is selected. The find function will only create one backup file, continuously saving backups to the same name. This saves on disk space but reduces the number of changes you'll be able to undo.

Option	Effect
Include Subfolders	The find function will search the specified folder and all folders contained in the specified folder.

TIP: *Although Multi-File Find and Replace can be set to automatically make backup files for each changed file, it cannot automatically restore the files. You'll have to open each individual file you want to restore, and then save it with the extension .htm (overwriting the changed file). An alternative is to copy the entire project folder to another location before you begin the Find and Replace process.*

8. Click the **Find** button. The Find and Replace window enlarges to show a list of the names of files containing the text string and a preview of the first instance of the text string along with the surrounding text, as shown in Figure 9-6.

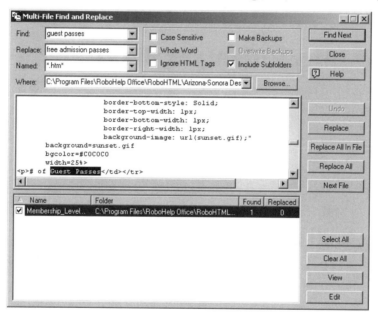

Figure 9-6: Displaying the specified text in the Find and Replace window

9. To change the text to the Replace text, do one of the following:

    ■ Click **Replace** to change the highlighted text and display the next instance of the Find text.

    ■ Click **Replace All in File** to change all instances of the Find text in the current file (indicated by highlighting in the list of filenames), and display the first instance of the text in the next file. While working in a file, the Undo button becomes active. Once you've finished with a file, you can no longer undo changes to that file within the Find and Replace tool.

    ■ Click **Replace All** to change all instances of the Find text in all files with check marks. You can click a check mark to omit a listed file from the change operation.

10. To search for the next instance of the text without making any changes, click either the **Find Next** button or the **Next File** button.

11. As you make changes, the check mark is removed from each file that you've viewed in the window. When you've finished replacing the text in all files, a status window appears, as shown in Figure 9-7. Click **OK** to close the status window.

Figure 9-7: Displaying the status of the Find and Replace operation

12. You can repeat steps 3 through 11 to search for and change other text strings. When finished, click **Close** to close the Find and Replace window.

Organizing Information for the User

When a user views your WebHelp Enterprise files, the left-hand pane of the browser displays a table of contents, an index, and a search feature. RoboHelp HTML comes with several tools that make it easy to create these navigation elements.

NOTE: *See the section on skins in Chapter 10 for more information about customizing the user's browser window.*

Working with a Table of Contents

A table of contents lists the topics in a logical order so that your users can easily find the information they're seeking. RoboHelp HTML comes with a TOC Composer that lets you quickly create and edit the table of contents for your project. It displays each topic as a page and each folder as a book. Books work just like folders that contain the topic pages. Pages can be topics, or they can point to bookmarks within a topic. You can add or remove books and pages, choose the order in which books and pages display, and choose the icon that represents each element.

Creating a Table of Contents

The easiest way to create a table of contents is to use the automatic table of contents feature. This will create a table of contents based on your existing folder and topic structure. You can edit or make changes to the table of contents later.

To create a table of contents, follow these steps:

1. In the left-hand pane, click the **TOC** tab ( ).

2. With the cursor in the left-hand pane, click the **Auto Create TOC** button at the bottom of the TOC pane to display the Auto-create TOC window, as shown in Figure 9-8.

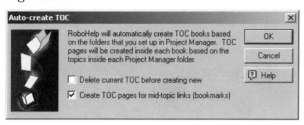

Figure 9-8: Using the existing folder structure to create a table of contents with the Auto-Create TOC window

3. Set the following options. Remember, you can always go back and add or remove books or pages later.

   ■ Select **Delete current TOC before creating new** to start a new table of contents. If this check box is not selected, the new table of contents will include existing entries as well as a new entry for each folder and topic. Depending on your existing structure, this may create duplicate entries.

   ■ Select **Create TOC pages for mid-topic links (bookmarks)** to create a TOC page for each bookmark in your topics. If you have a lot of bookmarks, this may make your table of contents very large.

4. Click **OK** to create the table of contents. Existing folders will be displayed as books; topics will be displayed as pages. When displayed on the Topics tab in the right-hand pane, the topic icons are blue, indicating that they're included in the table of contents, as shown in Figure 9-9.

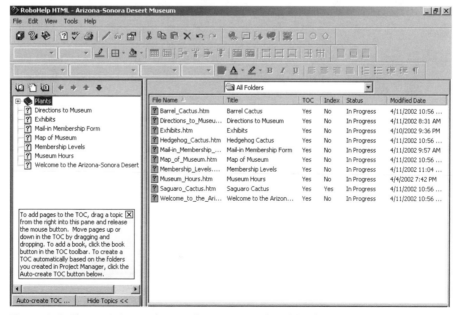

Figure 9-9: Blue topic icon indicating that topic is in the table of contents

5. You must compile the project before you can view the table of contents. From the **File** menu, choose **Generate**, and then specify the output format you want.

6. The view option only lets you preview one topic at a time, so to test the table of contents, you'll need to open it in a browser. From the **File** menu, choose **Run**, and then choose the output format you want.

NOTE: *If your output format is WebHelp Enterprise, you'll have to generate the files and publish them to the server before you can test the table of contents.*

Editing a Table of Contents

Once you've created a table of contents, you can make changes to it at any time. The default table of contents displays existing folders as books and lists each topic as a page within the book or at the root folder level. By default, the pages are displayed alphabetically. You can add or remove pages, add or remove books, and rearrange the order in which books and pages are displayed.

1. Topics are in alphabetical order within each folder. The first topic at the top of the list will be the first topic the user sees. You can rearrange the topics in one of the following ways:

   ■ Click the page or book and drag it to a new location. For example, you might drag the Welcome to the Arizona-Sonora Desert Museum topic to the top of the Table of Contents pane.

   ■ Click the page or book, and then click the up or down arrow at the top of the TOC pane.

   ■ Click the page or book, and then click the right arrow to move the item into the previous book. Or click an item, and then click the left arrow to move it out of a book. You can use this method to place books inside each other. For example, within the plant book you might create a book for cacti and a separate book for flowering plants.

2. To add a book, open the book properties window in one of the following ways:

   ■ Click the **New TOC Book** icon (📖) on the TOC pane just above the existing books and pages.

   ■ Click the right mouse button and choose **New**, then **Book**.

   ■ From the **File** menu, choose **New** and then **Book**.

3. Enter the name of the new book in the title section of the New TOC Book window, as shown in Figure 9-10.

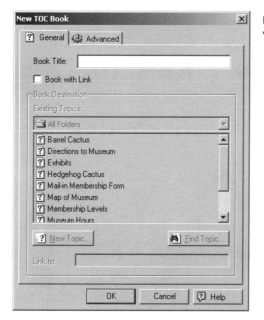

Figure 9-10: The New TOC Book window

4. Books work just like folders. While you're working in RoboHelp HTML, a plus sign indicates there are pages in a book, and a minus sign is displayed when the book is open and all pages are displayed. In the completed help file, book icons will be displayed. To change the displayed icon, click the **Advanced** tab in the New TOC Book window, and then choose a new icon from the displayed list.

5. Click **OK** to add the book to the table of contents.

6. You must add at least one topic to the book, or it won't appear in the table of contents when you generate the file. Add pages to the new book in one of the following ways:

   ■ Click and drag a table of contents entry into the new book. This will move the topic from the old table of contents location.

   ■ Click and drag a topic from the **Topics** tab on the right-hand pane into the book. This will leave existing table of contents entries for the topic, if any, in place.

   ■ Click the book name, and then click the right mouse button and choose **New Page**. You'll have to enter the page name in the properties window, just as you did for the new book.

7. You must compile the project before you can view the table of contents in a browser. From the **File** menu, choose **Generate**, then **WebHelp Enterprise**.

8. The view option only lets you preview one topic at a time, so to test the table of contents, you'll need to open it in a browser, as shown in Figure 9-11. From the **File** menu, choose **Run**, and then choose the output format you want.

> **NOTE:** *If your output format is WebHelp Enterprise, you'll have to generate the files and publish them to the server before you can test the table of contents.*

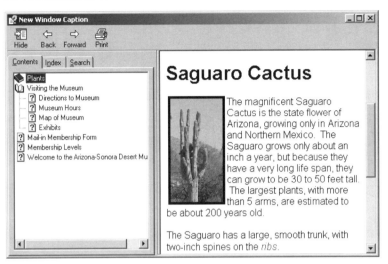

Figure 9-11: Previewing the table of contents in a browser

Creating an Index

The table of contents displays your topics in a predefined, logical order. For example, you may display the plant topics together and the animal topics together. The index will display your topics in order by keyword. For example, the membership level Coati Club for Kids would be displayed next to the animal Coati Mundi. By giving your users multiple ways to find information, they'll be able to find information more quickly.

This is true within the index as well. Give your users several words with which to find each topic, and you'll make it more likely that they'll find what they want. For example, the map topic might be in the index under "map," but also under "directions" and "location."

To create an index, you'll need to specify the keywords for the index in each topic. When you generate or run the help system, RoboHelp HTML creates the index file from the keywords.

You can add index keywords to individual topics manually, or you can use the Smart Index Wizard to automatically scan your topics and suggest keywords. If you use Smart Index, you can refine the way that it suggests keywords.

> **NOTE:** *If your output format is HTML Help, you must select the Binary index check box in order to properly display the finished index. From the File menu, select Project Settings. Then choose the Index tab to verify that the Binary index check box is selected.*

Adding Keywords in the Index Tab

To add keywords in the Index tab, you'll have to first add the keyword and then specify topics which will contain the keyword. Follow these steps:

1. In the left-hand pane, click the **Index** tab to display a list of existing keywords.

2. Click the right mouse button and select **New**, then **Keyword**. An empty text box will be displayed in the keyword list.

3. Type the new keyword, and then press **Enter**. The new keyword is displayed in the list in alphabetical order.

4. In the right-hand pane, click the **Topics** tab to display a list of topic names.

5. Click the name of a topic to which you want to link the new keyword, and then drag the topic name to the **Topics** box in the lower portion of the **Index** tab on the left-hand pane. The topic will be displayed in the Topics box and the keyword will be added to the topic.

Adding Keywords with Smart Index

The Smart Index tool automatically adds keywords to topics based on criteria you specify. To use the Smart Index tool, follow these steps:

1. In the left-hand pane, click the **Keyword** tab ( ).

2. Open the Smart Index window shown in Figure 9-12 in one of the following ways:

   - Click the **Smart Index** button at the bottom of the Index pane.

   - From the **Index** tab, click the right mouse button and choose **Smart Index**.

   - From the **Tools** menu, choose **Smart Index Wizard**.

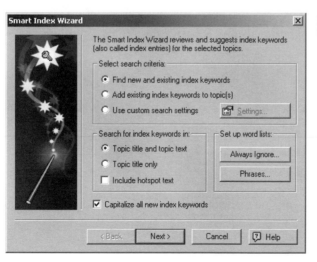

Figure 9-12: The Smart Index Wizard

3. Choose the search criteria by selecting one of the check boxes.

   ■ **Find new and existing keywords:** Select this option to have Smart Index suggest words and phrases that are likely index keywords. Smart Index will suggest new words that it finds as well as all words that are already in the index keyword list.

   ■ **Add existing keywords to topics:** Select this option to have Smart Index only display words that already exist as keywords in the project. This might be a good choice if you've generated the index at least once already and have just added a few topics.

   ■ **Use custom search settings:** This option refines the way that Smart Index identifies and suggests possible keywords. See the following section, "Specifying Custom Index Settings" for more information.

4. Choose the portion of the topic that you want Smart Index to search for potential keywords.

   ■ **Topic title and topic text:** Both the body and title of each topic will be searched.

   ■ **Topic title only:** Smart Index will search the title of each topic only (not from the body of the topic).

   ■ **Include hotspot text:** Text identified as hotspots or links will be searched. You can choose this option in addition to either of the other two keyword search options.

5. Specify whether or not Smart Index should capitalize the keywords it finds.

6. (Optional) The word lists specify certain words that Smart Index will ignore when searching for potential keywors (such as "a," "the," "or," etc.). See "Specifying Custom Index Settings" for more information on word lists.

7. Click **Next** to display the second Smart Index Wizard window, as shown in Figure 9-13.

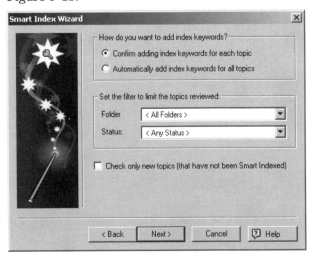

Figure 9-13: Specifying topics in the Smart Index window

8. Choose whether you want to confirm individual keywords for each topic or allow Smart Index to automatically enter the keywords it finds.

9. Specify which topics Smart Index should search by setting either or both of the following filters:

   ■ In the Folder box, choose **All Folders**, or limit the index search to a specific folder.

   ■ In the Status box, choose to check all topics (**Any Status**) or specify only those topics with a specific status (In Progress, Ready for Review, or Complete).

10. Check the **Check only new topics** check box to specify that the search for potential keywords should only occur in topics which have not yet been checked by the Smart Index Wizard. This option will still check topics to which you may have manually added keywords.

11. Click **Next** to begin the search for new potential keywords. If you chose "Automatically add keywords" in step 8, the Smart Index tool searches for keywords and adds them to each topic and then displays a status window. If you chose to confirm individual keywords in step 8, Smart Index displays the words found in the first topic, as shown in Figure 9-14. The topic name is displayed in the window and in the title of the window.

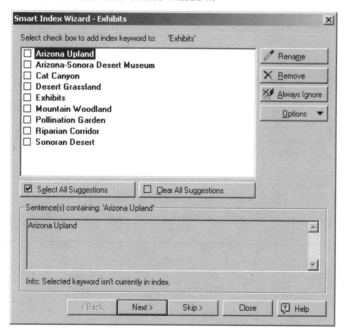

Figure 9-14: The Smart Index suggesting keywords

12. In the keywords box, click on the words you want to include in your index for the specified topic. If you aren't sure about a word, highlight it to display the sentence in which the word appears. You can also click the **Select All**

Suggestions button to include all suggested words in the index or the **Clear All Suggestions** button to exclude all the words.

13. Click the **Next** button to display the suggested keywords from the next topic.

14. Repeat steps 12 and 13 for each topic you've searched. When you've finished all the topics, click the **Next** button to display the status of your changes, as shown in Figure 9-15.

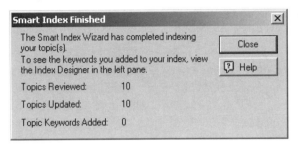

Figure 9-15: Search status display

15. Click **Close** to close the status window and the Smart Index window.

16. The view option only lets you preview one topic at a time, so to test the table of contents, you'll need to open it in a browser, as shown in Figure 9-16. From the **File** menu, choose **Run**, then choose the output format you want.

NOTE: *If your output format is WebHelp Enterprise, you'll have to generate the files and publish them to the server before you can test the table of contents.*

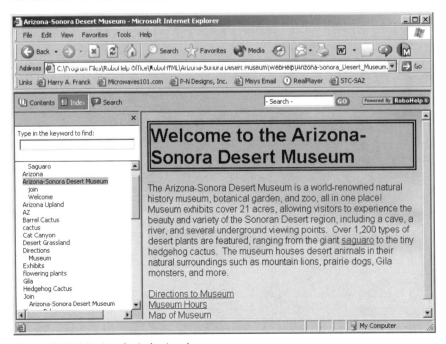

Figure 9-16: Viewing the index in a browser

Specifying Custom Index Settings

When Smart Index searches for potential keywords, it uses a combination of settings and word files to identify the words that it will suggest. You can change either the settings or the files to refine the lists of suggested keywords. In addition, the word lists specify those words that the final index will ignore during searches. For example, if a user types in "the desert," the word "the" will be ignored.

To change the index settings and lists to identify words you want Smart Index to suggest, follow these steps:

1. Open the Smart Index window in one of the following ways:

   ▪ Click the **Smart Index** button at the bottom of the Index pane.

   ▪ From the **Index** tab, click the right mouse button and choose **Smart Index**.

   ▪ From the **Tools** menu, choose **Smart Index Wizard**.

2. Click the **Use custom search settings** check box. This activates the Settings button.

3. Click the **Settings** button to display the Smart Index Settings window, as shown in Figure 9-17.

Figure 9-17: Refining the way Smart Index suggests keywords

4. Specify the types of words that will be included in the suggested keywords by choosing one or more of the check boxes in the **Include all** section. Note that the labels on the check boxes display examples of the type of word they're

describing. For example, to always suggest words that appear in the topics in all capital letters, select the check box with the label **Uppercase WORDS**.

5. Specify how you want Smart Index to suggest multiword phrases by selecting one of the phrase options:

   ■ Choose **Multiple words** if you want Smart Index to suggest phrases.

   ■ Choose **Single words** if you don't want Smart Index to suggest phrases.

6. For help systems in the English language, you can select any of the displayed check boxes in the English Settings area to include that type of word in the Smart Index keyword suggestions.

7. Click **OK** to store your changes, close the Options window, and return to the Smart Index Wizard.

8. RoboHelp HTML comes with several word lists. These lists identify words that the search feature will not display, either when suggesting keywords (Always Ignore) or when a user is searching the finished help (Stop List). To modify either of these lists, click the **Always Ignore** button to display the Localization window, shown in Figure 9-18.

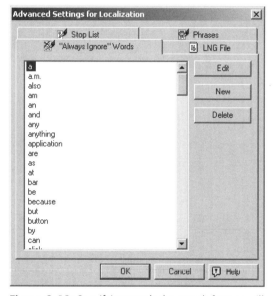

9. Click the **"Always Ignore" Words** tab to refine the list of words that will not appear when Smart Index is suggesting keywords. Click the **Stop List** tab to refine the list of words that will not appear when the user is searching the finished help file.

Figure 9-18: Specifying words the search feature will ignore

10. Click **New** to add a word to the list, or highlight a word and click **Delete** to remove it from the list. Click **OK** when you are done to return to the Smart Index Wizard.

11. From the Smart Index Wizard, you can click the **Phrases** button to add phrases that the Smart Index will always suggest. For example, you may want to add a phrase such as "Arizona-Sonora Desert Museum."

TIP: *The Phrases window works much like the Always Ignore and Stop List windows in that you can easily add and delete words or phrases. Remember, though, that the Phrases window specifies words you want to include in the search; Always Ignore and Stop List specify words you don't want to include.*

12. Click **OK** to close the Phrases window and return to the Smart Index Wizard.

13. You may continue with the Smart Index Wizard as described in the previous section, or you may click **Cancel** to stop the wizard, saving your changes for the next time you run Smart Index.

Adding Keywords to Individual Topics

If you choose not to use the Smart Index tool, you can add index keywords to each topic as you go along. The index words you enter will appear in the Index tab of the left-hand pane, as well as in the index you generate at the end of the project.

To manually add index keywords to a topic, follow these steps:

1. With the topic selected in the right-hand pane, click the **Properties** icon (📇) to display the Properties window.

2. Click the **Index** tab to display the list of existing keywords for the topic, if any, as shown in Figure 9-19.

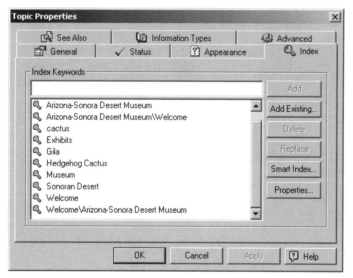

Figure 9-19: Displaying keywords for the topic in the Index tab

3. Type the keyword you want to add in the box at the top of the window or choose an existing keyword by clicking the **Add Existing** button.

4. If you chose to add an existing keyword, the list of existing keywords for the entire project is displayed in the Add Existing Index Keyword window, as shown in Figure 9-20 on the following page.

5. The left side of the window displays all of the keywords for the project. The right side of the window displays the keywords for the current topic. Click a keyword on the left side of the window, and then click the arrow to add it to the right side of the window and to the topic. Click **OK** when finished.

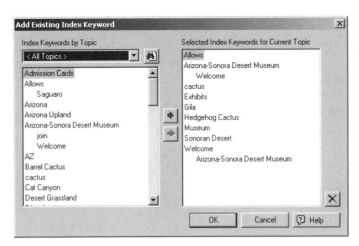

Figure 9-20: Adding existing keywords to the current topic

6. Click **Add** to add the new name. The name appears in the list.
7. Click **OK** to save the keywords and return to the topic display.

Creating a Multilevel Index

A multilevel index lets you create categories of information and then include index entries for each member of the group or category. For example, in addition to having index entries for ocotillo, saguaro, and prickly pear, you may want to list those three types of cactus under a generic cactus entry. The resulting index would look like this:

    cactus
        ocotillo
        prickly pear
        saguaro

Another common use for multiple levels in an index is to use verbs to break up long lists of topics. For example, if there are 20 topics that use the index word "prickly pear," you may want to split them up as follows:

    prickly pear
        characteristics
        cooking
        growing

The second level of the index (characteristics, cooking, and growing in the above example) is created by specifying *subkeywords*. Like regular keywords, subkeywords can be words or phrases. To add subkeywords, you can:

■ Add subkeywords to the keyword in the Index tab and then specify topics for the subkeyword.

■ Create a list of subkeywords in the Smart Index tool and then choose from the subkeyword list for each topic.

■ Manually add subkeywords to each topic.

Adding Subkeywords in the Index Tab

To add subkeywords in the Index tab, you'll have to first add the subkeyword and then specify topics to which the subkeyword will point. Follow these steps:

1. In the left-hand pane, click the **Index** tab to display a list of existing keywords.

2. Highlight the keyword to which you want to add subkeywords. For example, highlight "prickly pear."

3. Add the new subkeyword placeholder in one of two ways:

   ■ Click the **subkeyword** icon ( ) on the Index pane.

   ■ Click the right mouse button and select **New**, then **Subkeyword**.

   With either method, an empty text box will be displayed beneath the selected keyword.

4. Type the subkeyword, then press **Enter.** The new subkeyword is displayed beneath the keyword to which it is linked.

5. In the right-hand pane, click the **Topics** tab to display a list of topic names.

6. Click the name of a topic to which you want to link the new subkeyword. Then drag the topic name to the Topics box in the lower portion of the Index tab on the left-hand pane. The topic will be displayed in the Topics box, as shown in Figure 9-21, and the new subkeyword will be added to the topic.

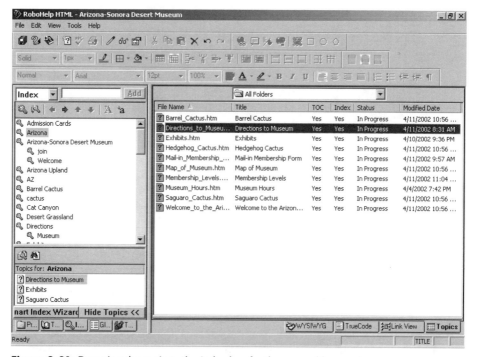

Figure 9-21: Dragging the topic to the Index box for the new subkeyword

Adding Subkeywords with Smart Index

As you add subkeywords, make sure that you are consistent from one topic to the next. For example, if you are "deleting" in one topic, don't use "deletes" or "delete" in another. The Smart Index Wizard helps you stay consistent by creating a list of words, usually verbs, that can be used as subkeywords in many topics.

To use the Smart Index tool to add subkeywords, you'll need to create the list and choose from the list when adding keywords. Follow these steps:

1. Open the Smart Index window in one of the following ways:

   ▪ From the **Index** tab, click the right mouse button and choose **Smart Index**.

   ▪ From the **Tools** menu, choose **Smart Index Wizard**.

2. From the first Smart Index window, click **Next** to display the second Smart Index window.

3. From the second Smart Index window, click **Next** to display the Smart Index topic display, as shown in Figure 9-22.

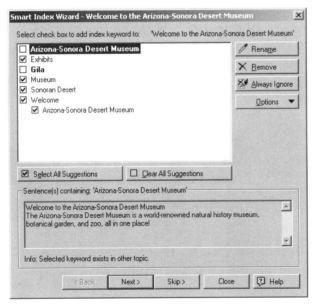

Figure 9-22: Smart Index displaying suggested keywords

4. Highlight the word for which you want to add a subkeyword.

5. Click the **Options** button, and then choose **Verbs** to display the list of available subkeywords, as shown in Figure 9-23 on the following page.

TIP: *Although this window is accessed by the word "Verbs," you can specify other parts of speech for the subkeywords.*

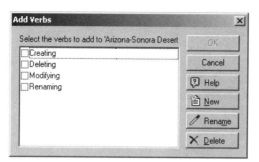

Figure 9-23: The verbs list

6. To add a word to the list, click **New** to display the window shown in Figure 9-24.

Figure 9-24: Entering a new word for the Subkeyword list

7. Enter a new word and click **OK**. The new word is displayed in the Verbs list.

8. Choose the subkeywords you want to add to the keyword you selected back in step 4. Then click **OK**. The new subkeyword is added to the topic.

9. You can continue using Smart Index, adding subkeywords to other topics, or you can click **Cancel** to close the Smart Index window.

Adding Subkeywords to Individual Topics

If you choose not to use the Smart Index tool, you can add subkeywords to each topic as you go along. This gives you more control over the keywords and subkeywords, but it is also more difficult to maintain consistency from one topic to the next.

TIP: *Remember, the index considers each spelling of a word as a separate keyword or subkeyword. For example, if you use "visit" in one topic, "visiting" in another, and "visits" in a third, the entries will each display as separate index entries. To prevent this, pick one form of the word and stick to it.*

To manually add index subkeywords to a topic, follow these steps:

1. With the topic selected in the right-hand pane, click the **Properties** icon ( ) to display the Properties window.

2. Click the **Index** tab to display the list of existing keywords for the topic, if any, as shown in Figure 9-25.

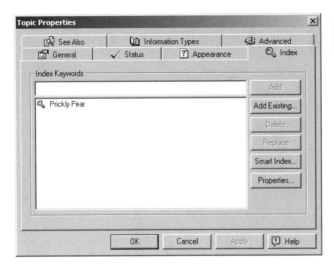

Figure 9-25: Displaying keywords for the topic on the Index tab

3. Type a keyword <u>and</u> a subkeyword separated by a backslash (such as "prickly pear\recipes") in the keywords box.

4. Click **Add** to add the new subkeyword. The name appears in the list, as shown in Figure 9-26.

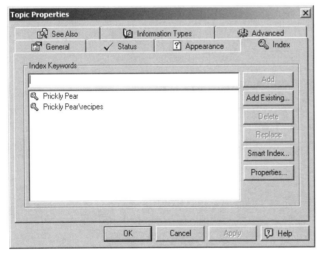

Figure 9-26: Displaying the new subkeyword in the Index tab

6. Click **OK** to save the keywords and return to the topic display. The keyword and subkeyword will display in the Index tab.

Embedding Navigation in a Topic

The standard output displays the table of contents and index entries on the side of the topic pane. If, however, you choose not to use the tri-pane mode, you can still include a table of contents in an HTML Help project using an ActiveX control. Like other ActiveX controls included with RoboHelp, the table of contents control can only be added to HTML Help output.

Both the table of contents and index controls use the same wizard—only the title bar is different. To include a table of contents or index in a topic instead of in a separate pane, follow these steps:

1. In the WYSIWYG Editor, click where you want to add the control in the topic.

2. From the **Insert** menu, choose **HTML Help** and then either **Table of Contents** or **Index** to start the wizard, as shown in Figure 9-27.

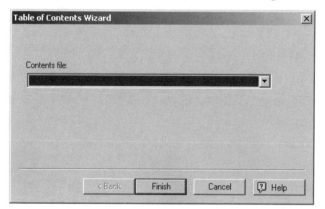

Figure 9-27: Specifying the name of the contents file

3. Choose the **contents** (*.hhc) or **index** (*.hhk) file from the drop-down menu.

4. Click **Finish** to close the wizard and insert the table of contents or index into your topic.

Summary

In this chapter, you saw how to use folders to organize the project as you are working on it. You also learned how to create and edit a table of contents and discovered a variety of ways to create an index for the RoboHelp HTML output.

The next chapter will discuss how to maintain consistent output with templates and create custom viewer elements with skins.

Chapter 10

Maintaining Consistency with Templates and Skins

A help system should have a consistent look and feel across all of the topics in the system. Although RoboHelp HTML stores each topic in a separate file, you can use *templates* to ensure that the topics have some elements in common. For example, you could create a template with a header that appears at the top of every topic. If you make changes to the header later, all topics that use that template would automatically be updated.

RoboHelp HTML also lets you define how the final help topic will be displayed through the use of *skins*. Skins let you specify how the menu bar and navigation pane will appear around each topic. In addition to ensuring that the topics are displayed like each other, you can use skins to make the help look more like other components of your product or system. Once defined, you can share skin files with other help authors to ensure consistency throughout your help system.

Working with Templates

A template looks much like a topic in that it has an area for text (the body of the topic) and can have a header and a footer. Like topics, templates can also use a specific style sheet and have associated background sounds. Unlike a regular topic, however, templates can be used to create new topics or applied to other topics.

Templates can contain any type of element that topics can have, including images, color, multimedia, links, and DHTML effects. Elements in the header or footer will be stored with the template and referenced by each topic that uses the template. This lets you make one change (for example, to a link in the template footer) and have that change apply to many topics. Similarly, the template properties (style sheet and background sound) are stored with the template and apply to all topics that use the template.

> **NOTE:** *Elements in the body of the template will only be copied to a topic if you are creating a new topic with the template. These elements will be overridden by changes you make to the topic and will not be updated if the template changes.*

Creating Topic Templates

All templates for your project are stored in the Template Gallery and are included in the Templates folder for your project. Template files have an extension of .htt. You can create new templates from the Templates folder, or you can create a template based on an existing topic.

Creating a New Template from the Templates Folder

To create a new template, follow these steps:

1. Click the **Folders** tab to display the Templates folder in the left-hand pane of the RoboHelp HTML window.

2. Highlight the **Templates** folder. Then click the right mouse button and choose **New Topic Template** to display the New Template.

3. Enter a name for the new template. Like other names, make it distinctive enough so that you'll know what the template contains. For example, you may create a template just for pages that describe desert plants. In this case, name the template "Desert Plants" rather than "Template 1."

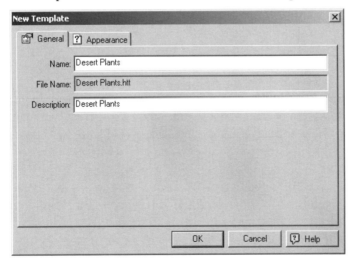

Figure 10-1: Entering a name and optional description for the new template

4. Enter an optional description. The description defaults to specifying the style sheet. You may add to the description or replace it entirely.

5. Click the **Appearance** tab to set the template style sheet and background sound settings. The Appearance tab for the template is the same as the Topic Properties Appearance tab, as shown in Figure 10-2.

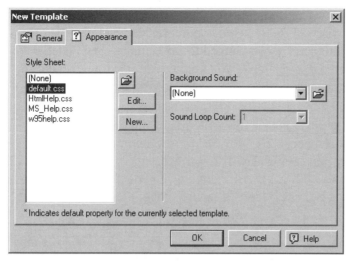

Figure 10-2: Setting the template properties in the Appearance tab

6. Choose a style sheet, if necessary. Style sheets are discussed in more detail in Chapter 6.

7. If you want, you can also specify a background sound that will play whenever the topic is displayed. See Chapter 8 for more information about background sounds and other types of multimedia.

8. Click **OK** to close the New Template window and display the template. The template looks just like a new topic, except the word "Template" is displayed in a dark banner across the top of the WYSIWYG pane, as shown in Figure 10-3.

Figure 10-3: Displaying a new template in the WYSIWYG pane

9. Make changes to the template just as you would to a topic. Remember, the elements in the body of the topic will be overridden by the topic body. Elements in the header and footer will be linked to the template and updated when the template is updated. For example, you might want to include an outline for plant pages in the sample template. This will act as a guide for the help authors who use the template.

10. Templates are most powerful when you include headers or footers. For example, to add a header, choose **Header** from the **View** menu, and then insert whatever elements you want to display. The example in Figure 10-4 shows a header that contains a table with custom borders and a hyperlink that goes to the "Welcome to the Arizona-Sonora Desert Museum" page.

Figure 10-4: Adding headers and footers to the template

11. To see what the topics using the new template will look like, you can click the **View** icon (🔍) to open the template as if it were a topic, as shown in Figure 10-5.

Figure 10-5: Previewing the template to see headers and footers

Creating a Template from an Existing Topic

To create a template from an existing topic, follow these steps:

1. Open an existing topic.

2. Ensure that the topic uses the style sheet, background sound, and header and footer information you want in the template, and thus on every page. For example, if you're creating a template for all plant pages, you wouldn't want text about the Saguaro in the header (just in the body of the topic). You can use any of the elements discussed throughout the rest of this book. For example, you could add See Also buttons, as shown in Figure 10-6.

Figure 10-6: Adding See Also buttons to the template

3. You may want to edit the body of the topic to reflect the text that you want to appear in new topics. For example, rather than use an entire page of text about Saguaros in the template, you might want to take out most of the text and leave only the headings.

CAUTION: *If you edit the body of an existing topic to reflect what you want in a template, the topic will be stored with the edited information (and you'll lose whatever text you may have entered). To prevent this, either create a new template or leave the existing text in the template.*

4. Display the Add to Template Gallery window shown in Figure 10-7 in one of the following ways:

   ■ From the **File** menu, choose **Add to Template Gallery**.

   ■ In the WYSIWYG pane, click the right mouse button and choose **Add to Template Gallery**.

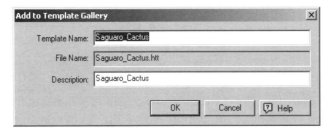

Figure 10-7: The Add to Template Gallery window

5. The filename of the existing topic is the default name for the template, but you can change this. As you enter a name for the new template, the filename also changes. Like other names, make it distinctive enough so that you'll know what the template contains. For example, you may create a template just for pages that describe desert plants. Name the template "Desert Plants" rather than "Template 1."

6. Enter an optional description. The description defaults to the description of the topic you started with. You may add to the description or replace it entirely.

7. Click **OK** to save the topic, close the Add to Template Gallery window and add the new template to the Template Gallery.

Importing Templates

You can import templates from one project to another or use templates that someone else has created as a starting point for your own templates. When you import a template, you also copy all of the associated files for that template (such as images or style sheets).

> **TIP:** *Copying a template .htt file to your project folder is not enough to let your project use the template. You must use the import template function in order for your project to recognize the template and ensure it has access to all the template's files.*

To import a template, follow these steps:

1. From the **File** menu, choose **Import** and then **Topic Template**.

2. In the **Open** window, enter the name and location of the template. You can also use the browse feature to point to the location of the template file (.htt). Click **OK** when you are done.

3. RoboHelp HTML displays a series of windows that ask if you want to copy files referenced by the new style sheet (style sheets, graphics, sound files, etc.). A sample window is shown in Figure 10-8.

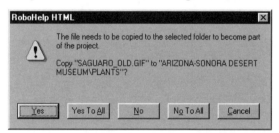

Figure 10-8: Copying the template files to your project

- Click **Yes** or **Yes To All** to copy the files to your project.

- If you are sure that all required files are already in your project, you can click **No** or **No To All.** You can also click No or No To All if you know that you are going to change the template and won't need the specified file. For example, you might have a template where you want to use the header and footer but don't want to use the template's background sound. You don't need to copy the sound file into your project.

4. Repeat step 3 for each window that is displayed (one window for each file associated with the template). RoboHelp HTML copies the files, which will be displayed in the appropriate folders (such as images, multimedia, style sheets, and template folders).

Once you've imported a template, you can edit it as described earlier in this chapter or use it as you would any other template, as described in the following sections.

Using Templates

Once you have a template that you like, you can use it when you create new topics, or you can apply it to existing topics. When you create new topics, the entire template will be used, including the body text. When you apply a template to existing topics, you'll overwrite any header, footer, or style sheet information the topic may have, but the template won't change the text in the body of the topic.

Creating New Topics with a Template

To create a new topic with a template, follow these steps:

1. Open the New Topic window (shown in Figure 10-9) in one of the following ways:

    ■ Click the **New Topic** icon (🎲).

    ■ From the **File** menu, choose **New** and then choose **Topic**.

    ■ Press **Ctrl+T**.

    ■ With the cursor in the HTML Files (Topics) folder of the left-hand pane or the Topics tab of the right-hand pane, click the right mouse button and choose **New Topic** to create the topic in the default HTML editor.

    ■ With the cursor in the HTML Files (Topics) folder of the left-hand pane or the Topics tab of the right-hand pane, click the right mouse button and choose **New Topic With**. Choose one of the available HTML editors from the list to create a topic using that editor.

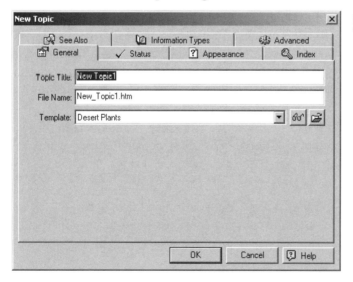

Figure 10-9: The New Topic window

2. Enter a title for the topic. The title will appear in the title bar of the finished help window and will be the default heading for the topic.

3. As you enter the title, RoboHelp enters the title as the filename (with under-scores replacing spaces). While this is sometimes convenient, the filenames can get very long. If you want to use a shorter filename, enter the new name in the File Name box. Remember, you cannot use spaces or special characters in a filename.

4. Click the down arrow next to the Template box to display a list of templates for the project. Click on a template name to display it in the Template box.

5. Once the template name is in the Template box, you can click the **View** icon () to see what the template contains.

6. Click **OK** to create the topic with the specified template. The topic opens in the specified editor (or the default editor) with the title you entered as heading of the topic. The body of the topic contains the text from the body of the template.

7. Add and edit text in the new topic just as you did in the first topic.

> **NOTE:** *Text that you enter or change in the body of the new topic will remain as you enter it, even if a new template is applied to the topic later.*

8. The topic retains its connection to the template. If you change the header or footer information for the topic, a message will be displayed when you save the file, as shown in Figure 10-10.

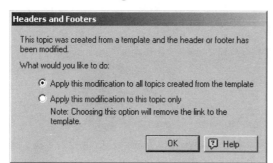

Figure 10-10: Changing the header or footer in the template

9. You must either change the template to match the header or footer or remove the template from the current topic. If you change the template later, this topic will not be updated. Click **OK** when you've chosen an option to close the message window and display the topic.

Applying Templates to Existing Topics

When you apply a template to an existing topic, the topic's header and footer will be replaced by the template's header and footer (if any). In addition, the style sheet and background music will be updated to those of the applied template. Body text will not be changed.

To apply a template to an existing topic, follow these steps:

1. Display the Topic Properties window, as shown in Figure 10-11, in one of the following ways:

   ■ Open the topic in the WYSIWYG pane, then click the **Properties** icon (🖺).

   ■ Open the topic in the WYSIWYG pane, then click the right mouse button and choose **Topic Properties**.

   ■ Open the topic in the WYSIWYG pane, then choose **Properties** from the **Edit** menu.

   ■ Highlight the topic name in the left-hand pane, then click the right mouse button and choose **Properties**.

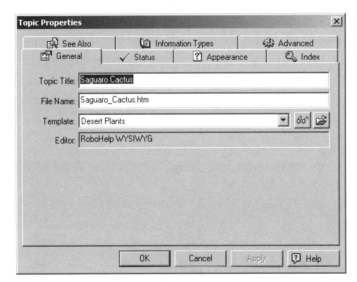

Figure 10-11: Displaying the topic properties to apply to a new template

2. Click the down arrow next to the Template box to display a list of templates for the project. Click on a template name to display it in the Template box.

3. Once the template name is in the Template box, you can click the **Preview** icon (👓) to see what the template contains.

4. Click **OK** to close the property window and apply the template to the current topic.

Working with Skins

A skin in RoboHelp defines the way the finished help topics appear in the browser. A skin replaces the default browser navigation with customized elements, such as icons, tabs, and toolbars to the left and across the top of your topics. You can also specify the labels for tabs, background images, and logos.

RoboHelp HTML comes with a gallery of predefined skins. Figure 10-12 shows a few of these skins.

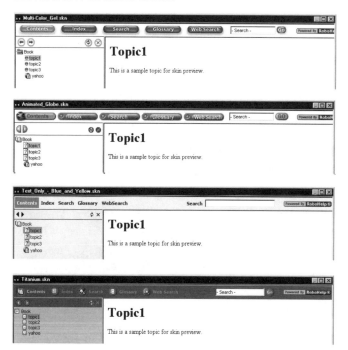

Figure 10-12: Sample skins from the RoboHelp HTML gallery

You can start with any of these skins and modify them for your needs, or you can make your own skin by editing the default skin that is automatically associated with each project. Once you create a skin, you can use it for multiple projects and share it with other help authors for a consistent look and feel across your product line or your whole company. Skins are applied to the help system when you generate it. The default skin is also used when you preview the help.

Customizing a RoboHelp HTML Skin

To create a set of navigation tools and icons for your help system, you can edit existing skins or start a new one. If you create a new skin, you'll start with the default skin settings. However you choose to begin, you'll always edit the skin with the RoboHelp HTML Skin Editor tool. The Skin Editor has three primary areas:

- The Preview area lets you see what your skin will look like as you make changes.

- The Toolbar tab lets you changes elements across the top of the window, such as the contents and index icons and labels, as well as background colors and images. You can also add items to the toolbar, such as links to other web pages.

- The Navigation tab lets you change the elements in the left-hand pane, such as topic and book icons, colors, and background images

Opening, Viewing, and Saving a Skin

To open the RoboHelp HTML Skin Editor, follow these steps:

1. Start by choosing one of the following methods:

   - Double-click the name of the skin in the **Skins** folder. The Skin Editor opens and displays the specified skin (and you can skip to step 4).

   - Right-click in the **Skins** folder and choose **New Skin**. A window appears, as shown in Figure 10-13.

   - From the **File** menu, choose **New** and then **Skin**. A window appears, as shown in Figure 10-13.

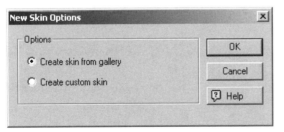

Figure 10-13: The New Skin Options window

2. If you want to start with the default skin settings, choose **Create custom skin** and then click **OK** to display the Skin Editor (and skip ahead to step 4). If you want to start with a predefined skin, choose **Create skin from gallery** and then click **OK** to display the list of available skins, as shown in Figure 10-14.

3. Highlight the name of the skin in the gallery. Once a name is highlighted, you can click the **Preview** button to see what the skin looks like. When you've chosen the skin you want, click **OK** to close the gallery window and display the specified skin in the Skin Editor.

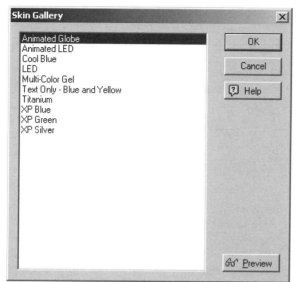

Figure 10-14: Choosing a skin from the gallery

4. The specified skin is displayed in the Skin Editor. Figure 10-15 shows the Skin Editor with the default skin settings. The left-hand pane shows what the skin will look like. Click the tabs across the top of the pane to see how each tab will look (contents, index, search, and glossary). The right-hand pane lists the elements you can change and gives you access to the various editing windows.

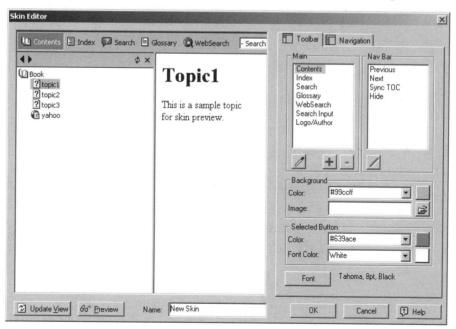

Figure 10-15: The Skin Editor

5.   Make changes as necessary, as described in the following sections of this chapter. As you edit the various skin elements, click the **Update View** button to see what the skin will look like. If you want to see what the skin looks like without the Skin Editor, you can click the **Preview** button at any time.

6.   The Name box at the bottom of the window displays the name of the skin you selected or the words "New Skin," if you chose to create a new skin back in step 1.

   ■   If it is a new skin, enter a name for the skin in the **Name** box.

   ■   If you are working with an existing skin, you may type a new name for the skin.

CAUTION: *Entering a new name for an existing file in the Skin Editor will change the name that appears in the list of skins when you generate the file. It does not change the filename. For example, if you double-clicked the default skin to begin the process and then changed the skin name to "Colorful," the default skin will be listed as "colorful," but the file name will remain default.skn.*

7.   Click **OK** to save your changes to the specified skin name and close the Skin Editor. If you are editing an existing skin, your changes will be stored to the existing skin name in the Skins folder. If you started by creating a new skin, clicking **OK** displays the window shown in Figure 10-16.

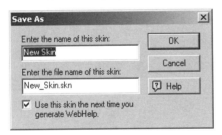

Figure 10-16: Saving the skin to a new name

8.   The top box displays the name you entered in the Name box. The system automatically copies the name into the file name box, replacing spaces with underlines. You can change the filename if you like, but it is best to keep the skin name (that appears in a list from which you choose the skins) and the filename (the name the skin is stored under on your disk) very closely related.

9.   If you want RoboHelp to use the skin you are saving as the default skin for this project, click the check box. Whether you check this box or not, you'll have an opportunity to select a different skin when you generate the files.

10. Click **OK** to close the Save As window and the Skin Editor.

Changing the Main Toolbar Elements with the Skin Editor

Once you have the Skin Editor open, you can change any of the elements across the top of the skin with the Toolbar tab. You can also add elements or remove them. Default elements are listed in Table 10-1.

Table 10-1: Default toolbar elements

Element	Description
Contents	Displays the table of contents entries as defined in the TOC tab within RoboHelp HTML
Index	Displays the index entries indicated by keywords within each topic
Search	Displays a box into which users can enter criteria to search for topics within the help system
Glossary	Displays any glossary entries that you entered on the Glossary tab in the left-hand pane
WebSearch	Displays a box into which users can enter criteria to search for information across the World Wide Web
Search Input	The box that appears for the WebSearch option
Logo	Displays information about the generation date and software used to build the system (like an "About" button)

To change elements in the toolbar, follow these steps:

1. Open the skin in the Skin Editor as described in the previous section.

2. Click the **Toolbar** tab to display the Toolbar options, as shown in Figure 10-17.

3. To change any of the default tabs (Contents, Index, Search, Glossary, WebSearch), double-click the tab name in the Main box or highlight the name in the Main box and click the **Edit** button ( ). The appropriate editing window will display for that tab. The tab editing windows all look and work the same way. The only difference between them is the title bar. For example, Figure 10-18 shows the WebSearch tab editing window.

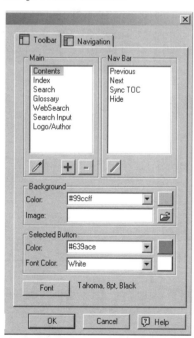

Figure 10-17: Changing the toolbar items with the Toolbar tab

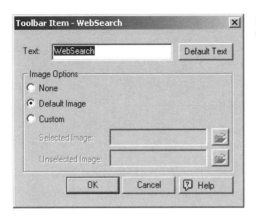

Figure 10-18: Editing window for WebSearch tab

4. To change the text of the toolbar item, type new text in the **Text** box or click the **Default Text** button to return to the default text. This is particularly useful if you want the help to match other features of your product. For example, you could rename the Search toolbar item "Find in Help." You can also delete text from the Text box to display only an image for this tab. This is useful when you have an image that contains text on it already, as in some of the skins in the Skin Gallery.

5. To change the image that is displayed next to the toolbar text, choose one of the items in the Image Options area.

Table 10-2: Image options

Option	Description
None	The text will appear on the tab with no image or icon.
Default Image	The image that comes with RoboHelp HTML will be used for the selected tab. For example, this will be a book icon for Contents and a globe with a magnifying glass for WebSearch.
Custom	When you select Custom, the two image boxes become active. Enter a name for the image you want to have appear next to the tab text when the user clicks the tab (and displays the tab information in the navigation pane). You may also specify an image that will display on this tab when it is not selected. If you enter only one image name, that image will display whether the tab is selected or not. You can also use the browse feature to point to image files. If you haven't used the image within the project before, RoboHelp HTML will copy it into your project for you.

TIP: *You may use any of the images that come with RoboHelp HTML for icons and buttons by browsing to the RoboHelp HTML folder and then to \gallery\ images\Skin_Toolbar.*

6. A Search Input box appears next to the WebSearch tab in the toolbar and also in the Search navigation pane. You can modify the default text that displays inside the input box or the size of the input box. Open the Search Input box editing window, shown in Figure 10-19, in one of the following ways:

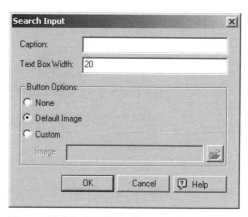

    ■ Double-click on the **Search Input** name in the Main box of the Skin Editor.

    ■ Highlight **Search Input** and click the **Edit** button (✎).

Figure 10-19: Specifying the input box appearance

7. Enter the Search Input parameters:

    ■ Specify a caption that will appear inside the search box in the toolbar. This caption will not apply to the search box within the navigation pane.

    ■ Enter the width of the text box in characters. Valid widths are from 10 to 40 characters long. This is the maximum number of characters displayed at once. Users may still type longer strings than this.

    ■ Enter the button options. These are the same as the options for the other tab editing windows, as described in Table 10-2, except you only get to enter one image name for the Custom option. This image will be displayed next to the input box regardless of which tab is selected.

8. A logo is displayed in the far right-hand side of the toolbar. The default is a logo that says "Powered by RoboHelp," but you can change this to any image you want. When a user clicks the logo, a window displays the version information about the help system. You can also include an author or company name, as shown in Figure 10-20.

Figure 10-20: Displaying information about WebHelp when the user clicks the logo

To change the logo on the toolbar and the author's name that is in the About box, open the Logo editing window shown in Figure 10-21 in one of the following ways:

- Double-click on the word **Logo** in the Main box of the Skin Editor.
- Highlight **Logo** and click the **Edit** button.

Figure 10-21: Entering logo parameters

9. Enter the Logo parameters:

    - Enter the name of an image you want to use instead of the RoboHelp logo. If you don't specify an image, the default will be used.
    - Enter whatever text you want to display in the About box next to Author.

10. In addition to the default tabs, you can include custom items on the toolbar, such as a link to an external web page or custom elements using JavaScript. To display the Custom Toolbar Item window shown in Figure 10-22, click the **Add** button (➕).

11. You must enter a name in the **Item Name** box (which will be displayed in the Main box with the other item names). You must also enter either the text (which will be displayed on the toolbar) or the name of an image to display on the toolbar. You may enter both, if you like. To specify an image, click the **Custom** check box and enter the image name.

12. Click the **Action** tab (shown in Figure 10-23) to define what happens when the custom tab is selected.

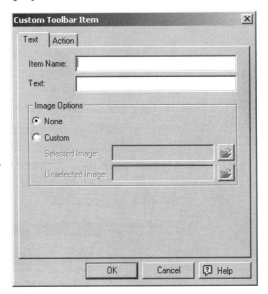

Figure 10-22: The Custom Toolbar Item window Text tab

13. Specify what the custom tab will do in one of the following ways:

   ■ Click the **Link** button and enter a URL or topic name. For example, you might create a toolbar item that points to the URL of your corporate home page.

   ■ Click the **JavaScript** button, and then enter functions for the button. You must also specify either inline JavaScript or point to an external JavaScript file. While this will be of interest only to a small percentage of HTML Help developers, it's a powerful feature. For more information about JavaScript, a good place to start would be *Learn JavaScript* by Chuck Easttom. For more detailed information, try *Advanced JavaScript, 2nd Edition*, also by Chuck Easttom (both available from Wordware Publishing).

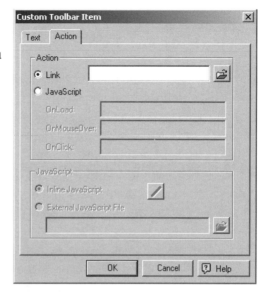

Figure 10-23: The Custom Toolbar Item window Action tab

14. Click **OK** to close the Custom Toolbar Item window. The Skin Editor displays the custom item in the Main box with the default items. To delete a custom item, highlight the item name and then click the custom item **Delete** button (**-**).

15. To view your changes, click **Update View**. To see what the skin would look like without the Skin Editor, click **Preview**.

Changing the Navigation Toolbar Elements with the Skin Editor

There is also a second menu near the top of the skin, but this one does not go across the topic, just the navigation pane. You can edit the images that represent each element on this menu in the box marked Nav Bar.

Table 10-3: Navigation toolbar options

Option	Description
Previous	Displays the previous topic as defined by the browse sequence
Next	Displays the next topic as defined by the browse sequence
Sync TOC	Displays an image indicating where the currently displayed topic appears in the table of contents
Hide	Allows the user to turn off the navigation pane entirely, using the full width of the help window to display the topic. The user can redisplay the navigation pane by clicking any of the tabs in the toolbar.

CAUTION: *Some versions of Netscape Navigator will not display the Hide button. Always test your help on the browser your users are likely to have.*

To change the Navigation toolbar images, follow these steps:

1. Open the skin in the Skin Editor as described in "Opening, Viewing, and Saving a Skin" earlier in this chapter.

2. Click the **Toolbar** tab to display the Toolbar options, as shown in Figure 10-24.

3. To change any of the Navigation toolbar images (Next, Previous, Sync TOC, or Hide), double-click the tab name in the **Nav Bar** box, or highlight the name in the Main box and click the **Edit** button. The appropriate editing window will display for that image. The image editing windows all look and work the same way. The only difference between them is the title bar. For example, Figure 10-25 shows the Index tab editing window.

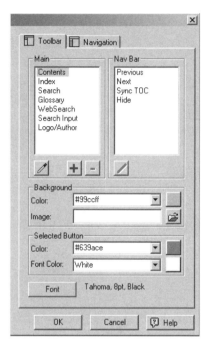

Figure 10-24: Changing the Navigation toolbar with the Toolbar tab

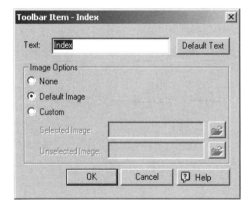

Figure 10-25: Editing window for Index tab

4. To change the image that is displayed for the selected toolbar item, choose one of the following options.

Table 10-4: Image options

Option	Description
None	The text will appear on the tab with no image or icon.
Default Image	The image that comes with RoboHelp HTML will be used for the selected item. For example, this will be a triangle pointing to the right for Next and an X for Hide.

Option	Description
Custom	When you select Custom, the two image boxes become active. For the Next and Previous items, you can specify an image to display when there is a topic available in that direction (enabled) and a different image when there is not (disabled). For example, at the last topic in a browse sequence, the Next button would display the "disabled" image because there is no "next" topic. For the Sync TOC and Hide items, there will only be one image box. You can also use the browse feature to point to image files. If you haven't used the image within the project before, RoboHelp HTML will copy it into your project for you.

TIP: *You may use any of the images that come with RoboHelp HTML for icons and buttons by browsing to the RoboHelp HTML folder and then to \gallery\images\ Skin_Toolbar.*

5. Click **OK** to close the Toolbar Item window.

6. Click **Update View** to see the changes you've made in the Skin Editor. Click **Preview** to see the changes in a sample browser window without the Skin Editor.

7. Click **OK** to close the Skin Editor and save your changes.

Changing the Colors and Fonts on the Toolbars

The Toolbar tab in the Skin Editor allows you to set the background behind the toolbars to any color you want. Or you could use a graphic as the background. You can also change the font in which the text appears on the toolbars.

NOTE: *Set the colors and fonts for the content of the tabs (where the topic lists appear) with the Navigation tab on the Skin Editor, not the Toolbar tab.*

To change toolbar images, follow these steps:

1. Open the skin in the Skin Editor as described in "Opening, Viewing, and Saving a Skin" earlier in this chapter.

2. Click the **Toolbar** tab to display the Toolbar options on the right-hand pane of the Skin Editor, as shown in Figure 10-26. It doesn't matter which tab is selected on the left-hand pane.

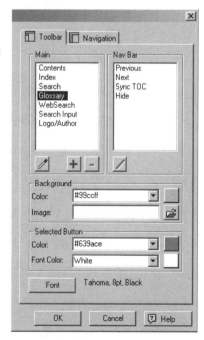

Figure 10-26: Changing the toolbar background with the Toolbar tab

3. Select the background of the toolbars in either of the following ways:

    ■ Choose a color from the Background Color drop-down menu. The square next to the drop-down menu displays the selected color. See "Creating Custom Colors" later in this chapter for more information about other color options.

    ■ In the Background Image box, specify the name of an image to appear as the background. Some of the skins in the gallery use images as backgrounds. You can browse to point to an image.

 TIP: *You may use any of the images that come with RoboHelp HTML for backgrounds by browsing to the RoboHelp HTML folder and then to \gallery\images\ Skin_Toolbar.*

When a user clicks one of the elements on the toolbar, the background of the text for that element changes to indicate that the element is selected.

 NOTE: *This has no effect if you are not using text labels in the toolbar (if you are using images to represent your toolbar elements).*

4. To specify a background color for selected text, choose a color from the **Selected Button Color** drop-down menu. The square next to the drop-down menu displays the selected color. See "Creating Custom Colors" later in this chapter for more information about other color options.

 TIP: *When selected, the text background will automatically be changed to the Selected Button Color. Although you should always give the user some indication of the selected button, you may have already indicated this with the Selected and Unselected Images. If you don't want the background text to change when the element is selected, specify the same color for both the background and selected button colors.*

5. You may need to change the text color when the background color changes to maintain readability. To change the text color for the selected button, select a color from the Selected Button Font Color drop-down menu. The square next to the drop-down menu displays the selected color. See "Creating Custom Colors" later in this chapter for more information about other color options.

6. If you are using text labels on the toolbars, you can specify the font, size, and color of the text. Click the **Font** button to display a standard character formatting window, as shown in Figure 10-27.

7. Choose from the **Font** window to specify the font, size, style, and color of the text labels in the left-hand pane. The Preview box displays some text that reflects your font choices. Click **OK** when you're done.

NOTE: *This font box on the Toolbar tab applies only to text in the toolbars. Define text labels for the body of the left-hand pane with the Navigation tab.*

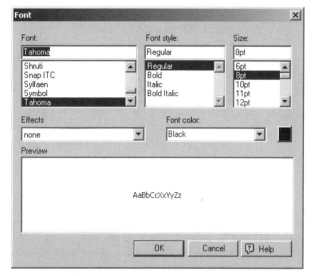

Figure 10-27: Using the Font window to change the text font, size, style, and color

8. Click **Update View** to see the changes you've made in the Skin Editor. Click **Preview** to see the changes in a sample browser window without the Skin Editor.

9. Click **OK** to close the Skin Editor and save your changes.

Changing the Body of the Left-hand Pane with the Skin Editor

The skin consists of both the toolbars and the elements that appear in the left-hand pane when the various toolbar elements are selected. For example, when a user clicks the Index tab, index entries are displayed in the left-hand pane. You can specify the background color or image for the pane. For the Contents pane, you can specify different images to represent the books and pages in your table of contents. For example, you may want to use folder icons instead of book icons.

To specify settings for the body of the left-hand pane, follow these steps:

1. Open the skin in the Skin Editor as described in "Opening, Viewing, and Saving a Skin" earlier in this chapter.

2. Click the **Navigation** tab to display the Navigation options on the right-hand pane of the Skin Editor, as shown in Figure 10-28. It doesn't matter which tab is selected on the left-hand pane.

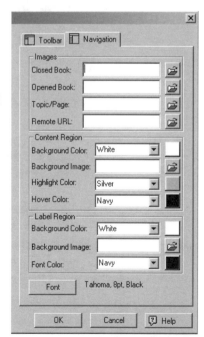

Figure 10-28: Defining the body of the left-hand pane with the Navigation tab

3. The Images area specifies the icons that will be used on the Contents pane. For more detail about books and pages, see "Working with a Table of Contents" in Chapter 9. If you don't specify an image, the default icons will be used. Specify any or all of the following images.

Table 10-5: Navigation icons

Image	Description	Default icon
Closed Book	When topics that make up the book are hidden	
Opened Book	When topics that make up the book are displayed	
Topic/Page	Once for each topic, whether in a book or not	
Remote URL	For each web page in the table of contents	

 You may use any of the images that come with RoboHelp HTML for books or topics by browsing to the RoboHelp HTML folder and then to \gallery\images\ Books_and_Pages.

4. The content region refers to the space on which the Contents, Index, Glossary, or Search is displayed. You can specify either a background color or a background image (but not both) in the Content Region area. Select the background of the content region in either of the following ways:

   ■ Choose a color from the **Background Color** drop-down menu. The square next to the drop-down menu displays the selected color. See "Creating Custom Colors" later in this chapter for more information about other color options.

   ■ In the **Background Image** box, specify the name of an image to appear as the background. Some of the skins in the gallery use images as backgrounds. You can browse to point to an image.

 You may use any of the images that come with RoboHelp HTML for backgrounds by browsing to the RoboHelp HTML folder and then to \gallery\images\ backgrounds.

5. The content region refers to the portion of the left-hand pane that displays the names of the topics for the Contents and Index tabs, individual words for the Glossary tab, and a search box for the Search tab. As the user moves the cursor around within the content region, you can specify the background behind the text item to change in either of the following ways:

   ■ In the **Highlight Color** box, specify a color for the background when the user clicks on an item such as a topic name or glossary word.

   ■ In the **Hover Color** box, specify a color for the background of the item when the user pauses the cursor over the item.

6. The label region is the portion of the Navigation pane that contains labels for the Index, Search, and Glossary tabs (there is no label region on the Contents tab). You can specify either a background color or a background image (but not both) for all label regions in the Label Region area. Select the background of the label region in either of the following ways:

   ■ Choose a color from the **Background Color** drop-down menu. The square next to the drop-down menu displays the selected color. See "Creating Custom Colors" later in this chapter for more information about other color options.

   ■ In the **Background Image** box, specify the name of an image to appear as the background. Some of the skins in the gallery use images as backgrounds. You can browse to point to an image.

TIP: *You may use any of the images that come with RoboHelp HTML for backgrounds by browsing to the RoboHelp HTML folder and then to \gallery\images\ backgrounds.*

7. In the **Font Color** box, specify a color for the text labels in the label region of the Index, Search, and Glossary tabs (optional). If you have changed the label region background to a dark color, you may want to change the label text to a lighter color.

8. You can specify the font, size, and color of the text that appears in the navigation panes. Click the **Font** button to display a standard character formatting window, as shown in Figure 10-29.

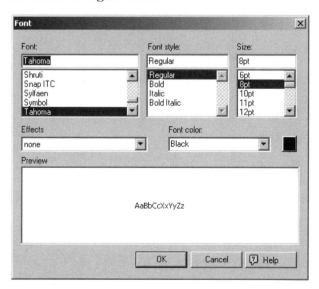

Figure 10-29: Using the Font window to change the text font, size, style, and color

9. Choose from the Font window to specify the font, size, style, and color of the Navigation pane text in the left-hand pane. The Preview box in the Font window displays some text that reflects your font choices. Click **OK** when you're done.

 NOTE: *This font box on the Navigation tab applies only to text in the selected panes. Define text labels for the toolbars with the Toolbar tab.*

10. Click **Update View** to see the changes you've made in the Skin Editor. Click **Preview** to see the changes in a sample browser window without the Skin Editor.

11. Click **OK** to close the Skin Editor and save your changes.

Importing and Exporting Skins

Once you've created a skin, you can share it with other help authors in your company. Or you can use skins that they created to give your product line a consistent look and feel. To share a skin, export the skin to a central location. The other authors can then import the skin into their own projects.

A good central location is the RoboHelp gallery, which already contains many of the elements that allow for a consistent look and feel (icons, backgrounds, buttons, etc.). RoboHelp gives you two ways to export a skin, by saving to the gallery or by exporting the skin to a central location.

Saving a Skin to the Gallery

To save a skin to the gallery, follow these steps:

1. In the left-hand pane of the RoboHelp HTML window, open the **Skins** folder to display a list of available skins.

2. Highlight the skin you want to save to the gallery.

3. Click the right mouse button and choose **Add to Gallery**. The skin and all its components will be saved so that other authors can use them. A message is displayed when the skin is successfully saved, as shown in Figure 10-30.

Figure 10-30: Confirming that the skin has been added to the gallery

4. Click **OK** to close the message window.

Exporting a Skin to a Central Location

If you don't want to store your skins in the Skin Gallery, you can store them any-where on your network that is accessible to all authors. When you export a skin, RoboHelp HTML creates one file from the skin (with extension .skn) and its component parts, such as images or JavaScript files. The resulting file will be a "zipped skin" file with an extension of .zkn.

To export a skin, follow these steps:

1. In the left-hand pane of the RoboHelp HTML window, open the **Skins** folder to display a list of available skins.

2. Highlight the skin you want to export.

3. Click the right mouse button and choose **Export** to display the Save As window shown in Figure 10-31.

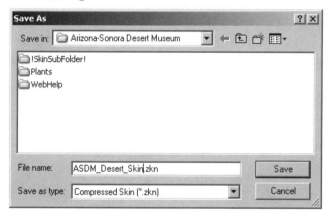

Figure 10-31: Saving a skin to the file type .zkn

4. Browse to the central location where you'd like to store the skin and click **Save**. The skin and all its components will be saved so that other authors can use them. A message is displayed when the skin is successfully saved.

Importing a Skin from a Central Location

You've already seen how to open skins from the gallery (see "Opening, Viewing, and Saving a Skin" earlier in this chapter). You can also import skins created by other authors on your network or skins they've exported to a central location.

To import a skin from a central location on your network, follow these steps:

1. In the left-hand pane of the RoboHelp HTML window, open the **Skins** folder to display a list of available skins.

2. Click the right mouse button anywhere in the Skins folder, and then choose **Import** to display the Import Skin window shown in Figure 10-32.

Figure 10-32: Displaying a list of available skins

3. Browse to the skin's location. This can be another project's skin folder (!SkinSubFolder!) or the central location for your company. Note that in the Files of type box, you can specify skins (*.skn), compressed skins (*.zkn), or both.

4. Highlight the skin you want to import and click **Open**. The skin and all of its components will be copied to your project and the skin will be opened in the Skin Editor.

5. Make any changes you'd like and click **OK** to close the Skin Editor and display the Save As window, as shown in Figure 10-33.

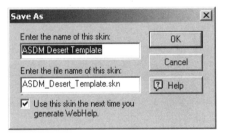

Figure 10-33: Saving the skin and making it the default

6. The top box displays the name you entered in the Name box. The system automatically copies the name into the filename box, replacing spaces with underlines. You can change the filename if you like, but it is best to keep the skin name (that appears in a list from which you choose the skins) and the filename (the name the skin is stored under on your disk) very closely related.

7. If you want RoboHelp to use the skin you are saving as the default skin for this project, click the check box. Whether you check this box or not, you'll have an opportunity to select a different skin when you generate the files.

8. Click **OK** to close the Save As window and save the skin.

Importing a Skin from the eHelp Online Help Community

Skins can be a powerful way to standardize the look and feel of your projects. You can make your help look just like your product or like other existing interfaces (such as windows or browsers). Some standard interfaces have already been duplicated by other help authors and are available to you through the eHelp Online Help Community. Members of the Help Community are always adding new skins to the Skins Collection, so you'll have to go online to see what's available on any given day.

NOTE: *By its very nature, the Help Community changes often. New skins may be added and others removed, and features of the community pages may be changed. The following instructions are accurate as of this printing, but if you have trouble, click the FAQs page, or use the online support features of the Help Community.*

To import a skin from the Help Community, follow these steps:

1. Make sure that your Internet connection is up and running.

2. In the left-hand pane of the RoboHelp HTML window, open the Skins folder to display a list of available skins.

3. Click the right mouse button anywhere in the Skins folder and choose **Import from Web**. RoboHelp HTML will open your default browser and automatically go to the eHelp RoboHelp Community Skins Collection page shown in Figure 10-34.

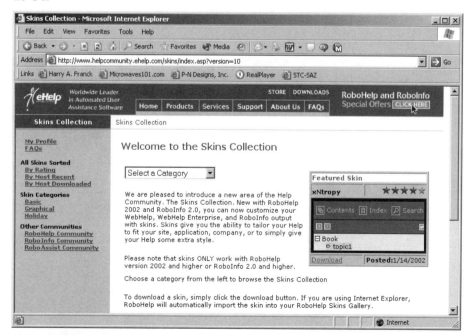

Figure 10-34: The eHelp Skins Collection

4. Specify the way you want to browse through available skins (by date, by most popular, etc.) in the Select a Category drop-down box. The Skins Browser appears, as shown in Figure 10-35.

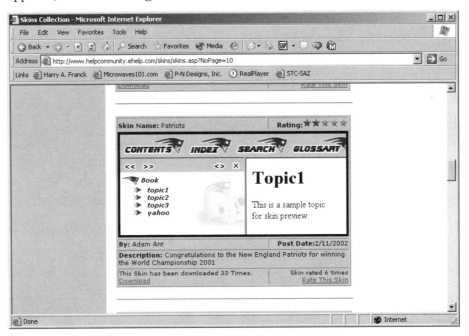

Figure 10-35: The Skins Browser with an example of a skin

5. Use the scroll bars to view additional skins on the page and the navigation buttons to view additional pages of skins.

6. When you've chosen a skin you like, click the **Download** link to import it to your current project. RoboHelp automatically stores the skin and all its components into your project.

7. You can select the skin to open it in the Skin Editor, make changes, or import or export the skin as described in the other sections in this chapter.

Working with Custom Colors

One of the easiest ways to make your help system look like it is part of your product is to use the same color scheme throughout. RoboHelp HTML comes with a variety of predefined colors, accessed by choosing from a drop-down menu. These colors may match your product colors exactly, but more likely you'll need custom colors. RoboHelp HTML lets you add custom colors as you go along, or you can add a custom color to the drop-down box. In both cases, you'll start from the color selection area on any RoboHelp window. These may vary slightly in the label, but they'll all have the word "color" in them and display a sample color box to the right of the drop-down menu. For example, the Skin Editor contains several color selection areas, as shown in Figure 10-36.

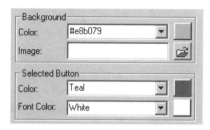

Figure 10-36: Color selection areas

Creating Custom Colors

To create a custom color, follow these steps:

1. From any window that has a color selection area, double-click on the sample color box to display the Color window shown in Figure 10-37.

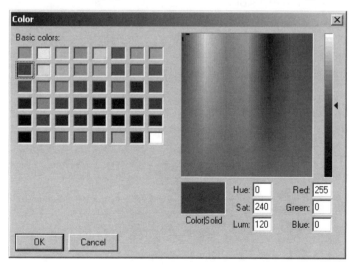

Figure 10-37: The Color window

2. The Color/Solid box shows the current color selection, and the boxes containing numbers show the values of the various color components. Colors can be defined in any of the following ways:

   ■ Click one of the colors in the **Basic colors** area.

- Click anywhere in the shaded color display.
- Enter Hue, Saturation, and Luminocity numbers. White is 239-240-240; black is 0-0-0.
- Enter Red, Green, and Blue values. White is 255-255-255; Black is 0-0-0. Make Yellow by combining Red and Green.

3. As you enter numbers or click on the color options, the Color/Solid box shows the results. The intensity scale (a vertical bar on the right of the window) shows how light or dark the color will be. You can move the black intensity marker up or down as needed.

4. When the Color/Solid box displays the color you want, click **OK**. The color will appear in the sample color box on the RoboHelp HTML window. In addition, a code for the color will appear in the text box portion of the drop-down menu. This code represents the color in hexadecimal format.

Adding a Custom Color to the Drop-Down Menu

The color drop-down menus display a list of predefined color names, such as Blue and Silver. You can add your own custom color to the drop-down menu, and it will be available to you any place RoboHelp HTML lets you enter color information (including font colors and other toolbar color options).

To add a custom color to the drop-down menu, follow these steps:

1. From any window that has a color selection area, choose **Custom** from the drop-down menu to display the New Custon Color window, as shown in Figure 10-38. The name should be something that lets other people identify the color easily.

Figure 10-38: The New Custom Color window

2. Click **OK** to close the Custom Color window and display the Color window shown in Figure 10-39.

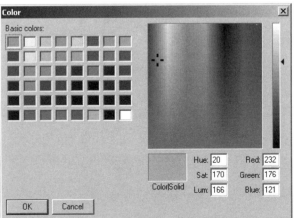

Figure 10-39: Creating a custom color in the Color window

3. The Color/Solid box shows the current color selection, and the numbered boxes show the values of the various color components. Colors can be defined in any of the following ways:

    ■ Click one of the colors in the Basic colors area.

    ■ Click anywhere in the shaded color display.

    ■ Enter Hue, Saturation, and Luminocity numbers. White is 239-240-240; Black is 0-0-0.

    ■ Enter Red, Green, and Blue values. White is 255-255-255; Black is 0-0-0. Make Yellow by combining Red and Green.

4. As you enter numbers or click on the color options, the Color/Solid box shows the results. The intensity scale (a vertical bar on the right of the window) shows how light or dark the color will be. You can move the black intensity marker up or down as needed.

5. When the Color/Solid box displays the color you want, click **OK**. The color will appear in the sample color box on the RoboHelp HTML window, and the color name will be in all color drop-down boxes.

Summary

In this chapter, you saw how to create and use templates to make topics look alike. You also learned how skins work and how to create, edit, and share skins with other authors in your company and on the web. Finally, you learned how to create custom colors that can be used to make your help system look and feel the way you want it to.

The following chapter discusses how to create various types of windows for your RoboHelp HTML output.

Chapter 11

Using Windows in RoboHelp HTML

When your users view the help system, they will view it in a *window*. In addition to your topic information, the window may include toolbars, navigation panes, or other elements. RoboHelp HTML lets you control some aspects of the way your output windows look. The output format you choose will determine how much control you have over the output windows.

Table 11-1: Output format window options

	HTML Help	WebHelp	WebHelp Enterprise
Where can I turn window elements on or off?	Windows Properties Editor	At generation time	Windows Properties Editor
Can I create and use a custom window as my output window?	Yes	No. Although the interface lets you define them, it won't use any window settings.	Yes. However, you can't preview window settings on the local drive; you must publish to the server and view them there.
Can I link different custom windows to TOC and index entries?	Yes	No. Although the interface lets you define them, it won't use any window settings.	No
Does the format allow the use of skins (to change the appearance of window elements)?	No	Yes	Yes

Although you can create many types of output from one RoboHelp HTML project, the tools, menus, and functions available to you at any time will be determined by your Primary Target setting. The rest of this chapter describes how to create, edit, and apply custom windows to Microsoft HTML Help and WebHelp Enterprise output targets. For information about modifying WebHelp output appearance using skins, see Chapter 10.

Working with Microsoft HTML Help Windows

If your primary target is Microsoft HTML Help, RoboHelp HTML lets you specify the location, size, and type of information displayed. For example, you may want to have a navigation pane but remove the Glossary tab if you have no glossary entries. Or you might specify that the navigation tabs appear on the bottom of the window instead of across the top. You can create up to 256 custom windows for HTML Help output, but only nine of them can be viewed at a time. To use the custom windows, specify one window for the default and separate windows to open when the user clicks the table of contents or index. For context-sensitive windows, you can create the custom windows within RoboHelp HTML, but a developer will have to assign the window to the links.

NOTE: *Windows created for HTML Help output cannot be used with WebHelp Enterprise output. You must create separate windows as described in "Working with WebHelp Enterprise Windows" later in this chapter.*

To create and use Microsoft HTML Help windows, you must do two things:

- Create the custom window (or edit the default window).
- Specify when you want the output to use the custom windows.

Creating and Editing a Custom Microsoft HTML Help Window

RoboHelp HTML automatically creates the first Microsoft HTML Help format window, giving it the name NewWindow. To create custom windows, you can edit NewWindow and specify a new name. To create or edit a Microsoft HTML Help window, specify the following types of information:

- The window name, caption, and location
- The buttons you want to display and the tri-pane elements and options (the tabs in the left-hand pane of the output window)

Specifying HTML Help Window Name, Caption, and Location

To specify the name, caption, and location of Microsoft HTML Help windows, follow these steps:

1. From the **File** menu, choose **Primary Target** and then **HTML Help**.
2. In the left-hand pane of the RoboHelp HTML window, open the **Windows** folder to see a list of existing window names.
3. Open the Window Properties (HTML Help) Editor shown in Figure 11-1 in one of the following ways:

- Double-click on a window name in the Windows folder to open the Properties window for that window type.

- Click the right mouse button anywhere in the Windows folder and choose **New Window**.

- From the **File** menu, choose **New**, and then choose **Window**.

- From the **File** menu, choose **Project Settings**. From the **Projects Settings** window, choose **Windows**. Then double-click the window name.

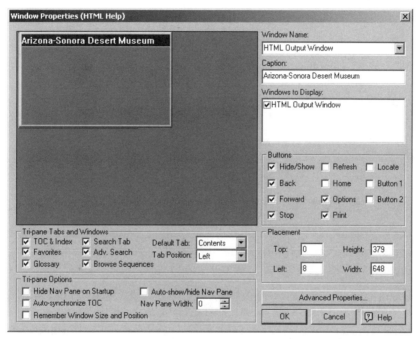

Figure 11-1: The Window Properties (HTML Help) Editor

4. Enter a name for the window in the **Window Name** box. This is the name that RoboHelp will display in the Windows folder and other areas where you can specify a window.

TIP: *If you are creating multiple help outputs, you may want to indicate the output format in the window name. This will make it easier to choose the correct window later. For example, you may want to call this window ASDM-HTMLHelp and the one you create for WebHelp Enterprise output ASDM-Enterprise.*

5. Enter a caption in the **Caption** box. This is the text that will be displayed in the title bar of the window. Remember, all topics get this caption, so make it fairly generic, such as "Arizona-Sonora Desert Museum."

6. The window name you entered is displayed in the window preview on the upper left-hand corner of the Window Editor. The large gray area represents your

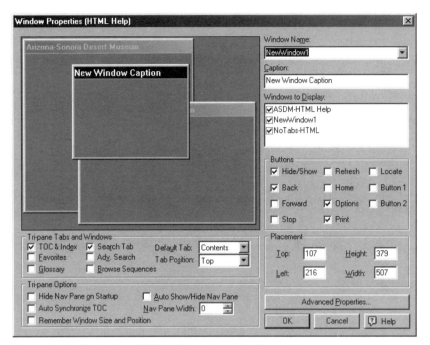

Figure 11-2: Displaying all HTML Help windows in the preview area

desktop, and the smaller rectangle with the caption represents the window you are creating. The only properties that will be reflected by this preview area are the size, location, and name of the window.

If you have more than one defined HTML Help window, a list of all the windows is displayed in the Windows to Display box, and all the windows are in the preview area, as shown in Figure 11-2. You can select which windows you want to see in the preview area by clicking the check boxes next to each name. If you click a box to remove the check mark, the window will be removed from the preview area (but not from the project).

7. Click a window in the preview area to select it, and then specify the location of the window on the desktop in one of the following ways:

   ■ Drag the window to a new location. For example, you may want the help window to always open on the lower left.

   ■ In the Placement area, specify a value in pixels for the distance between the window and the top of the desktop and between the window and the left of the desktop.

8. Specify the size of the window in one of the following ways:

   ■ Click on the window to display resizing handles (small squares on the edges of the window). Click on a handle and drag it to a new location to increase or decrease the window size. Use the corner handles to keep the window's aspect ratio (the proportion of height to width).

■ In the Placement area, specify a value in pixels for the height of the window. The window height must be between 110 and 695 pixels. Specify a value in pixels for the width of the window. Window width must be between 65 and 967 pixels.

9. At the bottom of the Editor in the Tri-pane Options area, check **Remember Window Size and Position** to open the current window with the placement the user last specified. Uncheck this option to always open the window in the size and position you've specified.

10. Specify the window buttons and tri-pane options as described in the following section. When done, click **OK** to save the custom window definition and close the Window Properties (HTML Help) Editor.

Specifying HTML Help Window Tri-Pane Options

Microsoft HTML Help can use a tri-pane format. This means that there are three distinct window areas:

■ The topic as you defined it on the right-hand pane

■ Navigation elements, such as search fields, index, and table of contents, on the left-hand pane

■ A menu bar across the top

You can modify the elements that appear in the navigation pane and menu bar, or you can turn the entire tri-pane option off and display only the topic.

To specify tri-pane buttons and options, follow these steps:

1. From the **File** menu, choose **Primary Target** and then **HTML Help**.

2. In the left-hand pane of the RoboHelp HTML window, open the Windows folder to see a list of existing window names.

3. Open the Window Properties (HTML Help) Editor, as shown in Figure 11-3, in one of the following ways:

■ Double-click on a window name in the **Windows** folder to open the Properties window for that window type.

■ Click the right mouse button anywhere in the **Windows** folder and choose **New Window**.

■ From the **File** menu, choose **New**, and then choose **Window**.

■ From the **File** menu, choose **Project Settings**. From the **Projects Settings** window, choose **Windows**, then double-click the window name.

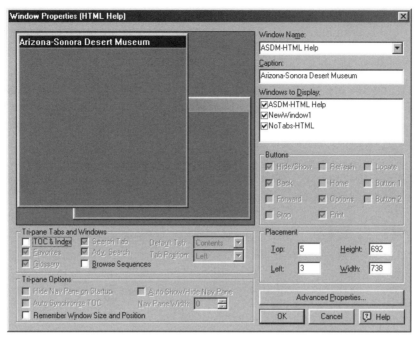

Figure 11-3: Activating tri-pane mode

4. To use the tri-pane mode, click **TOC & Index** in the Tri-pane Tabs and Windows area to activate the other tri-pane options. If you don't want to use the tri-pane mode for your output, clear the check mark from the TOC & Index check box. If you don't use tri-pane mode, many of the check boxes in the Tri-pane Tabs and Windows and Tri-pane Options areas will be disabled. Only Browse Sequences and Remember Window Size and Position will be available.

5. Choose the tabs you want to display by selecting or clearing the check boxes. Each tab will display different content in the navigation pane.

Table 11-2: Navigation pane tabs

Tab	Description
Favorites	Displays a list that the user builds by adding topics to the Favorites pane. The top portion of the pane displays the list, and the bottom portion of the pane displays a text box and Add button with which the user can add topics to the list.
Glossary	Displays the glossary created in the RoboHelp HTML Glossary Designer. This tab must be selected for the user to access online glossary entries.
Search	Displays the search pane, which consists of a text box into which the user can enter words or phrases and a display area for the results of the search. There are also search options at the bottom of the search pane that allow the user to modify the search. When you select the Search check box, the Adv. Search check box is activated. Select Adv. Search if you want to allow your users to use wildcards (*.*) or Boolean operators (AND, OR, NOT, NEAR).

6. Specify the appearance of the tabs by choosing from the following drop-down menus:

   ■ Choose the tab that will be active when the user first opens the help system by choosing from the Default Tab drop-down menu.

   ■ Choose the location of the tabs in the Navigation pane by choosing from the Tab Position drop-down menu.

CAUTION: *Always test your help system with the configuration your users are likely to have. Some desktop settings won't display tabs on the left of the window correctly.*

7. If you have defined browse sequences, click Browse Sequence to activate them. Browse sequences specify a particular order in which the topics will be displayed and are described in more detail in Chapter 17. The sequence is displayed across the top of the topic area, and browse sequence arrows allow the user to move to the next or previous topic in the sequence, as shown in the sample output window in Figure 11-4. The Browse Sequence menu is independent of the tri-pane options and can be set whether the tri-pane mode is used or not.

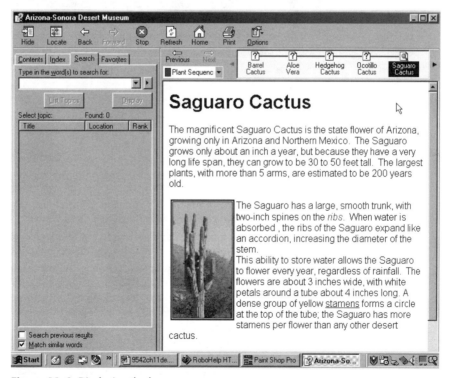

Figure 11-4: Displaying the browse sequence

8. Specify the elements you want to include in the menu across the top of the tri-pane window by checking or clearing the following boxes:

Table 11-3: Menu bar button options

Button	Description	Icon
Show	Displays the navigation pane (either Show or Hide will be displayed, depending on the status of the navigation pane)	Show
Hide	Closes the navigation pane (either Show or Hide will be displayed, depending on the status of the navigation pane)	Hide
Back	Opens the previously viewed topic	Back
Forward	Opens the next topic (only available if you've viewed topics, then used the Back button)	Forward
Stop	Stops the process of loading or displaying information (useful when loading information from a web page)	Stop
Refresh	Redisplays the current topic	Refresh
Home	Displays a predefined web page, specified in the Advanced Options	Home
Print	Prints the current topic. If clicked while the table of contents is displayed, the print feature allows the user to print either the topic or TOC elements.	Print
Options	Displays a drop-down menu that provides access to menu options such as back, forward, and home	Options
Locate	Highlights the current topic in the table of contents	Locate
Button 1	Opens a web page or topic as defined in Advanced Options	
Button 2	Opens a web page or topic as defined in Advanced Options	

9. Specify the additional tri-pane options in the Tri-Pane Options area.

Table 11-4: Tri-pane options

Check box	Description
Hide Nav Pane on Startup	When the user first opens the help, the navigation pane will not be displayed. The user must click the Show button to display the navigation pane. Clear this check box to display the navigation pane when the help system starts.
Auto Synchronize TOC	Highlights the displayed topic in the table of contents pane
Auto Show/Hide Nav Pane	When the user selects a program other than the help file, this option will automatically hide the navigation pane. When the user clicks on the help file again, the navigation pane will be displayed again. This is only useful if the help file is set to always display on top of other windows (Top-most Window option in Advanced Properties).
Nav Pane Width	Specifies the width in pixels of the navigation pane

10. When done, click **OK** to save the custom window definition and close the Window Properties (HTML Help) Editor.

Displaying Topics in Custom Windows

Once you've created Microsoft HTML Help custom windows, you can use the custom windows in the following situations:

■ As the default window

■ When a user clicks a topic in the Contents or Index tab on the navigation pane

■ When a user accesses context-sensitive help

Specifying the Default HTML Help Window

If you don't specify a default output window for HTML Help, RoboHelp will use the first valid HTML Help window that it finds in the Windows folder. The windows are listed in alphabetic order, so the default (unless you change it) will be the window with the name that comes first alphabetically. To specify a default HTML Help window, follow these steps:

1. From the **File** menu, choose **Project Settings** to display the Project Settings window.

2. Click the **Compile** tab, as shown in Figure 11-5.

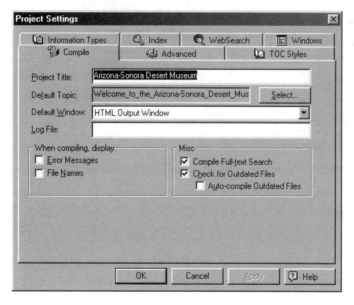

Figure 11-5: The Project Settings window Compile tab

3. Choose the custom window from the **Default Window** drop-down menu. Only HTML Help format windows will be displayed in this list.

4. Click **OK** to close the Project Settings window. The next time you compile the HTML Help, the specified custom window will be used as the default window.

Specifying Contents Windows for HTML Help

If you don't specify an output window for topics opened from the Table of Contents Navigation pane, RoboHelp will use the first valid HTML Help window that it finds in the Windows folder. The windows are listed in alphabetic order, so the default (unless you change it) will be the window with the name that comes first alphabetically. To specify an HTML Help window for topics selected from the Table of Contents, follow these steps:

1. From the **File** menu, choose **Project Settings** to display the Project Settings window.

2. Click the **TOC Styles** tab, as shown in Figure 11-6.

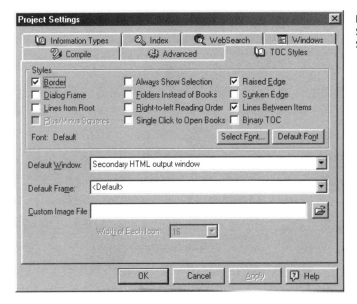

Figure 11-6: The Project Settings window TOC Styles tab

3. Choose the custom window from the **Default Window** drop-down menu.

CAUTION: *All types of windows appear in this list. Make sure you specify only HTML Help format windows, or you will encounter errors.*

4. Click **OK** to close the Project Settings window. The next time you compile the HTML Help, the specified custom window will be used when a user clicks a topic in the table of contents.

Specifying Index Windows for HTML Help

If you don't specify an output window for topics opened from the Index Navigation pane, RoboHelp will use the first valid HTML Help window that it finds in the Windows folder. The windows are listed in alphabetic order, so the default (unless you change it) will be the window with the name that comes first alphabetically. To specify an HTML Help window for topics selected from the Index pane, follow these steps:

1. From the **File** menu, choose **Project Settings** to display the Project Settings window.

2. Click the **Index** tab, as shown in Figure 11-7.

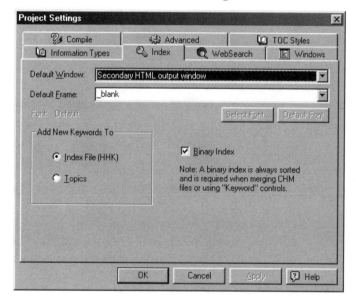

Figure 11-7: The Project Settings window Index tab

3. Choose the custom window from the Default Window drop-down menu.

CAUTION: *All types of windows appear in this list. Make sure you specify only HTML Help format windows, or you will encounter errors.*

---

4. Click **OK** to close the Project Settings window.

5. In the left-hand pane of the RoboHelp HTML window, click the **Index** tab to display the list of index keywords.

6. Highlight the keyword that the user will click to display the custom window, and then click the right mouse button and choose **Properties** to display the Keyword Properties window.

7. Click the **Advanced** tab to display the advanced portion of the Keyword Properties window, as shown in Figure 11-8.

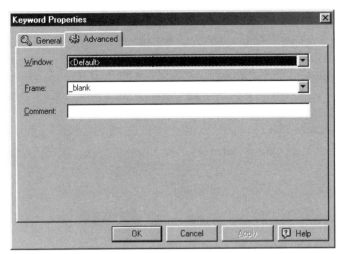

Figure 11-8: The Keyword Properties window Advanced tab

8. In the Window drop-down menu choose the window in which you want topics to display when the user clicks the topic name from the keyword in the index. Click **OK** when done to close the Keyword Properties window.

9. The next time you compile the HTML Help, the specified custom window will be used when a user clicks a topic in the Index tab of the navigation pane.

Working with WebHelp Enterprise Windows

Although you can create many custom windows for WebHelp Enterprise, you can only use one at a time within a WebHelp Enterprise output. The output will be displayed in the user's browser based on the window settings you specify. You can specify various toolbars on or off, define the location and size of the window in relation to the desktop, and specify toolbar buttons. You can also use skins with WebHelp Enterprise output, as discussed in Chapter 10.

NOTE: *Windows created for WebHelp Enterprise output cannot be used with Microsoft HTML Help output. You must create separate windows as described in "Working with Microsoft HTML Help Windows" earlier in this chapter.*

To create, edit, and use a WebHelp Enterprise window, you must:

■ Create the window, specifying the window name, caption, and location

■ Specify the elements you want to include in the window

■ Set the new custom window as the default window in the Project Settings

NOTE: *In order to see what your window settings look like, you must publish your WebHelp Enterprise project and view it on the server. Local preview functions will not reflect window settings.*

Specifying WebHelp Enterprise Window Name, Caption, and Location

To specify the name, caption, and location of WebHelp Enterprise windows, follow these steps:

1. From the **File** menu, choose **Primary Target** and then **WebHelp Enterprise**.

2. In the left-hand pane of the RoboHelp HTML window, open the **Windows** folder to see a list of existing window names.

3. Open the Window Properties (WebHelp Enterprise) Editor, as shown in Figure 11-9, in one of the following ways:

   ■ Double-click on a window name in the Windows folder to open the Properties window for that window type.

   ■ Click the right mouse button anywhere in the Windows folder and choose **New Window**.

   ■ From the **File** menu, choose **New**, and then choose **Window**.

   ■ From the **File** menu, choose **Project Settings**. From the Projects Settings window, choose **Windows**, then double-click the window name.

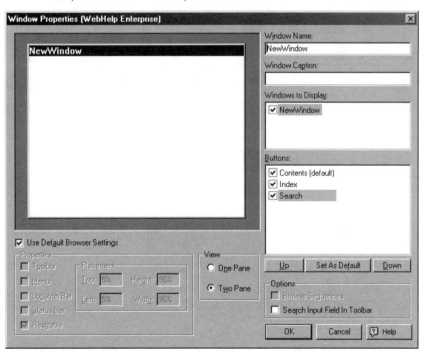

Figure 11-9: The Window Properties (WebHelp Enterprise) Editor

4. Enter a name for the window in the **Window Name** box. This is the name that RoboHelp will display in the Windows folder and other areas where you can specify a window.

If you are creating multiple help outputs, you may want to indicate the output format in the window name. This will make it easier to choose the correct window later. For example, you may want to call this window ASDM-Enterprise and the one you create for HTMLHelp output ASDM-HTML Help.

5. Enter a caption in the **Window Caption** box. This is the text that will be displayed in the title bar of the window. Remember, all topics get this caption, so make it fairly generic, such as "Arizona-Sonora Desert Museum."

6. The window name you entered is displayed in the window preview on the upper left-hand corner of the Window Editor. The large gray area represents your desktop, and the smaller rectangle with the caption is the window you are creating. The only properties that will be reflected by this preview area are the size, location, and name of the window.

   If you have more than one defined WebHelp Enterprise window, a list of all the windows is displayed in the Windows to Display box, and all the windows are in the preview area, as shown in Figure 11-10. You can select which windows you want to see in the preview area by clicking the check boxes next to each name. If you click a box to remove the check mark, the window will be removed from the preview area (but not from the project).

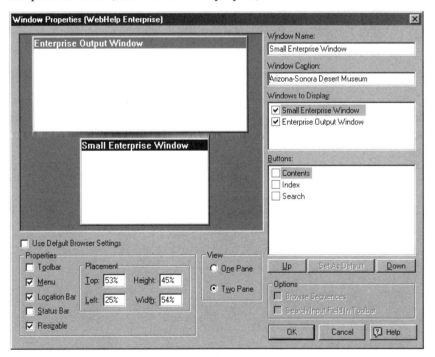

Figure 11-10: Displaying all available windows in the Windows Properties Editor

7. Click a window in the preview area to select it. If you want the window to use the default settings for each user's browser, click the **Use Default Browser Settings** check box. When this is selected, the window properties are inactive, and you can skip to step 9. If you want to control the window settings for your output, clear the Use Default Browser Settings.

8. Specify the location of the window on the desktop in one of the following ways:

   ■ Drag the window to a new location. For example, you may want the help window to always open on the lower left.

   ■ In the Placement area, specify values for the distance between the window and the Top and the Left of the desktop as a percentage of the total desktop area. Make sure you type percentage symbols (%) in the Placement boxes or RoboHelp HTML will assume you are entering a pixel value.

   ■ In the Placement area, specify a value in pixels for the distance between the window and the top of the desktop and between the window and the left of the desktop.

9. Specify the size of the window in one of the following ways:

   ■ Click on the window to display resizing handles (small squares on the edges of the window). Click on a handle and drag it to a new location to increase or decrease the window size. Use the corner handles to keep the window's aspect ratio (the proportion of height to width).

   ■ In the Placement area, specify values for the height and width of the window as a percentage of the total desktop area. Make sure you type percentage symbols (%) in the Placement boxes or RoboHelp HTML will assume you are entering a pixel value.

   ■ In the Placement box, specify a value in pixels for the height and width of the window. The window height must be between 110 and 695 pixels. Window width must be between 65 and 967 pixels.

10. Specify the window properties, views, and options as described in the following sections. When done, click **OK** to save the custom window definition and close the Window Properties (WebHelp Enterprise) Editor.

Specifying WebHelp Enterprise Window Options

The WebHelp Enterprise output is displayed in the user's default browser. To control which elements appear in the browser, follow these steps:

 NOTE: *If you are using a skin, these settings will be applied to the skin, which in turn will be applied to the window.*

1. From the **File** menu, choose **Primary Target** and then **WebHelp Enterprise**.

2. In the left-hand pane of the RoboHelp HTML window, open the Windows folder to see a list of existing window names.

3. Open the Window Properties (WebHelp Enterprise) Editor in one of the following ways:

   ■ Double-click on a window name in the Windows folder to open the Properties window for that window type.

   ■ Click the right mouse button anywhere in the Windows folder and choose **New Window**.

   ■ From the **File** menu, choose **New** then **Window**.

   ■ From the **File** menu, choose **Project Settings**. From the Projects Settings window, choose **Windows**, then double-click the window name.

4. Clear the **Use Default Browser Settings** check box, as shown in Figure 11-11.

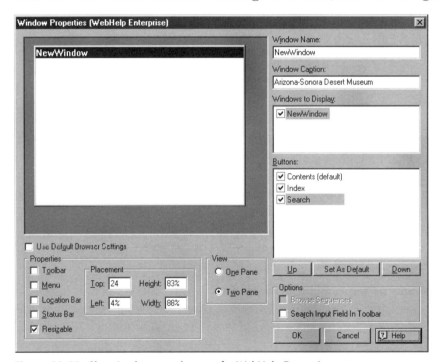

Figure 11-11: Choosing browser elements for WebHelp Enterprise output

5. Select one of the following check boxes to display the element, or clear the check box if you don't want the element displayed.

Table 11-5: WebHelp Enterprise output properties

Check box	Description
Toolbar	Displays icons, such as Back and Next, at the top of the browser window
Menu	Displays text representing the menus, such as File, Edit, and Tools, at the top of the browser window

Check box	Description
Location Bar	Displays a location bar across the top of the window
Status Bar	Displays progress indicators and other status messages at the bottom of the window

6. If you want the users to be able to resize your help window, select the **Resizable** check box. If you want the help window to remain at the size you specified, clear the Resizable check box.

7. You have the option of displaying a navigation pane to the left of your topics. To turn the navigation pane off, select the **One Pane** check box in the View area. To turn the navigation pane on and activate the button options, select **Two Pane**.

8. The Buttons box displays the available options for the navigation pane. Select the options you want included in the navigation pane of the output window (Contents, Index, Search, or WebSearch). This is the same functionality as choosing Tabs in the Tri-pane section of HTML Help Editor.

9. To change the order in which the buttons appear on the toolbar, highlight a button by clicking the button name (not the check box) and then click **Up** or **Down** to move the button within the list. The button at the top of the list will appear first in the toolbar (on the left). To return the button order to the original settings, click **Set As Default**.

10. If you have defined browse sequences, click **Browse Sequence** to activate them. Browse sequences specify a particular order in which the topics will be displayed and are described in more detail in Chapter 17. The sequence is displayed across the top of the topic area, and browse-sequence arrows allow the user to move to the next or previous topic in the sequence. The Browse Sequence menu is independent of the other window options and can be set for either one- or two-pane output.

11. Select **Search Input Field In Toolbar** to display a text box in the output window where users can enter expressions they'd like to search on.

 NOTE: *In order to see what your window settings look like, you must publish your WebHelp Enterprise project and view it on the server. Local preview functions will not reflect window settings.*

12. When done, click **OK** to save the custom window definition and close the Window Properties (WebHelp Enterprise) Editor.

Summary

This chapter described how to create and use custom windows for Microsoft HTML Help output and WebHelp Enterprise output.

The following chapter will discuss how to use RoboHelp HTML to create context-sensitive help links.

Chapter 12

Creating Context-Sensitive Help

Context-sensitive help is help that is directly linked to a program. When the user presses F1 or clicks on the Help button, the context-sensitive link between the program and the help file identifies the topic to display and then displays it.

In order to create this type of help, you'll need to work closely with the developers of the program. You'll create the topics using RoboHelp HTML as you normally would, and you can even create custom windows for the context-sensitive topics. The developers will build the links into the program windows or dialog boxes. Together, you and the developer will assign your topics to the program's links. The files that tell RoboHelp HTML which topics go with each link are called *map files*.

Map files contain information in different formats, depending on your target output. To assign context-sensitive topics to program links in Microsoft HTML Help, you'll need to create both map files and *aliases*. To assign context-sensitive topics to program links in WebHelp or WebHelp Enterprise, you'll need to create *context strings*. In either case, you should create your topics first, as described in earlier chapters. This means you'll need to have a good idea of what the program will look like so you can identify the windows or buttons that require dedicated topics. It's also a good idea to confirm terminology with the developers (such as the wording on the buttons or descriptive interface labels).

 TIP: *Although the topic files must exist first, you can create the context-sensitive links before you have content in those topics. This might be useful if your development process is lengthy. You'll be able to provide the developers with the input they need (the map numbers) and then go back and fill in the topic content later.*

Working with Developers

Because the context-sensitive help is so closely incorporated with the program, it is important that you as a help author work closely with the program developers. Since you'll need access to their code, you'll want access to whatever code control system they are using. This will ensure that they aren't making changes while you are working with the files.

You'll also want to ensure that you get the program updates as they are released during the program development process. One useful method is to get access to a shared drive where the developers can store the program source. You could also monitor the developer's email lists or bug reporting procedures.

Creating Context-Sensitive Help for Microsoft HTML Help Output

In Microsoft HTML Help, there are two basic kinds of context-sensitive help: Window-level help displays a standard HTML Help topic, and field-level or text-only help (also known as What's This? Help) provides simple text-based popup help to describe a screen item such as a field or a button.

 NOTE: *It is useful to review the elements for which you plan to create context-sensitive help with the developers. Ask the developers about things that the What's This? Help Composer may not catch, such as dynamic dialog boxes, custom class dialog boxes, unused dialog boxes, or dynamic controls. You'll then be able to create help for these elements manually.*

Creating Window-Level Topics for HTML Help

For window-level help, HTML Help uses two separate files to match up (or "map") topics to the buttons or keystrokes from the program. The *map file* contains the *map numbers* that the program uses to identify the button or keystroke. Each map number has a corresponding *topic ID*. The topic ID is similar to the topic name, except it must be unique across the whole program (topic names might be duplicated under separate folders). In addition, topic IDs cannot contain spaces or special characters. Each entry in the map file is called a *map ID* (map number + topic ID).

The second file contains all of the topic IDs with corresponding topic names. You can reuse the topic names as often as you need in order to display the same topic from different locations in the program. This second file is called the *alias file*, and the entries are called *aliases*. Note that a single topic can be associated with many topic IDs, and thus have several aliases. Each topic ID, however, can only be associated with one topic name.

When the user of the program clicks on a button or presses a key, the program sends the map number for that program location to the HTML Help Engine. There, the map number is converted to a topic ID, the topic ID is converted to the topic name, and the topic name is sent to the HTML Help Viewer for display, as shown in Figure 12-1. Simple, right?

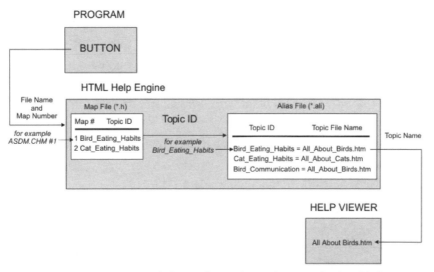

Figure 12-1: Context-sensitive help translates a keystroke into a displayed help topic

To create context-sensitive help for HTML Help output, you must match up the topics you create with the links for each window in the program. To do this, you'll have to perform the following general steps:

1. Create your topics as described earlier in this book.

2. Create a unique map ID (topic ID + map number) for each button or control in the program. You can do this in any of the following ways:

    ■ Assign map numbers that you choose to each topic ID. This approach will let you specify ranges tied to categories you define. For example, you may want to use map numbers 1-99 for buttons on administrative portions of the program, 100-199 for printing topics, 200-299 for data entry, etc.

    ■ Let RoboHelp HTML assign map numbers as you enter the topic IDs.

    ■ Outside of RoboHelp, create a map file, and then import it into the project. This may be the best approach if your developer gives you a list of predefined codes that you need to use. You'll still have to assign topics to each map ID.

3. Create an alias for each map ID by assigning a topic name to it.

4. Provide a list of the map IDs to the program developer, who will incorporate them into the program windows.

5. Compile the help project and test with the program.

The earlier chapters in this book described how to create topics for step 1. Step 4 will vary greatly depending on your corporate procedures and happen outside the scope of RoboHelp HTML. The following sections of this chapter focus on steps 2 and 3 in the context-sensitive help process.

Creating Map IDs and Assigning Aliases in RoboHelp HTML

To create map IDs in RoboHelp HTML, follow these steps:

1. In the left-hand pane of the RoboHelp HTML window, open the **Context-Sensitive** folder.

2. Open the Edit Map IDs window, as shown in Figure 12-2, in one of the following ways:

   ■ In the Context-Sensitive Help folder on the left-hand pane, double-click the **Aliases** icon.

   ■ From the **Edit** menu, choose **Map IDs**.

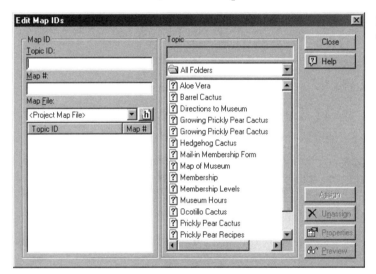

Figure 12-2: The Edit Map IDs window

3. Enter a topic ID in the Topic ID box. As you enter the Topic ID, RoboHelp automatically changes spaces, special characters, and punctuation to underscores. If you enter a Topic ID that exists in the project already, the Map Number for that Topic ID is displayed in the Map # box. If it is a new Topic ID, the word <auto> is displayed in the Map # box.

4. Enter the map number in either of the following ways:

   ■ Leave the word <auto> in the Map # box. RoboHelp HTML will assign the next available map number, starting with 1.

   ■ Type a new number in the Map # box.

NOTE: *If you received a list of map numbers from a developer, the numbers may be in hexadecimal format (a combination of letters and numbers, preceded by 0x). RoboHelp HTML will accept either hexadecimal or standard decimal numbers.*

5. If you aren't sure which topic you want, you can highlight the topic and click **Preview** to see what the topic looks like before you assign it to the map ID. You

can also click **Properties** to display a list of topic IDs, if any, that are already assigned to the highlighted topic.

6.   To assign a topic to the displayed map ID, highlight a topic name from the list on the right of the window, then click **Assign**. The Map ID (both Topic ID and associated Map #) is displayed in the lower-left portion of the Edit Map IDs window. The icon next to the Topic ID is blue, indicating that a topic name has been assigned to it.

7.   To see which topic is assigned to each listed topic ID, move the cursor over the topic ID to display a screen tip that lists the topic ID, the map number, and the assigned topic filename, as shown in Figure 12-3.

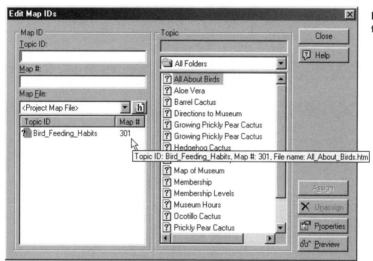

Figure 12-3: Assigning topics to each map ID

8.   Repeat steps 3 through 6 for each topic ID you need to add. Remember that you can assign the same topic name to any number of topic IDs, but each topic ID can point to only one topic name. Click **Close** when you are done to close the Edit Map IDs window.

As soon as you create the first map ID, RoboHelp HTML creates a map file (BSSCDefault.h). When you save the project, RoboHelp HTML creates the alias file (*<projectname>*.ali). In most cases, you won't need to access these two files directly; you can add to them or edit them with the Edit Map IDs window.

Importing Map Files into RoboHelp HTML

In some cases, you may start with a file that already contains a list of map numbers and their associated topic IDs. If there are a lot of map numbers, you might just find it easier to create all of the topic IDs in a regular text file instead of through the Edit Map IDs window. Or you might be able to get the map file directly from the program developers. Many development projects automatically generate a map file, though they may call it a header file or use some other ter-minology. The file you want usually has an extension of .h, .hh, or .hm.

The map file contains a list of all of the topic IDs as well as the map numbers associated with each, as shown in Figure 12-4. Note that the format of the actual topic ID will vary with each project. For example, many programs use prefixes to indicate the portion of the program that uses each ID (e.g., RPT_help_button). Some may use longer map numbers to encode information, such as two digits for the program, two for the module, and two for the screen (for example, 234061 even though there aren't 200,000 entries).

```
#define CSS_dialog_box                      1052
#define CSS_Selection_Dialog_Box            1033
#define CSS_Log_On_dialog_box               1014
#define CSS_CSS_taskbar                     1015
#define CSS_Inquiry_Window                  1028
#define CSS_Billing_Modifiers_Dialog_Box    1040
#define Queue_Window_CSS                    44
#define Preauthorization_Window_CSS         45
#define Preauthorization_Dialog_Box_CSS     46
#define Details_Window_CSS                  47
#define Cancel_Dialog_Box                   27
#define CSS_Startup_window                  1036
```

Figure 12-4: The map file contains topic IDs and map numbers

When you import a map file, you'll still have to create the alias file to identify which topic name should be associated with the topic IDs. To import a map file to your project, follow these steps:

1. Copy the map file into the project folder.

2. Import the map file into the project in one of the following ways:
   - From the **File** menu, select **Import** and then **Map File**.
   - Open the **Context Sensitive** folder on the left-hand pane. Then open the **Map Files** folder. Click the right mouse button and choose **Import Map File**.
   - From the open **Edit Map IDs** window, click the **New Map File** icon (🏠), then type the map filename or use the Browse feature to point to the map filename.

3. The map file you added will be displayed in the Map Files folder. If you've cre-ated any map IDs manually, the file BSSCDefault.h will also be in the Map Files folder. To assign topics to the new map IDs, open the Edit Map IDs window shown in Figure 12-2 in one of the following ways:
   - In the Context-Sensitive Help folder on the left-hand pane, double-click the **Aliases** icon.
   - From the **Edit** menu, choose **Map IDs**.

4. Use the drop-down menu to choose the map IDs you want to display. Choose one of the following:

Table 12-1: Map ID display options

Option	Description
a map filename	Displays only those map IDs in the specified file
<All Map Files>	Displays map IDs from all the map files in the project
<Project Map File>	Displays only the map IDs you've manually entered (from BSSCDefault.h)

The specified topic IDs and map IDs appear in the lower-left corner of the window. Figure 12-5 shows the Edit Map IDs window with <All Map Files> chosen. Blue icons with a question mark indicate that the map ID has been assigned a topic name. Yellow icons without the question mark indicate that the map ID has not yet been assigned a topic name.

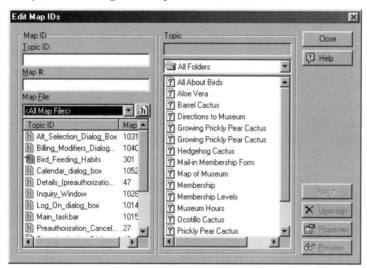

Figure 12-5:
Displaying the imported map IDs

5. To assign a topic name to the topic ID (or change the existing name), highlight the topic ID you want to work with or type the name in the Topic ID box.

NOTE: *If you mistype by even one character, the Edit Map IDs window will create a new topic ID. You'll know this happened when the default <auto> appears in the Map # box.*

6. If you aren't sure which topic you want, you can highlight the topic and click **Preview** to see what the topic looks like before you assign it to the map ID. You can also click **Properties** to display a list of topic IDs, if any, that are already assigned to the highlighted topic.

7. To assign a topic to the displayed map ID, highlight a topic name from the list on the right of the window, then click **Assign**. The Map ID (Topic ID and associated Map #) is displayed in the lower-left portion of the Edit Map IDs window. The

icon next to the topic ID is blue, indicating that a topic name has been assigned to it.

8. To see which topic is assigned to each listed topic ID, move the cursor over the topic ID to display a screen tip that lists the topic ID, the map number, and the assigned topic filename, as shown in Figure 12-6.

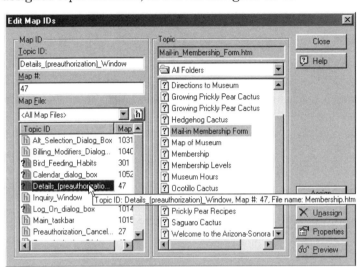

Figure 12-6: Assigning topic names to imported map IDs

9. Repeat steps 5 through 7 for each map ID in the file. Remember that you can assign the same topic name to any number of topic IDs, but each topic ID can point to only one topic name. Click **Close** when you are done to close the Edit Map IDs window.

Editing Context-Sensitive Files

As you work on topics, sometimes you need to change titles or topic names. Similarly, sometimes the developers change the windows or buttons in the program. When either of these things happen, you'll have to update your context-sensitive help files. Some common changes you might have to make are listed in the following table.

Table 12-2: Editing options for context-sensitive files

Change	Procedure	Section
Add a button/field/ window to the program	1. Get the new topic ID and map number (or assign them yourself). 2. Create the new topic, if necessary. 3. Add the topic ID to the map file and point it to the new topic.	"Creating Map IDs and Assigning Aliases in RoboHelp HTML"

Change	Procedure	Section
Delete a button/field/window from the program	1. Unassign the topic name from the map ID. 2. Remove the map ID from the help.	"Removing Context-Sensitive Help Links"
Change a few map numbers or topic IDs	1. Remove the old map IDs. 2. Remove unused map IDs from the help. 3. Enter the new map IDs. 4. Assign topic names to each map ID.	"Removing Context-Sensitive Help Links" "Creating Map IDs and Assigning Aliases in RoboHelp HTML"
Reorganize the help topics into or out of folders or rename topics	1. For each old topic name, identify the topic IDs that point to the topic name and unassign the topic name from each map ID. 2. Remove unused map IDs from the help. 3. Delete the old topics (optional).	"Removing Context-Sensitive Help Links"
Add new topics that will be accessed by existing context-sensitive links	1. Create the topic. 2. Identify the topic ID you want to change. 3. Assign the new topic name to the topic ID.	"Creating Map IDs and Assigning Aliases in RoboHelp HTML"
Remove topics that were accessed by context-sensitive help, without changing the program.	1. Assign a new topic name to the existing map ID.	"Creating Map IDs and Assigning Aliases in RoboHelp HTML"

In all cases, it is very important that you compile and test your help with the compiled program. This is the only way you'll know for sure whether the changes work or not.

Removing Context-Sensitive Help Links

When programs change, you'll sometimes need to get rid of topics and links that you've created. For context-sensitive help, it isn't enough to simply delete the topic; you need to change the map and alias files as well. Do this through the Edit Map IDs window by following these steps:

1. In the left-hand pane of the RoboHelp HTML window, open the Context-Sensitive folder.

2. Open the Edit Map IDs window in one of the following ways:

   ■ In the **Context-Sensitive Help** folder on the left-hand pane, double-click the **Aliases** icon.

   ■ From the **Edit** menu, choose **Map IDs**.

3.   If you are removing the context-sensitive link because the program changed, skip to step 4. However, if you are removing the context-sensitive link because the help topic changed, highlight the help topic name and click the **Properties** button to display a list of all topic IDs that point to the highlighted topic as shown in Figure 12-7. Make sure you remove all of these links or you will get errors when you try to compile the help.

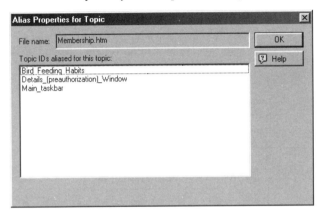

Figure 12-7: Displaying the topic IDs associated with a topic name

4.   Highlight the topic ID you need to remove to activate the Unassign button, as shown in Figure 12-8.

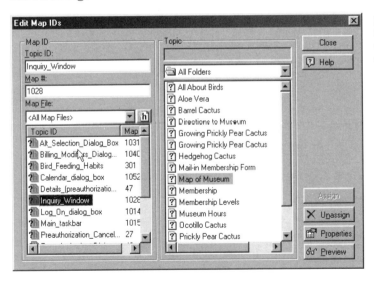

Figure 12-8: Unassigning the topic to remove it from the alias file

5.   Click **Unassign** to remove the topic ID from the topic name. The icon next to the topic ID turns yellow to indicate that it no longer has an assigned topic name. This will also remove the specified entry (topic ID + topic name) from the alias file.

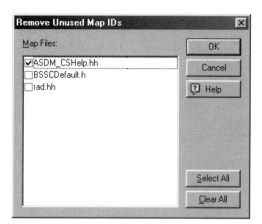

Figure 12-9: Removing the unused map IDs from the map file

6. Click **Close** to close the Edit Map IDs window.

7. With the cursor anywhere in the Map Files folder on the left-hand pane, click the right mouse button and choose **Remove Unused Map IDs** to display the Remove Unused IDs window, as shown in Figure 12-9.

8. Select the map file from which you'd like to remove the unused IDs, and then click **OK**. RoboHelp HTML removes all entries (topic ID + map number) from the map file that do not have corresponding alias file entries.

Creating Field-level Topics for HTML Help

Another option for context-sensitive help is to create text-only topics that can be accessed when a user needs information for a specific field or button. Also called What's This? Help, this type of context-sensitive help requires close coordination with the software developers.

RoboHelp includes a tool for creating context-sensitive help and associating it with individual fields in a program. What's This? Help allows the user to display a text box containing information for any field or control on any window in a program. The What's This? Help Composer automatically identifies all of the controls in a program, creates help topics for them, matches up the topic IDs and map numbers, and provides an editing environment where you can edit the resulting help topics.

NOTE: *A What's This? Help project is independent of other RoboHelp projects you may create. The What's This? Help output is a single file with the extension .dll which the developer calls from within the program.*

You can also create field-level help using the standard RoboHelp HTML windows and the Text-Only topic functionality.

Using the What's This? Help Composer

Before you begin, you'll have to make sure that users understand when and how to call What's This? Help. This is often determined by the program interface, so check with your developers to see what they have available. There are three options:

- The user clicks the question mark in the upper-right corner of a screen to change the mouse pointer to a question mark pointer and then clicks an item on the screen.

- The user positions the mouse pointer on an item on the screen and presses F1.

- The user clicks the right mouse button and chooses What's This?.

For HTML Help output, the What's This? Help Composer creates context-sensitive field-level help for C or C++ program files (.exe). If your program is a different type of file, you'll have to create text-only topics with the normal RoboHelp HTML tools (see "Manually Creating Field-Level Topics for HTML Help" later in this chapter).

The What's This? Help Composer looks at a C or C++ file to create a list of controls and fields that might need context-sensitive help. It then creates suggested text for each control or field that it finds. You can create stand-alone What's This? Help projects or you can link What's This? Help to existing HTML Help projects in RoboHelp.

Follow these general steps to create What's This? Help with the What's This? Help Composer:

1. The developers create a program.

2. The developers pause while the help author checks out the program files and uses the What's This? Help Composer to create the initial help files. When this is done, the help author checks the program files back in so that the developers can continue working on them.

3. The help author works on the help files, testing and compiling the What's This? Help and refining the text for the various controls.

4. The help author sends the completed help files back to the developers for incorporation in the program.

Creating a New What's This? Help Project

When you create a new What's This? Help project, the What's This? Help Composer creates map numbers for each dialog box control that it finds and can be set to automatically include text for each one.

NOTE: *You can only attach one What's This? Help project to each HTML Help project.*

To create a new What's This? Help Project, follow these steps:

1. Open an HTML Help project. You may start with an existing HTML Help project, or you may open an empty HTML Help project to create stand-alone What's This? Help.

2. From the File menu, choose **New**, then **What's This? Help Project** to display the What's This? Help Composer New Project Wizard, as shown in Figure 12-10.

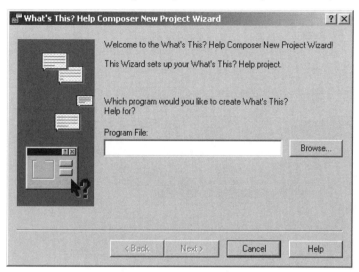

Figure 12-10: The What's This? Help Composer New Project Wizard

3. Enter the name of the program for which you want to create What's This? Help. You can use the Browse button to search for the program. When finished, click **Next** to display the second What's This? Help Composer Wizard screen, as shown in Figure 12-11.

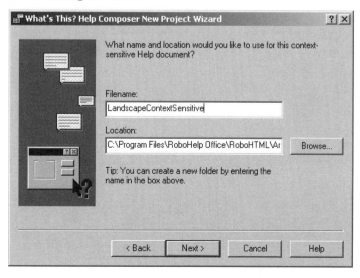

Figure 12-11: Specifying the filename and location of the completed What's This? Help

4. Enter information in the fields as follows:

■ The default filename is Context. You can either leave this or enter a new file-name for the What's This? Help file. Most files the system generates will use the entered filename. However, the text file that the Composer creates will always be called context.txt.

■ Enter the directory where you want to store the completed What's This? Help. This is typically the same directory as the other help files for the project.

When you have completed the filename and location, click **Next** to display the next What's This? Help Composer Wizard screen, as shown in Figure 12-12.

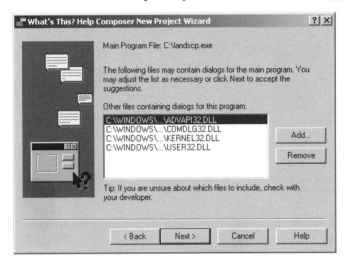

Figure 12-12: Identifying potential dialog boxes with the What's This? Help composer

5. To add a file containing elements that require context-sensitive help, click the **Add** button, then point to the filename. To remove a file from the context-sensi-tive help, highlight the filename, and then click **Remove**. When finished, click **Next** to display the next What's This? Help Composer Wizard screen, as shown in Figure 12-13.

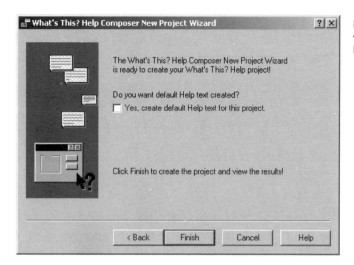

Figure 12-13: Specifying whether you want default help text

6. The What's This? Help Composer can include default text for each dialog box, field, or other element. This is very useful if you have a lot of similar fields. It also ensures that there is some text for every context-sensitive entry. Check the box if you want the What's This? Help Composer to create default help text for the project.

7. Click **Finish** to generate the What's This? Help files and display the What's This? Help Composer Project Results window, as shown in Figure 12-14.

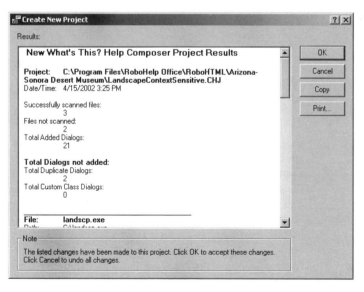

Figure 12-14: The What's This? Help Composer Project Results window

8. The project results include information about the number of files checked and the total number of dialog boxes found. If you scroll down the report, there is additional information about each scanned file. Click the **Print** button to print this report (a good idea for auditing purposes) or click **Copy** to store the report

to a new filename. Click **OK** to close the What's This? Help Composer Project Results window. The wizard is now complete, and the newly created project appears in the What's This? Help Composer window, as shown in Figure 12-15.

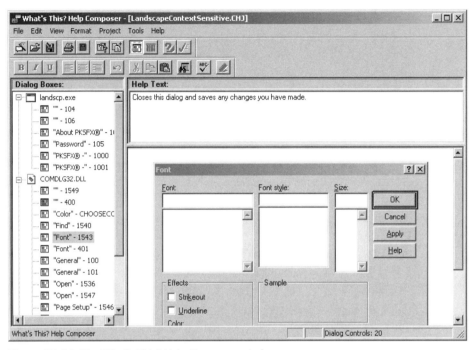

Figure 12-15: The What's This? Help Composer window

9. The What's This? Help Composer window consists of three panes that work together to display the various controls and associated help text.

Table 12-3: What's This? Help Composer components

Pane	Description
Dialog Boxes	Lists the dialog boxes and windows that the Composer found in the specified program. Click one of the dialog box items to view it in the Composer window Preview pane.
Help Text	Displays the text for the selected item. If you checked the default text button back in step 6, there will be a text entry for every dialog item. Note that some of these entries are quite generic and not very much help to the user. For example, many of them will say "Enter your input here."
View (Dialog mode)	Choose Dialog from the View menu to display the Dialog mode. The Dialog mode lets you see what the window looks like. For windows with several items, as shown in Figure 12-15, you can click on each item to display its text. The area will be surrounded by a dark blue line. This is the area the user will click to access the specified help text. In the example in Figure 12-15, the OK button is highlighted, and the default text for the OK button is in the Help Text pane.

Pane	Description
View (Control mode)	Choose Control from the View menu to display the Control mode. The Control mode displays a list of all the controls found in the highlighted dialog box. It also displays the topic IDs assigned by the Composer, and the associated dialog box name.

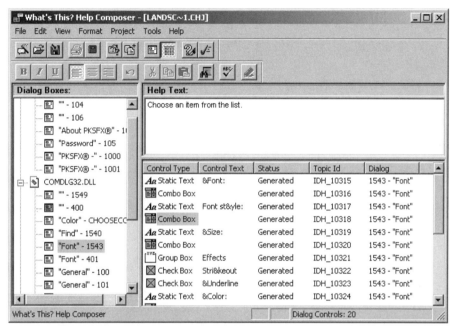

Figure 12-16: Displaying the Control view to see topic IDs

10. Edit the text for each control as needed by clicking in the Help Text box and typing new text or deleting text you don't want. For HTML Help files, you won't be able to use formatting such as bold or italic, but you can still use the following text editing icons.

Table 12-4: Text editing options

Icon	Description
✂	Cuts the selected text and stores it in memory
📋	Copies the selected text and stores it in memory
📋	Pastes the text from memory to the cursor location
🔍	Opens a standard find and replace window
✓	Checks the spelling of the entire project or just the open dialog help text

11. From the **File** menu, choose **Generate HTML files**. The RoboHelp HTML What's This? Help Composer creates the following files:

Table 12-5: What's This? Help project files

File	Description
filename.cdx	One of the What's This? Help database indexing files
filename.chj	The What's This? Help project file
filename.dbf	The What's This? Help database file
filename.dto	The default font and color information
filename.fpt	One of the What's This? Help database indexing files
filename.h	The What's This? Help map file
context.txt	The source file for the What's This? Help. This will always be called context.txt regardless of the filename you enter.

NOTE: *When you ship the finished help, you'll only need to provide the file with the .chj extension (the help file itself). You'll also need to include the CSHTML.dll file in the end user's windows/system directory.*

12. From the **File** menu, choose **Exit** to close the What's This? Help window. The What's This? Help Composer saves your work as you go along, so it is not necessary to save it separately.

Editing Existing What's This? Help Text

If you've already created the What's This? Help project, you will periodically need to go in and edit it. This might be to add or edit text, add or edit the elements for which you've created text, or delete the What's This? Help completely.

To edit an existing What's This? Help project, follow these steps:

1. Ensure that you have the most recent version of the software for which you are writing the help.

2. Open the RoboHelp HTML project associated with the What's This? Help.

3. From the **File** menu, choose **New**, and then **What's This? Help Project**. The What's This? Help Composer checks the associated files and displays a message, as shown in Figure 12-17.

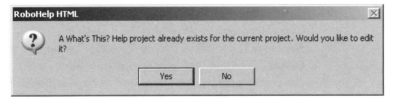

Figure 12-17: Opening an existing What's This? Help project with the New menu item

4. Click **Yes** to open the What's This? Help Composer window with the project displayed, as shown in Figure 12-18.

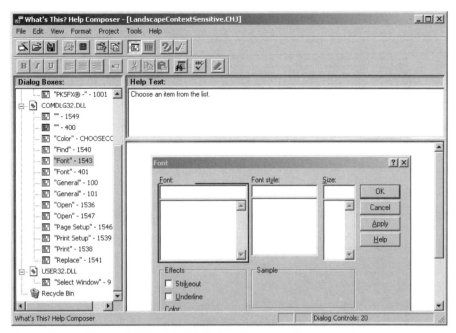

Figure 12-18: Opening a What's This? Help project in the Composer window

5. Highlight the item in the **Dialog Boxes** pane that you want to edit. Then click the element in the **View** pane to display the existing text. Add, edit, or delete text as necessary.

6. From the **File** menu, choose **Generate HTML files** to update all of the files you'll need for the completed help.

Adding and Removing Dialog Boxes

Because What's This? Help is so closely associated with a program, it is important to update the help whenever the software changes. If the program files with which the What's This? Help is associated have changed since the last time you opened the project, the Composer software will automatically update the help files using the default text setting. When you open the Composer (by choosing New and then What's This? Help from the File menu), you'll see a series of windows that allow you to either accept or cancel the automatic update.

You can also update the dialog boxes manually. For example, you may need to add a program file that wasn't part of the original or remove the help from specific fields or buttons. To update the What's This? Help dialog boxes manually, follow these steps:

1. Open the RoboHelp HTML project associated with the What's This? Help.

2. From the **File** menu, choose **New** and then **What's This? Help Project**. The What's This? Help Composer checks the associated files and displays a message telling you that the What's This? Help file exists already.

3. Click **OK** to close the message box and display the help project in the What's This? Help Composer window, as shown in Figure 12-19.

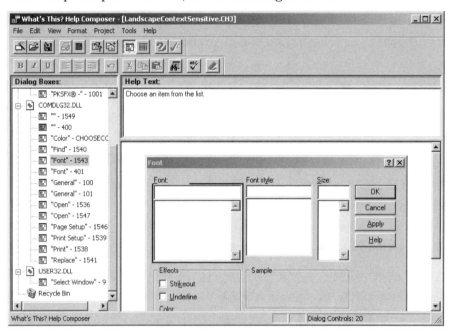

Figure 12-19: Displaying the project in the What's This? Help composer

4. To add a dialog box to the help project, choose **Add File** from the **Project** menu. The What's This? Help Composer displays a standard browser window.

5. At the bottom of the window, you can specify whether you want to display .exe, .dll, or .ocx files. You can also choose to display all files, even those that can't be included in the project. Browse to the file that you want to add, highlight the filename, and then click **OK**. The What's This? Help Composer displays a dialog box with information about the file that you just added, as shown in Figure 12-20.

6. Click **OK** to include the listed changes in your What's This? Help project and close the window.

7. To remove a file from the project (and all of its associated fields and buttons), highlight the name of the file in the left-hand pane. Then choose **Remove File** from the **Edit** menu. The entire file will be removed from the project.

8. To remove a single field or button from the project, highlight the dialog box in the left-hand pane. Then click on the field or button you want to delete in the **View** pane.

9. From the **Edit** menu, choose **Delete Dialog** to display a warning about deleting entries.

10. Click **OK** to delete the item. That item will be removed from the project.

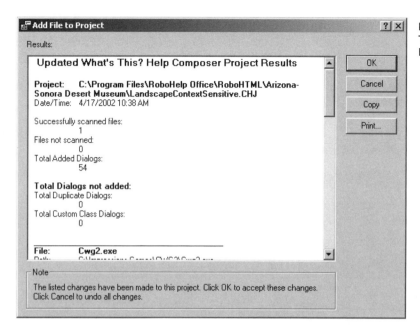

Figure 12-20:
The Add File to
Project dialog

11. From the **File** menu, choose **Generate HTML files** to create the What's This? Help files.

NOTE: *When you delete files or elements from a What's This? Help project, the Composer stores the files in the Recycle Bin displayed in the Dialog Boxes pane. Like other Recycle Bins, this folder stores the deleted files until you empty it. You can also restore deleted files from the Recycle Bin if you need to.*

Configuring the What's This? Help Composer

While much of the What's This? Help functionality is automated, you do have some options in how the help project is built. You can change the software program that the What's This? Help project is documenting, the format of the map IDs, or whether to use the default text when updating with the Configuration window.

1. With the project displayed in the What's This? Help Composer, choose **Configuration** from the **Project** menu to display the Configuration window, as shown in Figure 12-21 on the following page.

2. To change the program for which you are building this What's This? Help project, enter a new executable in the **Run Command** box. You may use the Browse button to point to the file if necessary.

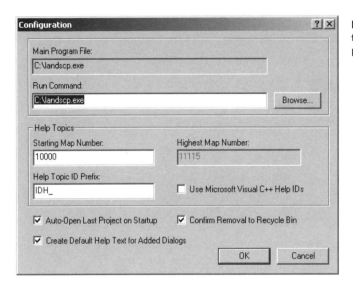

Figure 12-21: Configuring the What's This? Help project settings

3. To specify the format of the map IDs, you can specify any of the following options:

   ■ Specify the first number you want to use in the **Starting Map Number** box.

   ■ Specify the prefix, if any, for the map IDs. The default is IDH_, but you can change it to any prefix you like.

   ■ Select the check box labeled **Use Microsoft Visual C++ Help IDs** if you want the Composer to use the IDs that it may find in a Visual C++ project.

CAUTION: *The Visual C++ Help IDs are not verified within RoboHelp, and thus may contain IDs that duplicate other topics. Using this option may cause duplicate map ID errors.*

4. Select the check box labeled **Create Default Help Text for Added Dialogs** if you want the What's This? Help Composer to automatically generate default help text when creating or updating the What's This? Help project. Unselect this box if you would rather start with blank text for each topic.

5. Select the check box labeled **Confirm Removal to Recycle Bin** if you want to display a warning message before dialog boxes, fields, or buttons are removed from the project.

6. Select the check box labeled **Auto-Open Last Project on Startup** if you want the What's This? Help Composer to automatically open the most recent project you used.

7. When you are finished with your changes, click **OK** to close the Configuration window.

Editing the Default Text Entries

The What's This? Help Composer has a set of default text entries for many types of fields and buttons so that you don't have to manually enter the text for each one. This is useful, for example, if you have a lot of OK buttons. However, the default text is quite generic. In many instances you may want to change the default, but you can't do it from within the What's This? Help Composer or RoboHelp HTML. You'll have to use the Registry Editor that comes with windows to change the default text entries.

 CAUTION: *Registry files are a key component of your operating system. If you make changes to any of these files incorrectly, you might irreversibly corrupt your system. Before doing anything with registry files, make a backup.*

To edit the default text entries for each category of control through the Windows Registry, follow these steps:

1. Start the Registry Editor by typing **Regedit.exe** in the **Run** box of the Start menu. The exact method of starting the editor will vary by the type of operating system you have. A typical registry is displayed in Figure 12-22.

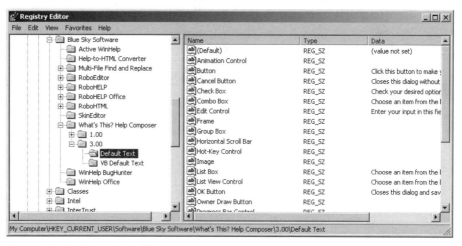

Figure 12-22: The Registry Editor

2. Open the following folders until you get to the default text for the What's This? Help Editor: \Hkey_Current_User\Software\Blue Sky Software\What's This? Help Composer\3.00\Default Text.

3. Double-click the entry that you want to change to display that entry's Edit String window, as shown in Figure 12-23.

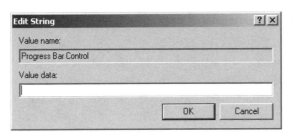

Figure 12-23: The Edit String window

4. Edit or enter the text for the entry and then click **OK.**

5. From the **Registry** menu, choose **Exit** to close the Registry Editor. The Registry Editor saves your changes. The next time you create or update a What's This? Help project, the new text will be used as the default. You may need to restart your computer for the changes to take effect.

Deleting a What's This? Help Project

Sometimes you'll need to remove a What's This? Help from a project. This might happen if you decide to approach the context-sensitive help in a different way, you want to start the What's This? Help over from scratch, or you simply want to test the project and run reports without the What's This? Help topics.

To delete What's This? Help from an HTML Help project, do the following:

1. In the right-hand pane Project tab of the main RoboHelp HTML window, open the **Context-Sensitive Help** folder.

2. Open the **Text-Only Topic Files** folder. The What's This? Help project appears as a file named context.txt.

3. Right-click the **context.txt** file and then choose **Delete.** The context.txt file and associated dialog.cid file will be removed from the project.

Manually Creating Field-Level Topics for HTML Help

While the What's This? Help Composer can be useful in many instances, there are also times when it is easier to create the field-level help manually. For example, the What's This? Help Composer automatically assigns map IDs to each topic. If you have a list of map IDs from the developers that you have to use, it is easier to create and maintain the project within the standard RoboHelp HTML interface.

To create context-sensitive field-level help topics for HTML Help output, follow these steps:

1. In the right-hand pane Project tab of the main RoboHelp HTML window, open the **Context-Sensitive Help** folder. If you have already created a What's This? Help for this project, you'll see the context.txt file.

2. Right-click **Text-Only Topic Files** in the Context Sensitive Help folder and choose **Create/Import Text-Only Topic File** to display a browser, as shown in Figure 12-24.

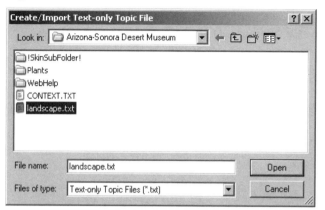

Figure 12-24: The Create/Import Text-only Topic File window

3. Enter a name for the new TXT file (or browse to an existing file). Then click **OK** to display the Context-Sensitive Text-Only Topics window, as shown in Figure 12-25.

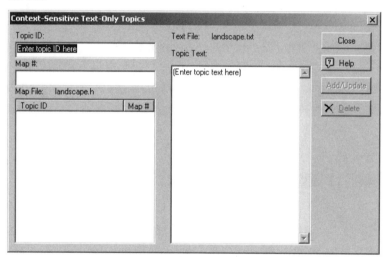

Figure 12-25: Entering text and IDs in the Context-Sensitive Text-Only Topics screen

3. Enter a topic ID in the Topic ID box. As you enter the topic ID, RoboHelp HTML automatically changes spaces, special characters, and punctuation to underscores. If you enter a topic ID that exists in the project already, the map number for that topic ID is displayed in the Map # box. If it is a new topic ID, the word <auto> is displayed in the Map # box.

4. Enter the map number in either of the following ways:

   ■ Leave the word <auto> in the Map # box. RoboHelp HTML will assign the next available map number, starting with 1.

   ■ Type a new number in the Map # box.

5. Enter the text for the field in the **Topic Text** box. This text will be stored with the map IDs, so it is not necessary to worry about aliases.

6. Click **Add/Update** to store the text and map ID.

7. Repeat steps 3 through 6 for each topic ID you need to add. Click **Close** when you are done to close the Context-Sensitive Text-Only Topics window.

Notes for Developers

When the context-sensitive help is complete, you'll still need to incorporate the help topics with the program. To enable What's This? Help in the program, keep the following in mind:

- The What's This? Help Composer expects the controls to have a logical tab order. Controls with an ID of –1 will not get help text.

- The cshuser.h file contains calls that you can use in C or C++ programs. The cshtml.dll file contains run-time communications. Both files are in \RoboHELP Office\RoboHTML\WhatsThs\ProgDlls and documented in the What's This? Help Composer documentation.

- eHelp Corporation provides a number of specific examples of code for various environments and the eHelp Developer's Forum and Knowledgebase on their web site at http://www.ehelp.com.

Creating Context-Sensitive Help for WebHelp and WebHelp Enterprise Output

For WebHelp and WebHelp Enterprise output formats, like HTML Help output, it is critical that you work closely with the program developer to ensure that the links work correctly. The developer can use the RoboHelp API or point directly to individual .htm files. This section discusses the methods used when the developer is going through the RoboHelp API and using the supplied functions. These support programs are written in the following:

- Visual Basic, Visual C++, web pages (HTML/JavaScript), or Java applets
- Visual C++
- Web-based HTML (including JavaScript)
- Java applets

WebHelp and WebHelp Enterprise outputs do not make a distinction between window-level and field-level help. In either case, the call from the program opens the specified topic in a window. You'll have to create topics for each of the fields and buttons—there is no separate text-only interface. This means that even for field-level help, you can use lists, images, links, and other elements in your topics. For WebHelp Enterprise output, you can also specify different windows for each topic.

As with other types of context-sensitive help, you need to assign each topic a code so that the program can find it. Rather than use aliases, though, WebHelp and WebHelp Enterprise use context strings. The Context String Editor lets you associate each context string (similar to a map ID) with the name of a topic and an optional window name.

NOTE: *Since the field-level topics are treated the same way as other topics, make sure that you've created them before beginning this process. Also, if you're going to use different windows for WebHelp Enterprise output (such as one window for lists and a different window for text entries), make sure you've created the window definitions first. See Chapter 11, "Using Windows in RoboHelp HTML" for more information about windows.*

To create context-sensitive help, follow these steps:

1. In the right-hand pane, open the context-sensitive **Help** folder. You will see various files based on the types of context-sensitive help you may have created for this project.

2. Double-click on the **Context Strings** entry to open the Context Strings window.

3. To add a new context string, click the **New** button. A new line will be added at the top of the window, and the list of available topics becomes visible, as shown in Figure 12-26. The default string will be "New_Context_String." The new context string will default to point to the first topic in the list.

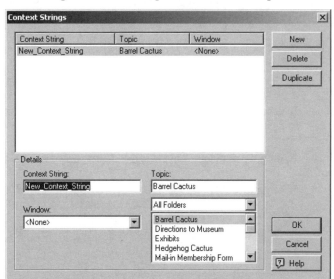

Figure 12-26: Entering the context string information in the Context Strings window

4. In the **Context String** box in the Details area at the bottom of the window, enter the context string you want to assign to the topic. This can be numeric, use prefixes, or be whatever format your developer needs it to be.

5. Choose a window in which to display the topic by selecting from the drop-down list under the label Window. You must specify a window in which to display each context-sensitive topic.

 NOTE: *Although you can specify a window for WebHelp output, it will only be used by WebHelp Enterprise output. WebHelp output will ignore the window settings.*

6. Click on a topic in the **Topic** box to assign it to the current context string.

7. Click **OK** to save your context strings.

8. Generate the help project and test with the program.

 NOTE: *For WebHelp Enterprise output, you must publish the files to the server before you can test the context-sensitive help.*

Notes for Developers

RoboHelp HTML provides support files for programming context-sensitive help. Which file you'll need depends on the programming language you're using. The files are stored in the following directory: C:\Program Files\RoboHelp Office\ RoboHTML\WebHelp5Ext\template_csh\rh_cshapi.

In addition, the RoboHelp HTML help includes code samples for each supported language. The topic titled "Examples for using context-sensitive support files" includes several, plus links to the language-specific help files.

Table 12-6 lists the supported languages, the associated files, and the name of the help file within RoboHelp HTML that describes how to use them.

Table 12-6: Where to find files for different programming languages

Language	Filename	Help topic
Visual Basic	rh_cshapi\RoboHelp_CSH.bas	Context-Sensitive Help for Visual Basic Applications
C or C++	rh_cshapi\RoboHelp_CSH.cpp and rh_cshapi\RoboHelp_CSH.h	Context-Sensitive Help for Visual C++ Applications
Web applications (HTML/JavaScript)	rh_cshapi\RoboHelp_CSH.js	Context-Sensitive Help for Web Pages
Java (applets only)	rh_cshapi\RoboHelp_CSH.java	Context-Sensitive Help for Java Applets

Summary

In this chapter, you learned about the different types of context-sensitive help. For HTML Help, you saw how to create map files and aliases and how to create both window-level and field-level help using several different tools. For WebHelp and WebHelp Enterprise, you saw how to create context strings and link them to the context-sensitive topics.

The next chapter will discuss how to create forms for HTML Help, WebHelp, and WebHelp Enterprise output.

Chapter 13 | *Creating Forms*

Forms allow your users to enter data into an HTML or web-based window. They are often used to get customer information from users, such as name and address. You'll see forms when you make online purchases, when you submit contest entries, and sometimes when you download information from web sites.

In addition to the standard text, links, and images, each form can contain several types of elements:

Table 13-1: Types of form elements

Element	Description
Text boxes	The user enters a text string consisting of numbers, letters, spaces, and special characters. You can define the maximum length of the string. There are several types of text boxes, also called *text fields*.
Radio buttons	The user clicks on a button to select it. There can only be one selected radio button at a time.
Check boxes	The user clicks on a box to select it. The user can select as many check boxes as necessary.
Drop-down menus	The user clicks the down arrow to display a list of options and then clicks on an option to select it. Only those options in the list may be selected.
Buttons	The user clicks the button to perform an action. There are several predefined buttons, or you can create a button for a custom action. You can also use a custom image as a button.

Form elements are also sometimes called fields or controls. In addition to the form elements, you'll need to think about what the help system will do with the entered information. This is usually handled by a separate program called a *CGI script*. The script specifies which action to take with each piece of data that the user enters.

For example, if you have a form that registers user software, you might have text boxes for name, address, and email information, a drop-down selection box for product name, and maybe some radio buttons that allow users to sign up for email notifications of upcoming releases. You'd also include a Submit button. When the user clicks the Submit button, the CGI script might store the name and address information in a database and send the email address to the list that manages the upcoming release announcements based on the selection of radio buttons.

Designing a Form

Before you begin to create a topic that will have a form in it, you need to make some decisions about the form and the script you'll use with it.

First, select or create a script. Make sure you know what data names the script is expecting. If, for example, your form has a text box for "FirstName" and another for "LastName," and the script is expecting to get a single "Name," the entered data will not be processed.

Decide which types of elements you're going to use for each piece of information. If you are using a drop-down menu, you'll need to know all of the options that might appear on the menu.

NOTE: *While you can use drop-down menus to limit a user to a specified list of options, it is a good idea to avoid drop-down menus for lists that are likely to change over time. For example, if you use a drop-down menu for a version number, you'll have to edit the list of version numbers every time you release a new version. This might be better as a text box.*

Decide where you want the elements on the topic and where you'll put descriptive labels. Keep in mind that the form should be easy to use. Remember to include text labels that specify how to use the form and what to enter in each field, if necessary. For example, you may want to indicate the limit, if any, for text entries. You don't want to make the user hunt for a Submit button. Remember, different browsers will display things in slightly different ways, so be sure to test your form on all browsers that your user is likely to have.

TIP: *Draw your form out on paper first, so you'll see where the various elements go and how much room you have for labels. This sometimes helps to determine which type of element you want to use. For example, a drop-down menu takes up a lot less room than a series of radio buttons. It is also useful to mark the element name (the name that the CGI script is expecting) right on the printout for easier entry later.*

Creating a Form

Once you've made all the decisions about your form, you're ready to create it. Each form must be in a topic. The topic itself can have any or all of the elements discussed throughout this book. To create the form, follow these general steps:

1. Create the topic that will contain the form.
2. Insert the form elements.
3. Specify the element properties (these vary by type of element).
4. Specify the form properties.

Inserting Form Elements

After you've decided which elements you want in the form, follow these steps to insert the elements into your topic.

1. Display the topic to which you want to add a form.

2. Place the cursor where you want the form to begin. From the **Insert** menu, choose **Form** to display a box that represents where the form will be, as shown in Figure 13-1.

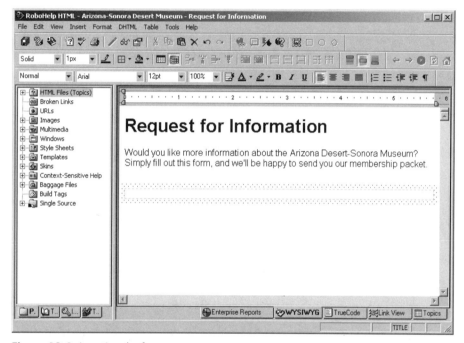

Figure 13-1: Inserting the form

3. Click anywhere on the form outline and drag the outline to the size you want it to be. Although you can create a form that fills several screens, or include several forms in a single topic, it is best to keep forms simple. The example form will only have a few elements in it, so the box can be about half the size of the window.

NOTE: *If you don't yet know how big you'll want the form, you can skip this step and enlarge the form box as you go along.*

4. With the cursor inside of the form box, open the **Insert** menu and choose **Form Element** to display the list of available form types, as shown in Figure 13-2.

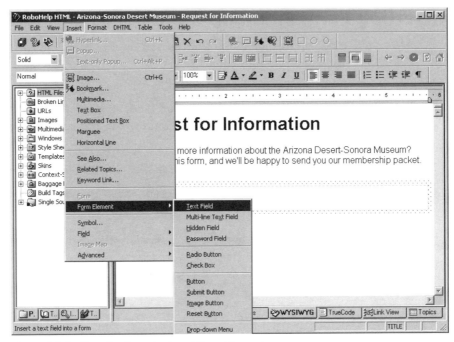

Figure 13-2: Choosing from the Insert Form Element menu

5. Select one of the available form elements. The element will be placed inside the form box.

Table 13-2: Form element functionality

Element	Appearance	Description
Text Field		The user enters information into the box.
Multi-line Text Field		The user can enter many lines of text information into the box and use the scroll bar on the right of the box to move up or down within the text.
Hidden Field		This type of text box does not appear in the form when it is on the web. You might use this to store information that you don't want the user to see but that you still want to pass to the CGI script.
Password Field		The user can enter text, just like a text box, but the typed characters all appear on the screen as asterisks.
Radio Button		The user clicks a radio button to select it. There are usually several radio buttons, but only one can be checked at a time. When the user clicks a different radio button, the first selected button is deselected.
Check Box		The user clicks a check box to select it or clicks a selected check box to deselect it. There may be only one or several check boxes. A user can select any number of check boxes at the same time.

Element	Appearance	Description
Button	Button	The user clicks the button to perform an action that you specify. You can modify the text label to something more specific to the action performed by the button.
Submit Button	Submit Query	The user clicks the button to send the data from the form to the CGI script. You can modify the text label if you need to.
Image Button	ENTER	The user clicks the image to send the data from the form to the CGI script. Typically, this image will look like a button, with and appropriate text label, though you can use any image. The sample image shown here is from the set of buttons that comes with RoboHelp Enterprise.
Reset Button	Reset	The user clicks the button to remove all data from the form and return it to the original state.
Drop-down Menu	a	The user clicks the down arrow and then chooses from a list of available options. You must specify the options.

6. After you select the form element, the element is displayed at the cursor location in the form box. Each element has its own shape. Add whatever label is appropriate for your form. For example, a text field is shown in Figure 13-3 with the label "Type your first and last name."

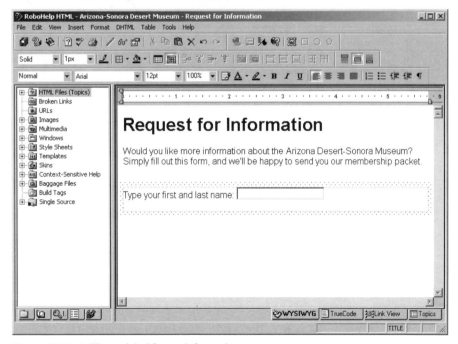

Figure 13-3: Adding a label for each form element

CAUTION: *Some browsers are not able to display paragraph styles within forms. It is best to use inline styles or character styles if you want the labels to be bold, italic, etc.*

NOTE: *The users may not understand what you expect them to enter in each field, so your labels need to be descriptive and clear. For example, if you are using radio buttons, tell the users that they can only choose one of the options. If it is a drop-down menu, let the users know that there are more options within the menu. For password fields, tell them that the asterisks are for security purposes, and they are supposed to look that way.*

7. Double-click on the form element to display the Properties window for that element and enter the properties. This will vary by type of element. The following section, "Specifying Element Properties," describes each of the form element property windows and how to fill them out.

8. Repeat steps 4 through 7 for each element you want to add to the form. Figure 13-4 shows a form with many types of elements in it.

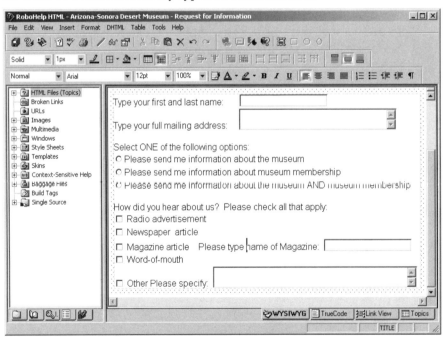

Figure 13-4: A form containing many form elements

9. Test the form by clicking the **View** icon ( ) to display the topic with the form as it will appear in the user's browser. Hidden fields, if any, will not appear. You can click the radio buttons and/or check boxes or type information into the text boxes. You won't, however, be able to test the Submit button until you've linked the form to a CGI script.

Specifying Element Properties

Though they vary with each type of element, all element properties must have a unique name that identifies it to the CGI script. Within RoboHelp, these are called the *control identifiers*. These names must be unique, and should be as simple as possible so that anyone who looks at it will know which field is which. For example, rather than have Name1 and Name2, you might use FirstName and LastName for identifiers. Other common properties include a default value or field size properties.

Although there are eleven different elements listed in the RoboHelp HTML interface, these elements use only five different property windows.

Table 13-3: Where to find information about element properties

Field type	Section
Text box (multiple lines with scroll bars)	"Specifying Multi-line Text Field Properties"
Text box (single line) Hidden fields Password field	"Specifying Text Field Properties"
Radio button Check box	"Specifying Radio Button and Check Box Properties"
Button Submit button Reset button Image button	"Specifying Button Properties"
Drop-down menu	"Specifying Drop-Down Menu Properties"

Specifying Text Field Properties

Text boxes (also called *text fields*) store textual data that the user enters.

 NOTE: *Multi-line text fields use a different type of properties window described in the following section, "Specifying Multi-line Text Field Properties."*

To specify text field properties, follow these steps:

1. Double-click the text field, password field, or hidden field to display the Text Field properties window, as shown in Figure 13-5 on the following page.

2. Depending on which type of element you originally inserted, the Control type will be plain text, password, or hidden. You can change the current text box to any of the other types.

   - Plain text (text field) indicates a single line of text.

   - The Password option specifies a single line of text that appears in the window as asterisks.

- Hidden indicates a single line that doesn't appear in the browser window at all.

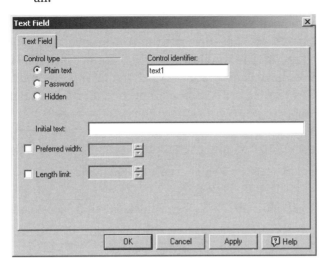

Figure 13-5: The Text Field properties window

3. Enter the name for the field in the **Control identifier** box. Remember, this is the unique name that the CGI script uses to identify the data entered in this field. It must match the name that the CGI script expects exactly.

4. Enter default text (such as "type your text here"), if any, in the **Initial text** box.

5. Specify the size of the text box by checking the **Preferred width** box and entering a value (in number of characters) in the box to the right. This is just the width of the box, not the number of characters the user can enter.

6. Specify the maximum number of characters the user will be allowed to enter by checking the **Length limit** box and entering a value in the box to the right. If the length limit is longer than the preferred width, the characters will scroll as the user enters them. Only the number of characters specified in the Preferred width box will be visible at any one time.

7. Click **OK** to save your changes and close the Text Field window.

Specifying Multi-line Text Field Properties

Text fields store text data that the user enters. A multi-line text field allows the user to enter more text and use scroll bars to move around and view different parts of the text. Use this type of text field for entries such as comment fields or other lengthy unstructured text data.

NOTE: *Single-line text fields use a different type of properties window, described in the previous section, "Specifying Text Field Properties."*

To specify multi-line text field properties, follow these steps:

1. Double-click the multi-line text field to display the properties window, as shown in Figure 13-6.

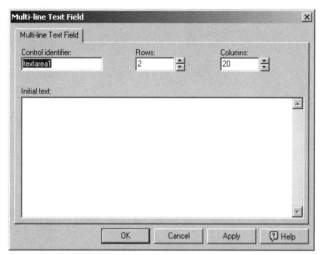

Figure 13-6: Entering property information in the Multi-line Text Field window

2. Enter the name for the field in the **Control Identifier** box. Remember, this is the unique name that the CGI script uses to identify the data entered in this field. It must match the name that the CGI script expects exactly.

3. Enter default text (such as "type your text here"), if any, in the **Initial text** box.

4. Specify the size of the text box by entering values in the Rows and Column boxes. This is just the width of the box, not the number of characters the user can enter.

NOTE: *You can also specify the size of the box by clicking the box in the WYSIWYG pane and then dragging the corners to create a new size/shape. This will override any properties you may have set.*

5. Click **OK** to save your changes and close the multi-line Text Field window.

Specifying Radio Button and Check Box Properties

Both radio buttons and check boxes use the same properties window. Use radio buttons when there is a list but the user can only choose one option. You'll be able to specify which of the radio buttons is selected when the window is first opened (the default).

Use check boxes when the user has a list from which to choose and can choose any number of the options (some, all, or none). Each check box is treated individually and must have a unique name (control identifier).

Radio buttons and check boxes are linked into sets by the control identifier (or name). Each button or box has a unique value, but they share the control identifier with the others in the set. For example, you might set up radio buttons with the following control identifiers and values:

Table 12-4: Sample radio button properties

Control identifier	Value
MembershipLevel	Gold
MembershipLevel	Silver
MembershipLevel	Turquoise
CurrentMember	Yes
CurrentMember	No

For this example, users would be able to choose any one of the membership level radio buttons <u>and</u> any one of the CurrentMember buttons. They would not, however, be able to choose both Gold and Silver membership levels.

Like the control identifiers, the values must be exactly what your script expects. If it is looking for the words "Yes" and "No" in the CurrentMember control, simply entering values of Y and N would not work. You'll need to check with the developer of your script for the valid values for each control.

To specify radio button or check box properties, follow these steps:

1. Double-click the Radio Button or Check Box to display the properties window shown in Figure 13-7.

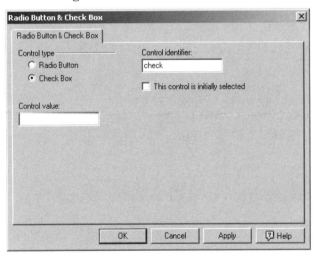

Figure 13-7: The Radio Button & Check Box window

2. Depending on which type of element you originally inserted, the Control type will be Radio Button or Check Box. You can change the current control to the other type.

   ■ Select **Radio Button** when the user can choose only one of the options.

   ■ Select **Check Box** when the user can choose any number of the options.

3. Enter the name for the field in the Control identifier box. Remember, this is the unique name that the CGI script uses to identify the data entered in this set of radio buttons. It must match the name that the CGI script expects exactly. Also, you must make all entries in the set the same. For example, radio buttons with a control identifier of MembershipLevel will not be in the same set as buttons with the control identifier of MemberLevel.

4. If you want this radio button or check box to be selected when the form is first opened, then select the **This control is initially selected** box.

 NOTE: *You can specify that all of the check boxes are initially selected, but only one radio button can be initially selected.*

5. Enter the specific value for the control. Each value must be unique within the set of buttons or boxes with the same control identifier.

6. Click **OK** to save your changes and close the properties window.

Specifying Drop-down Menu Properties

Drop-down menus contain a predefined list of options from which the user must choose. You have to enter the list of options, including a default if you like.

To specify drop-down menu properties, follow these steps:

1. Double-click the drop-down menu to display the properties window, as shown in Figure 13-8.

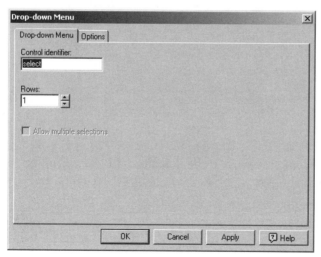

Figure 13-8: The Drop-down Menu window

2. Enter the name for the field in the **Control identifier** box. Remember, this is the unique name that the CGI script uses to identify the data entered in this field. It must match the name that the CGI script expects exactly.

3. Specify the size of the displayed drop-down menu by entering a number in the **Rows** box. This is only the size of the visible portion of the drop-down menu,

not a limit to the number of options you can have within the menu. If you specify more than one row, the menu will automatically display as a scrollable list.

 NOTE: *You can also specify the size of the box by clicking the box in the WYSIWYG pane and then dragging the corners to create a new size/shape.*

4. If you display more than one row of the drop-down menu, you can specify whether the user will be allowed to choose more than one option. Click the check box labeled **Allow multiple selections** to select it and let the user choose any number of options (like the check boxes). Click the check box to deselect it if you want to limit the user to selecting only one option (like radio buttons).

5. To specify the list of options for the drop-down menu, click the **Options** tab to display the Options window, as shown in Figure 13-9. The Options window contains the default list items "a" and "b."

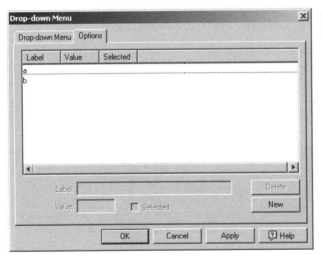

Figure 13-9: Entering a list of options for the drop-down menu

6. To add an option to the list, click the **New** button. The text boxes on the bottom of the window become active, and the default text ("New Caption" and "New Value") appears in the boxes, as shown in Figure 13-10 on the following page.

7. Enter the wording you want to display to the user in the **Label** box. For example, if you are entering membership levels, you could use "Silver Level." Enter the code that the form will pass to the CGI script in the Value box.

8. Click **Apply** to store the new information to the list.

9. To remove an entry from the list, click the entry and then the **Delete** button.

10. Repeat steps 6 through 8 for additional options.

11. Click **OK** when you are done to close the Drop-down Menu property window.

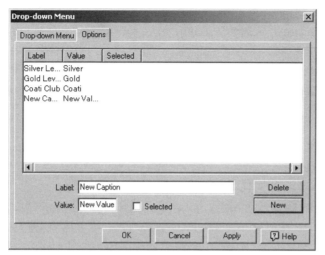

Figure 13-10: Changing the default label and value information

Specifying Button Properties

When a user clicks a button, he is actually requesting that an action be performed. You can create custom buttons using the standard Button shape or a custom image or using either of the two predefined buttons (Submit and Reset).

NOTE: *Radio buttons are not really buttons and are not covered in this section. See "Specifying Radio Button and Check Box Properties" earlier in this chapter.*

To specify the button properties, follow these steps:

1. Double-click the button to display the properties window shown in Figure 13-11.

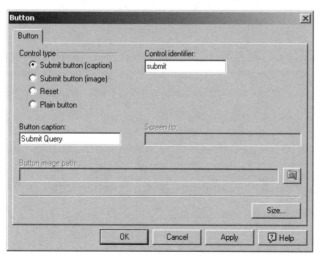

Figure 13-11: Entering property information in the Button window

2. Depending on which type of element you originally inserted, the Control type will be Submit (caption), Submit (image), Reset, or Plain. You can change the current button to any of the other types.

   ■ Choose **Submit button (caption)** to send the entered data to the CGI script when the user clicks the button. You must also specify the text label that appears on the button.

   ■ Choose **Submit button (image)** to send the entered data to the CGI script when the user clicks the image that you specify.

   ■ Choose the **Reset** option to remove the entered data, if any, and the form will display the default settings.

   ■ Select **Plain button** to specify the action that is performed when the user clicks on the button. You must also specify the text label that appears on the button.

3. Enter the name for the button in the **Control identifier** box. Remember, this is the unique name that the CGI script uses to identify each element in the form. It must match the name that the CGI script expects exactly.

NOTE: *The Reset button does not require a control identifier, since it does not interact with the script.*

4. Enter a caption in the **Button Caption** box. This is the text that will appear on the button itself. Default text (such as "Submit" for the Submit button) will be used if you don't change it.

NOTE: *Image buttons do not have a caption. If you want text on an image button, you must add it directly to the image with your graphics software.*

5. If you are creating an image button, you may enter an optional screen tip. The screen tip will appear when the user holds the cursor over the image. It will also display if the user has graphics turned off, which is very useful for Section 508 compliance.

6. If you are creating an image button, you must specify the location of the button. You can either type in the path or use the Browse button to point to the button image.

7. Click **OK** to save your changes and close the properties window.

Specifying Form Properties

Once you have defined the form, entered all of the elements, and specified properties for each element, you still have to set the properties for the form. In general, the form properties define what the form will do with the information it gathers.

Follow these steps to set form properties:

1. With the cursor anywhere within the form, click the right mouse button and choose **Form Properties** to display the Form window shown in Figure 13-12.

Figure 13-12: The Form window

2. Enter the location of the CGI script in the **Action** text box. This will typically be on your server and have an address like http://www.asdm.org/cgi-bin/membershipform.cgi.

3. In the **Method** box, choose either **POST** (sends just the entered data to the specified action address) or **GET** (appends the data from the form to the specified action and then attempts to open that address). The form in the example will POST to the script.

4. Enter the name of the form you've just created in the **Name** box. Remember, this must match the name that the script is expecting. For example, this might be the Membership form.

5. You can specify the size of the form by clicking the Size button to display the Size window. Enter a width (as a percentage of the browser window) and/or a height (in pixels), as shown in Figure 13-13 on the following page. Click **OK** to close the Size window.

Figure 13-13: Specifying the form size

6. You can specify how close the form elements can be to the edge of the form by clicking the Margin button. Enter margin values in points, as shown in Figure 13-14. Click **OK** to close the Margins window.

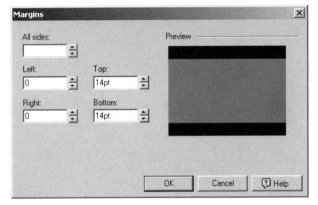

Figure 13-14: Entering margin values

7. You can add various types of borders in different widths, patterns, and colors around the edge of the form box by clicking the Border button to display the Borders window, as shown in Figure 13-15. This works the same way as the borders for text and paragraphs described in Chapter 6. Click **OK** to close the Borders window.

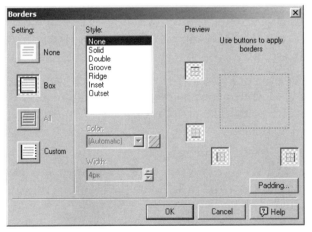

Figure 13-15: Entering border values

6. You can specify background fill or pattern by clicking the Shading button to display the Shading window, as shown in Figure 13-16. This works the same way as

the shading for text and paragraphs as described in Chapter 6. Click **OK** to close the Shading window.

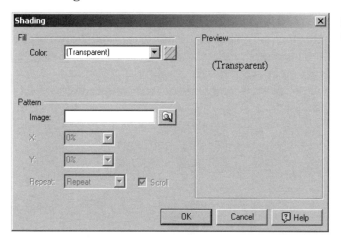

Figure 13-16: Entering shading values

A Few Words about CGI Scripts

A CGI script is simply a type of program that takes information from a form and sends it to your server. There are scripts for signing up for newsletters, submitting address information, managing passwords, and creating message boards. Scripts are written in a scripting or programming language, such as JavaScript, VBScript, or Perl.

RoboHelp HTML does not come with any prewritten scripts. Although you could write your own CGI script, it may not be necessary. There are several places you can get free or low-cost scripts.

Many Internet service providers (ISPs) and hosting services have a library of CGI scripts that they allow their customers to use for free. Even if they don't have a script that does exactly what you want, you may be able to make a few simple modifications to an existing script. Check with your provider for details.

There are also a number of web sites that offer CGI scripts. Some are free; others cost anywhere from $10 to hundreds of dollars.

You could also write your own script. There are many books available on scripting, such as *Learn JavaScript* and *Advanced JavaScript, 2nd Edition*, both by Chuck Easttom and available from Wordware Publishing.

Finally, you could have a developer create a script for you. You'd get exactly what you want and have control over which identifiers the script would use.

Summary

This chapter explained forms and CGI scripts. You learned what they do and when to use them. You learned to add text boxes, radio buttons, check boxes, and other types of form elements to a topic and saw several suggestions on how to find a script that meets your needs.

The next chapter discusses how to create frames and framesets for your topics.

Chapter 14

Using Frames and Framesets

A *frame* in RoboHelp HTML, like a picture frame, defines the space around a help topic. A *frameset* combines two or more frames into a single window. Each frame (usually referred to as panes) in the set can have its own design, buttons, images, and scroll bars. They can be connected to each other (as when a user clicks in one frame to display content in a second frame), but they don't have to be. For example, the default HTML Help browser uses frames.

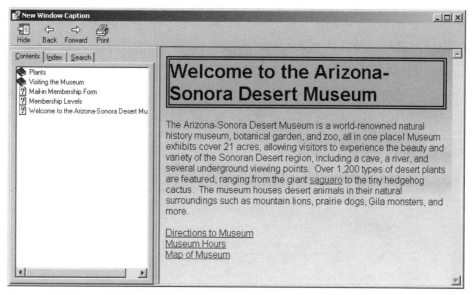

Figure 14-1: Frames in the HTML Help browser

Most framesets that you'll see on the web are either two side-by-side frames or one above the other.

 TIP: *While frames can be very useful, too many frames can be distracting. They also can use up computer resources, since you're loading a topic into each frame. Depending on your user's system configuration and connection speed, frames may load very slowly. Use only what you need to accomplish the organizational task you're attempting. Remember, too, that some older browsers may not be able to display frames properly, if at all.*

To implement frames in a topic, perform the following general steps:

1. Design your frameset.
2. Create the frameset.
3. Create topics for each frame.
4. Insert the links from one frame to another.
5. Create the links that will open the frameset.

Designing a Frameset

Most framesets that you'll see on the web are either two side-by-side frames or two frames with a third frame across the top of the window. The first thing you'll need to do when creating a frameset is to break up your window into frames.

RoboHelp HTML comes with a number of predefined framesets, as shown in Figure 14-2. These layouts work well for most help projects.

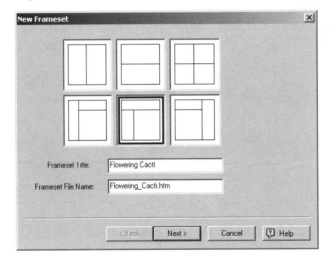

Figure 14-2: Choosing from the predefined RoboHelp HTML framesets

Before you begin to create your frameset, decide which layout suits your needs the best. For each frame, you'll have to make a series of decisions.

- How big will the frame be relative to the window?
- Will the contents of the topic need to scroll in the frame?
- Which topic will appear in each frame when the frameset is first opened?

Creating a Frameset

RoboHelp HTML comes with a variety of predefined framesets. For each frameset you create, you'll have to specify the frameset attributes to control the size of the frames within each set and the topics that will be displayed when the frameset first opens. Once you've created the frameset, it will appear as an .htm file in the project listing. You can preview the frameset to ensure it is what you expect and edit existing framesets.

Specifying Frameset Attributes

When you're ready to create the frameset, follow these steps:

1. From the **File** menu, select **New** and then **Frameset** to display the New Frameset window, as shown in Figure 14-3.

2. The six graphics represent the available basic framesets. Click a frameset to select it and highlight it with a blue border.

3. Enter a name for the frameset in the **Frameset Title** box. This is the name that will appear on the project tab and in topic lists. As you type, the filename will automatically be entered, substituting underscores for spaces.

4. Click **Next** to display the Frameset-Frame Attributes window, as shown in Figure 14-4.

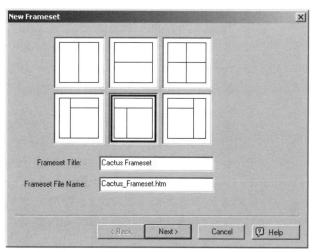

Figure 14-3: Displaying available configurations in the New Frameset window

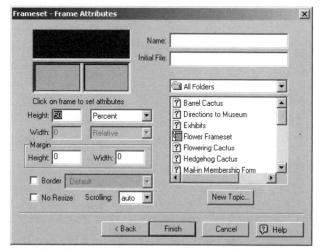

Figure 14-4: Specifying attributes for each frame

5. The individual frames are represented by boxes in the upper left-hand corner of the Attributes window. The attributes apply to only the selected frame (indicated by blue). You must finish specifying properties for each frame before you can select another frame. To specify attributes for each frame, click on the frame to select it.

6. Enter a name for the selected frame in the **Name** box. The name will appear in lists of frames throughout RoboHelp, so make it unique and descriptive. For example, use "TOCFrame" or "LowerLeft" rather than "FrameA."

7. Choose the topic that will appear when that frame is first opened from the list of topics. If the topic doesn't exist yet, you can click the **New Topic** button to create the topic. The topic you specify is automatically entered in the Initial File box.

8. Depending on the frame configuration, you'll be able to specify either a height or width for each frame. For both height and width, use any of the following methods:

   ■ Choose **Pixels** from the drop-down menu. Then enter the height or width in pixels.

   ■ Choose **Percent** from the drop-down menu. Then enter the height or width as a percentage of the window.

   ■ Specify that side-by-side frames have equal width (or top and bottom frames have equal height) by selecting **Relative** from the drop-down menu. You must select Relative for both frames.

   ■ Click the edge of the frame in the preview on the upper left-hand corner of the Attributes window and drag the border to a new location. The height or width numbers will display the change.

9. Enter the height and width of the distance between the topic content and the edge of the frame in the Margin area. You can specify either pixels (for an exact margin distance) or percentage of the frame.

10. To specify a border, click the **Border** check box. Then specify a border color by choosing from the drop-down menu.

11. Click the **No Resize** box to prevent users from changing the size of the frame within the output window. If No Resize is not selected, the user will be able to change the size of the frame.

12. Choose one of the following scrolling options:

    ■ Choose **Auto** to display scroll bars only when the topic content is too big for the frame.

    ■ Choose **Yes** to always display scroll bars, even if the topic content fits in the frame.

    ■ Choose **No** to prevent the display of scroll bars, even if the topic content is too big for the frame.

13. Repeat steps 5 through 12 for each frame in the frameset.

14. When you've finished specifying frameset attributes for all of the frames, click **Finish**. The new frameset will be listed in the Project tab with an extension of .htm.

Working with a Frameset

The frameset appears in the Project tab with an extension of .htm, just like the other topics. You can tell it is a frameset because it has a Frameset icon (), as shown in Figure 14-5.

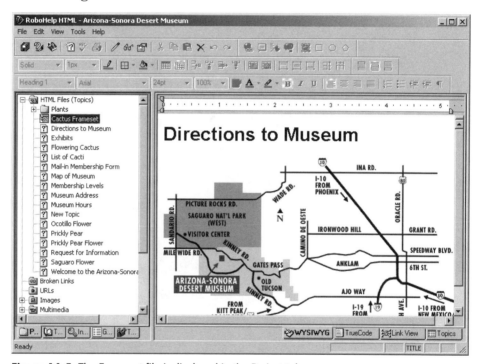

Figure 14-5: The Frameset file is displayed in the Project tab

In some ways, the frameset works just like other topics. You can point to it with hyperlinks, place it in a folder, or set it to be the default "topic" that is displayed when the project is opened. However, framesets are different from topics in several very important ways:

■ You cannot display a frameset in the WYSIWYG window. You must preview the frameset in order to see what it looks like and how it will work.

■ When you double-click the frameset in the Project tab on the left-hand pane, the Frameset-Frame Attributes window opens, not the WYSIWYG pane. This allows you to edit the frameset as necessary (described in the previous section).

Previewing a Frameset

To preview a frameset, first highlight the frameset name in either the left-hand Project tab or the right-hand Topics tab. Then do one of the following:

- Click the right mouse button and choose **View**.
- Click the **View** icon (👓).
- From the **View** menu, choose the frameset name (at the bottom of the menu).

The frameset and its default topics are displayed, as shown in Figure 14-6.

Figure 14-6: Using the preview function to look at framesets

Notice that in this example, there are three frames. Some of the attributes for each frame are:

Table 14-1: Sample frameset attributes

Frame	Scrolling	Border	Height/Width
Upper frame	No	Teal	Height 20%
Lower-left frame	Auto. There are no scroll bars because the topic fits within the frame.	Teal	Width 28%
Lower-right frame	Auto. There are scroll bars across the bottom and on the right-hand side of the lower-right frame because the topic, in this case a graphic, was larger than the frame.	None	Width 72%

Displaying Topics in the Frameset

Once you have your frameset, you'll need to set up the help to display the topics in the frames. Follow these basic steps:

1. Create the topics you're going to display in the frameset if you haven't already done so. Remember that the area for display will be less than a whole window. This is particularly important for frames with the scrolling turned off.

2. Create the links that open each topic, making sure you specify the correct frame. You can create these links in topics, in the table of contents, or in the index (or all three).

3. Display the frameset with the default topics. Once the frameset is open, the topics will display in the specified frames.

Creating Links that Open a Topic in a Frame

For each topic that you want to display in a frame, you will have to specify the frame name as part of the link that opens the topic. You can open topics in a frame using the following types of links:

■ Hyperlink from another topic

■ Link from the table of contents

■ Link from an index entry

CAUTION: *The specified frameset must be open before the link is clicked in order for the topic to appear. See "Opening a Frameset" later in this chapter.*

Opening a Topic in a Frame with a Hyperlink

You can specify that the results of any hyperlink be displayed in a frame. For more information on hyperlinks, see Chapter 5, "Linking Topics Together."

To create a hyperlink that causes a topic to appear in a frame, follow these steps:

1. Open the topic in which you want to include the link (the topic you are linking from). This may be a topic you intend to display in a frame or a regular window. Make sure the topic is showing in the WYSIWYG tab in the left-hand pane.

2. Highlight the text or image you want to convert to a link. The hyperlink icons become active.

3. Click the **Insert Hyperlink** icon () to open the Hyperlink window, as shown in Figure 14-7.

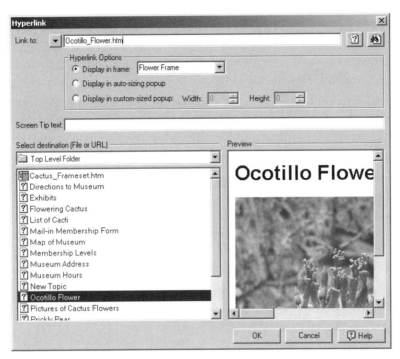

Figure 14-7: The Hyperlink window

4. Specify the information that will appear when the user clicks the link in one of two ways:

   ■ From the Select destination box at the bottom of the Hyperlink window, double-click one of the displayed topics for this project. For example, if you've highlighted the word "Saguaro," you might choose the topic "Saguaro Cactus."

   ■ From the **Link to** drop-down menu, choose the type of information that will display when the link is clicked, such as a URL. Note that if you are linking to one of the topics displayed in the lower part of the Hyperlink window, you don't need to fill in this box.

5. In the **Hyperlink Options** area, specify the frame in which the information should appear by choosing a frame from the drop-down list.

6. Click **OK** to close the Hyperlink window.

Opening a Topic in a Frame from the TOC

When a user clicks a table of contents entry, the default is to display topics in standard windows (without frames). If you want to display the topics in a frame, follow these steps:

1. Create the table of contents. See Chapter 9 for more information about tables of contents.

2. Select the **TOC** tab in the left-hand pane to display the table of contents entries.

3. Right-click on a table of contents entry and choose **Properties** to display the properties window.

4. Click the **Advanced** tab to display the Advanced properties, as shown in Figure 14-8.

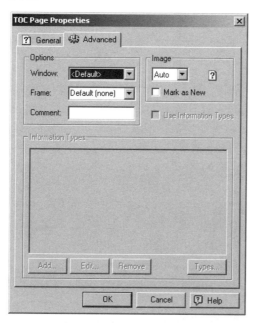

Figure 14-8: The TOC Page Properties window

5. From the **Frame** drop-down box, select the name of the frame in which you want this topic to be displayed.

6. Click **OK** to close the TOC properties window.

7. Repeat steps 3 through 6 for each TOC entry.

Opening a Topic in a Frame from an Index Entry

When a user clicks an index entry, the default is to display topics in standard windows (without frames). If you want to display the topics in a frame, follow these steps:

1. Create the index. See Chapter 9 for more information about creating an index.

2. Select the **Index** tab in the left-hand pane to display the index entries.

3. Right-click on an index entry and choose **Properties** to display the properties window.

4. Click the **Advanced** tab to display the Advanced properties, as shown in Figure 14-9.

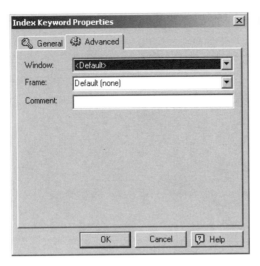

Figure 14-9: The Index Keywords Properties window

5. From the **Frame** drop-down box, select the name of the frame in which you want this topic to be displayed.

6. Click **OK** to close the Index Keyword Properties window.

7. Repeat steps 3 through 6 for each Index entry.

Opening a Frameset

Even if you have specified that a topic should open in a particular frame, the link won't work unless you first display the frameset that contains that frame. You can display a frameset through a regular hyperlink, TOC, or index entry, or you can set the frameset as the default topic.

Opening a Frameset with a Hyperlink

You can specify that the results of any hyperlink be displayed in a frameset. For more information on hyperlinks, see Chapter 5, "Linking Topics Together."

To create a hyperlink that causes a topic to appear in a frame, follow these steps:

1. Open the topic in which you want to include the link (the topic you are linking from). This may be a topic you intend to display in a frame or a regular window. Make sure the topic is showing in the WYSIWYG tab in the left-hand pane.

2. Highlight the text or image you want to convert to a link. The hyperlink icons become active.

3. Click the **Insert Hyperlink** icon to open the Hyperlink window, as shown in Figure 14-10.

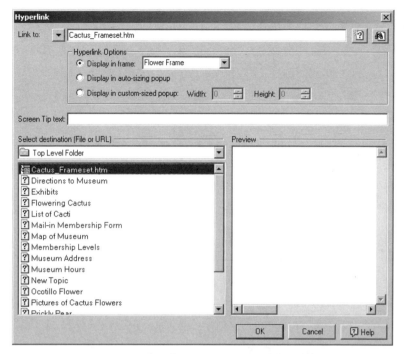

Figure 14-10:
Specifying a
frameset for the
hyperlink output

4. Choose the frameset from the list of topics. Remember, the framesets have a
    unique icon. You don't have to specify a frame at this point. When the link is
    clicked, the entire frameset will display with the default topics for that frameset
    as defined in the frameset properties.

5. Click **OK** to close the Hyperlink window.

Opening a Frameset from the TOC

When a user clicks a table of contents entry, the default is to display topics in
standard windows (without frames). If you want to display a frameset from a
table of contents entry, follow these steps:

1. Create the table of contents. See Chapter 9 for more information about tables of
    contents.

2. Select the **TOC** tab in the left-hand pane to display the table of contents entries.

3. Right-click on a table of contents entry and choose **Properties** to display the
    properties window, as shown in Figure 14-11 on the following page.

4. Choose the frameset from the Existing Topics list. When the link is clicked, the
    entire frameset will display with the default topics for that frameset as defined in
    the frameset properties.

5. Click **OK** to close the TOC properties window.

6. Repeat steps 3 through 5 for each TOC entry that will open a frameset.

Figure 14-11: The TOC Page Properties window

Opening a Frameset from an Index Entry

When a user clicks an index entry, the default is to display topics in standard windows (without frames). If you want to display the topics in a frameset, follow these steps:

1. Create the index. See Chapter 9 for more information about creating an index.
2. Select the **Index** tab in the left-hand pane to display the index entries.
3. Highlight the index entry that you want to use to display the frameset.
4. Display the list of topics in the right-hand pane with one of the following methods:
    - Click the **Show Topics** button in the Index tab.
    - Click the **Topics** tab at the bottom of the right-hand pane.
    - From the **View** menu, choose **Pane** and then **Topics**.
5. Drag the frameset topic from the right-hand pane to the Index tab. The frameset name will be associated with the index keyword, as shown in Figure 14-12.

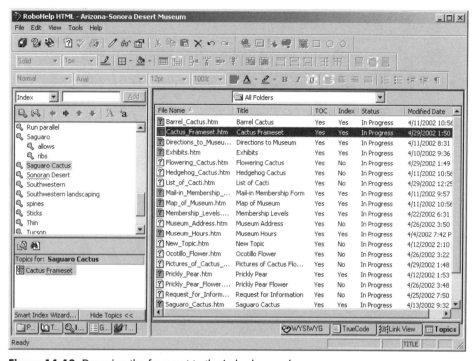

Figure 14-12: Dragging the frameset to the index keyword

Setting a Frameset as the Default Topic

If you've gone to all the trouble of setting up frames, you'll most often want to display the frameset all of the time. The easiest way to do this is to set the frameset as your default topic so that it is opened whenever the help is opened.

NOTE: *If you want the frameset to be displayed all of the time, make sure that you have defined all of the TOC and index entries to open in one of the displayed frames.*

To define the frameset as your default topic, follow these steps:

1. From the **File** menu, choose **Project Settings**.
2. Click the **Compile** tab to display the compile window, as shown in Figure 14-13.

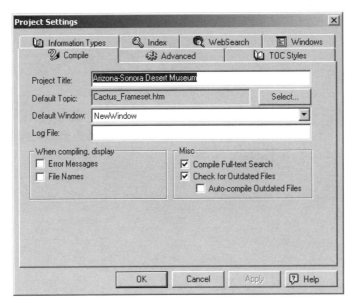

Figure 14-13: Setting the default topic in the Project Settings window

3. Click the **Select** button next to the current default topic to display a list of topics.

4. From the list of topics, select the frameset.

5. Click **OK** to close the list of topics and display the selected frameset in as the new default.

6. Click **OK** to close the Project Settings window.

Summary

In this chapter, you learned about frames and framesets. You saw the steps required to create a frameset, link to individual frames, and open framesets.

The next chapter will describe how to work with the variety of tools that ship with RoboHelp.

Chapter 15

Using Other RoboHelp Tools

RoboHelp Office and RoboHelp Enterprise come with a variety of tools that can help make your job as a help author easier. Some of these have already been described earlier in this book, such as the Graphics Locator and Resize tools in Chapter 8 and the Multi-File Find and Replace tool in Chapter 9. This chapter describes how to use some of the other tools that come with RoboHelp Office and RoboHelp Enterprise.

Table 15-1: Additional RoboHelp tools

Tool	Description
Find HTML Help Components	Searches the specified hard drive for dynamic link libraries (.dll), executable programs (.exe), and ActiveX controls (.ocx) associated with your .chm files.
Find HTML Help Files	Searches the specified hard drive for .chm files and identifies them on screen. This tool is useful if you need to locate, move, delete, or obtain more information about .chm files.
Help-to-Source	Converts a compiled WinHelp file (.hlp) into its component source files (decompiles it).
HTML Help Registration	Helps you register or identify compiled HTML Help files to your system.
HTML Help Studio®	Converts a compiled HTML Help file (.chm) into its component source files (decompiles it).
Smart Publishing Wizard™	Copies files and/or folders to a web server using various protocols. The Smart Publishing Wizard will only copy files that have changed since the last time you published them.
Software Video Camera®	Captures on-screen actions to create a video file. You can also record narration and view completed video files.

Finding HTML Help Files and Components

There are two tools that can help you find the compiled HTML Help files and associated components. The Find HTML Help Files tool displays a list of all of the compiled HTML Help files (.chm) on your system. The Find HTML Help Components tool displays a list of all of the .dll, .exe, and .ocx files associated with .chm files.

Using the Find HTML Help Files Tool

Use the Find HTML Help Files tool to display a list of all the .chm files on your system. Once displayed, you can access the directory where each file resides for maintenance tasks, such as deleting or moving files, or you can register the .chm so that your HTML Help engine can find it.

To use the Find HTML Help Files tool, follow these steps:

1. From the **Tools** tab, double-click the **Find HTML Help Files** icon (🔍) to display the Find HTML Help Files window.

2. Click **Search** to display a list of all the compiled HTML Help Files on your system, as shown in Figure 15-1.

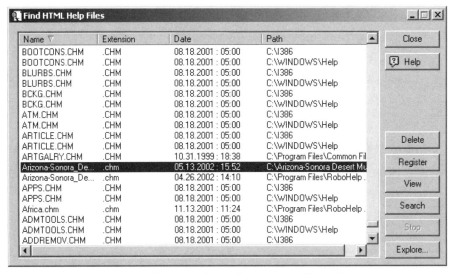

Figure 15-1: Displaying .chm files using the Find HTML Help Files tool

3. To perform any of the file functions, highlight a .chm in the list by clicking on it. Then click one of the following buttons:

Table 15-2: File functions in the Find HTML Help File tool

Button	Function
Delete	Removes the selected file from your system
Register	Stores the name and location of the .chm file in your system for later retrieval
View	Displays the selected file in the HTML Help viewer
Explore	Displays the contents of the directory where the file resides in the Windows Explorer. You can use Windows Explorer functions to move, copy, or delete the file.

4. Click **Close** when you are done to close the Find HTML Help Files window.

Using the Find HTML Help Components Tool

Use the Find HTML Help Components tool to display a list of all the files associated with the .chm files on your system. Once displayed, you can access the directory where each file resides for maintenance tasks, such as deleting or moving files.

To use the Find HTML Help Components tool, follow these steps:

1. From the **Tools** tab, double-click the **Find HTML Help Components** icon (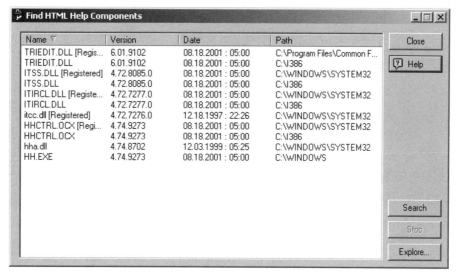) to display the Find HTML Help Components window.

2. Click **Search** to display a list of all the compiled HTML Help Components on your system, as shown in Figure 15-2. If a file is registered with the HTML Help engine, the word "Registered" appears beside the file name in brackets. This window also displays the version numbers and dates for each file.

Figure 15-2: Displaying .dll, .exe, and .ocx files with the Find HTML Help Components tool

3. To perform any of the file functions, highlight a file in the list by clicking on it. Then click one of the following buttons:

    ■ Click **Explore** to display the contents of the directory where the file resides in Windows Explorer. You can use Windows Explorer functions to move, copy, or delete the file.

    ■ Click **Close** when you are done to close the Find HTML Help Components window.

Registering and Unregistering HTML Help Files

Your computer has a system registry, which stores information about various files in binary form. This registry helps the operating system interact with the files. The stored information varies for each file, but it might include the version number, installation date, and uninstall information.

Most of the time, you won't need to worry about the registry. For example, when you installed RoboHelp, it was automatically registered. In some cases, though, you may need to manually register a compiled HTML Help file, depending on the way your developer chooses to have the program and help file interact. Stand-alone HTML Help does not need to be registered. Check with your developer to find out whether or not your compiled help needs to be registered.

Because the registry is an integral part of the way your system operates, you'll need to be very careful when making registration changes. The HTML Help Registration tool will let you register or unregister .chm files without harming the data in your registry.

 NOTE: *Although you may need to register the .chm file on your system, you don't need to register on your users' systems. The registration is only required on the system you are using to create or author the files.*

Registering .chm Files

To use the HTML Help Registration tool to register a .chm file, follow these steps:

1 From the **Tools** tab, double-click the **HTML Help Registration** icon ( ) to display the HTML Help Registration window, as shown in Figure 15-3.

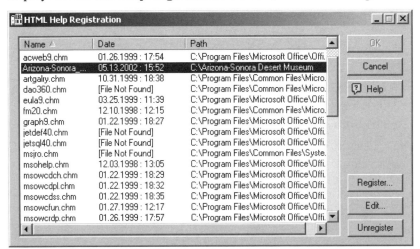

Figure 15-3: Displaying .chm files with the HTML Help Registration tool

2. The HTML Help Registration tool displays all of the registered compiled HTML Help files that it finds on your system. The display shows the filename, date, and path of the file. To perform any of the following file registration functions, highlight the filename and then click one of the buttons described in Table 15-3.

Table 15-3: File functions in the HTML Help Registration tool

Button	Function
Edit	Displays the filename and path of the selected file in the HTML Help viewer and allows you to change them
Unregister	Removes the selected file from your registry. This does not delete the file.

3. To register a file that does not appear in the list, click the **Register** button. A browse window will display the available .chm files, as shown in Figure 15-4.

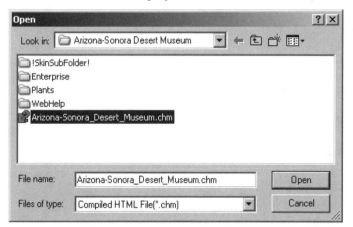

Figure 15-4: Choosing the compiled file to register

4. Select the compiled file you want to register. Then click **Open** to register the file and close the browse window.

5. Click **OK** to save the registry changes you've made and close the HTML Help Registration window.

Decompiling WinHelp to Create Source Files

The Help-to-Source tool *decompiles* a WinHelp file (.hlp), turning it back into its component source files and graphics. This is very useful if you don't have the original source files but want to convert the file to a different format, such as HTML Help or WebHelp.

CAUTION: *Most software licenses specifically prohibit decompiling help files, so make sure that you are authorized access to the source files before you use Help-to-Source. In some cases, the HTML coding and organization of the files as well as the content may be covered by copyright law.*

The Help-to-Source tool is a wizard that steps you through the conversion process. To decompile a WinHelp file, follow these steps:

1. In the RoboHelp Starter window, open the **Tools** pane.

2. Double-click the **Help-to-Source** icon (🖲) to display the first Help-to-Source
   Wizard window.

3. Enter the name of the WinHelp file you want to decompile and the location
   where the converted files will be stored.

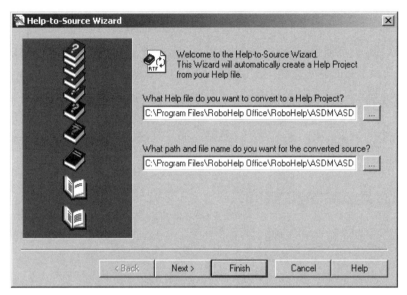

Figure 15-5: Specifying the WinHelp file to decompile

4. Click **Next** when finished to display the second Help-to-Source window.

5. Specify the options for the decompiled help by clicking any of the following
   options:

Table 15-4: Help-to-Source output options

Option	Description
Create Topic ID's based on topic titles	Creates topic IDs from the titles in the WinHelp file. This option may be easier to maintain but may cause some broken links if the original file used a lot of macros.
Create Topic ID's based on hash codes	Creates topic IDs from internal, hexadecimal codes created by the WinHelp compiler. Use this option if the WinHelp file has a lot of macros and is lacking a .cnt file.
Color hotspot text green	Displays hotspots as green text. If this option isn't selected, the hotspot text displays as black.
Do you want to create a map file that lists Topic ID's for context sensitive help?	Select the format you want for context-sensitive Help. You may choose any or all of the output formats.

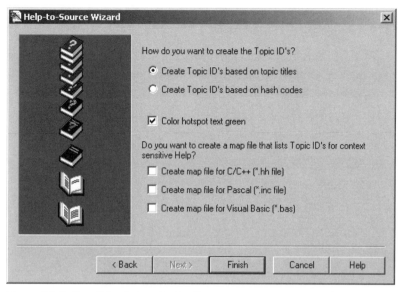

Figure 15-6: Specifying help output options

6. Click **Finish** to close the wizard and decompile the WinHelp file.

7. When the Help-to-Source tool has completed decompiling, a summary window will display, as shown in Figure 15-7.

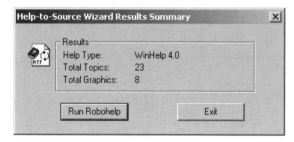

Figure 15-7: The Help-to-Source Wizard summary

8. Click **Run Robohelp** to use the newly decompiled files, or click **Exit** to close the summary window.

Decompiling HTML Help to Create Source Files

The HTML Help Studio tool *decompiles* a compiled HTML Help file (.chm) by separating the individual files that are included in it. This is very useful if you don't have the original source files but need to make changes to an existing .chm.

CAUTION: *Most software licenses specifically prohibit decompiling help files, so make sure that you are authorized access to the source files before you use HTML Help Studio. In some cases, the HTML coding and organization of the files as well as the content may be covered by copyright law.*

HTML Help Studio lets you look at the files in a compiled HTML Help file and copy them to your hard drive. You can extract a single file, an entire folder, or the whole help system. To decompile a compiled HTML Help file, follow these steps:

1. From the **Tools** tab, double-click the **HTML Help Studio** icon ( ) to display an empty HTML Help Studio window.

2. In the HTML Help Studio window, choose **Open** from the **File** menu. This will display a browse window.

3. Browse to the folder that contains the compiled help. Then double-click on the filename to display the HTML Help Studio with a list of all of the files included in the .chm file, as shown in Figure 15-8.

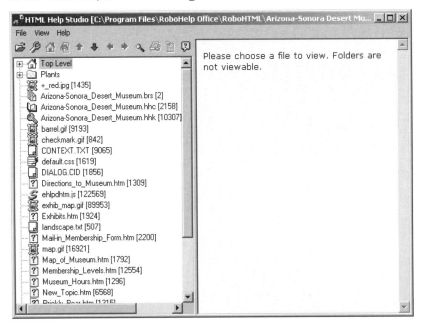

Figure 15-8: Displaying components of compiled HTML help in HTML Help Studio

4. The HTML Help Studio displays the files that are included in the .chm file in order by the existing folder structure. The size of each file is in parentheses next to each filename. To view the contents of a file in the HTML Help Studio, highlight the filename.

5. To extract files for editing or to use them in another project, highlight the file or folder you want to use. Then choose **Extract** from the **File** menu to display the Extract window shown in Figure 15-9.

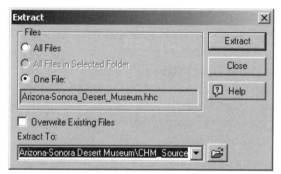

Figure 15-9: Extracting files from the compiled HTML help

6. If you had either a file or folder highlighted, the appropriate button will already be selected. To extract all files, click **All Files**.

7. In the **Extract To** box, specify the folder where you want the newly created source files to be stored.

8. If the specified folder already contains files with the same names as the ones you are extracting, select **Overwrite Existing Files**.

9. Click **Extract** to store the component files in the specified directory.

Software Video Camera

The Software Video Camera tool records videos of screen actions and then saves them as standard .avi movie files. You can then add these files to your help system (see Chapter 8). In addition to the video of whatever is happening on the screen, you can include narration through a microphone and sound card in the output .avi files.

Follow these basic steps to create a video with the Software Video Camera:

1. Set your system options to define the way you want the video to appear.

NOTE: The Software Video Camera only works with displays set to either 16 or 256 colors. For full-color movies, you'll have to use a different tool.

2. Define the area of the screen you want to include in the video by setting the recording area.

3. Record your screen actions.

4. View your completed video.

Setting the Software Video Camera Options

The Software Video Camera, though useful, does have some color limitations. It will only record videos in 16- or 256-color mode. Before you even start the Software Video Camera, it is a good idea to set your color mode using the Control Panel for your operating system. You may also want to set display options such as the wallpaper or background at this time.

Once your display looks the way you want it to, set up the Software Video Camera options. You'll only need to do this once—when you first use the tool. The options include the hotkeys for starting and stopping recording, the number of frames per second in the final video, and the audio settings.

NOTE: *Before defining hotkeys, make sure that the combination you intend to use for the Software Video Camera does not have an assigned function in the application you are recording.*

To set the video options, follow these steps:

1. From either the RoboHelp Starter or the RoboHelp HTML Tools pane, double-click the **Software Video Camera** icon (▣◉) to display the Software Video Camera window shown in Figure 15-10.

Figure 15-10: Displaying the Software Video Camera controls

2. Click the **Setup** icon on the Software Video Camera window to display the options window shown in Figure 15-11.

Figure 15-11: Setting the video options

3. To specify the combination of keystrokes that will start recording, enter the keystroke combination by selecting the **Alt** and/or the **Shift** check box and then choosing a key from the drop-down menu. You can use the Num Lock, Caps Lock, or Scroll Lock key with any combination of Alt and Shift. Whichever keys you specify must be pressed at the same time in order to start recording. The default is the Num Lock key.

4. To specify the combination of keystrokes that will stop recording, enter the keystroke combination by selecting the **Alt** and/or the **Shift** check box and then choosing a key from the drop-down menu. You can use the Num Lock, Caps Lock, Scroll Lock, or Escape key with any combination of Alt and Shift. Whichever keys you specify must be pressed at the same time in order to start recording. The default is the Escape key.

5. Set the remaining options for the Software Video Camera window.

Table 15-5: Software Video Camera display options

Option	Description
Hide during recording	Removes the Software Video Camera window from the screen while you are recording
Always on top	Displays the Software Video Camera window on top of all other application windows, even when it is not active
Maximum frames per second	Specifyies the number of frames to capture per second while recording. The default is ten frames per second, which gives the highest quality video but also takes up the most disk space.

6. To set the audio options, select the **Capture Audio with Video** check box to activate the Audio Settings button.

7. Click the **Audio Settings** button to display the Sound Selection window shown in Figure 15-12.

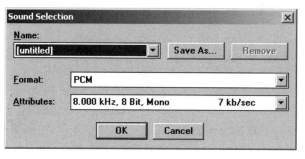

Figure 15-12: The Sound Selection window for setting audio options

8. The Software Video Camera stores the combination of format and attributes as Sound Selection names. The tool comes with several predefined selections. To choose an existing selection, such as CD quality or Telephone quality, choose from the drop-down menu. The attributes list the sampling in KHz, the bits per channel, and the number of channels (stereo or mono). Each attribute line also

specifies the amount of disk space required for each second of sound. For example, the 8.0000 KHz, 8-bit, mono setting requires 7 KB per second.

 NOTE: *The only available format is PCM, which is an uncompressed wave format.*

9. To create and store your own Sound Selection, choose an attribute from the drop-down menu. Then click **Save As**. Enter a new name for the selection and click **OK** to store the new name in the Name drop-down list.

10. Click **OK** when you are finished with the sound options to close the Sound Selection window.

11. Click **OK** to close the SoftwareVideo Camera Options window.

Setting the Capture Region

Although you could record a video of your entire monitor screen, the resulting video may be much larger than you need it to be. In most cases, you'll only need to capture a small portion of the screen or a single window. To specify the portion of the screen you want to include in the video, set the recording area.

To set the recording area, follow these steps:

1. From either the RoboHelp Starter or the RoboHelp HTML Tools pane, double-click the **Software Video Camera** icon to display the Software Video Camera window.

2. Double-click the **Area** icon (![icon]) at the top of the Software Video Camera window to display the Set Recording Area window shown in Figure 15-13. A large red rectangle will also appear that outlines the current recording area size and location.

Figure 15-13: Setting the recording area

3. Set the recording area in one of the following ways:

   ■ Click anywhere on the red outline and drag it to a new location. Click on a corner of the red outline and drag it to resize the recording area.

   ■ In the Set Recording Area window, specify the distance in pixels between the left and top edges of the window and the left and top edges of the recording area. Specify the height and width of the recording area in pixels.

4. Click **OK** to set the recording area and close the Set Recording Area window.

Recording Videos

Once you have set the options, you can record whatever happens on the computer screen. After you instruct the Software Video Camera to record a video, everything you do in the application(s) and on the desktop will be recorded until you stop the session. If you've got the audio option turned on, you can simply speak into your microphone while you perform the steps.

TIP: *It's a good idea to write down exactly what you want to do in your video and even create a script for your audio. Run through the entire series once or twice before recording for a smoother, more professional video.*

To record a video, follow these steps:

1. From either the RoboHelp Starter or the RoboHelp HTML Tools pane, double-click the **Software Video Camera** icon (📹) to display the Software Video Camera window.

2. Start recording in one of the following ways:

   ■ Click the **Record** icon (🔴) on the Software Video Camera window.

   ■ Press the hotkeys you defined during setup. The default hotkey to start recording is the Num Lock key.

3. Perform the keystrokes and other actions that you want to include in the video.

4. If you have set the audio option (selected Capture Audio with Video in the Setup menu), you can speak into your system microphone while performing the actions. The video and audio will be recorded together.

5. Stop recording in one of the following ways:

   ■ Click the **Stop** icon (⏹) on the Software Video Camera window.

   ■ Press the hotkeys you defined during setup. The default hotkey to stop recording is the Escape key.

6. When you stop recording, the Save window will open. In the **File name** box, enter the name of your video file.

7. Click **OK** to save the video file to the specified name and close the File Save window.

Viewing Videos

Once you've created a video file, you can also use the Software Video Camera to view it. To view any video file on your system, follow these steps:

1. From either the RoboHelp Starter or the RoboHelp HTML Tools pane, double-click the **Software Video Camera** icon to display the Software Video Camera window.

2. On the Software Video Camera window, click the **Play** icon (▶) to display a standard Open File window.

3. Choose the .avi file you want to view by double-clicking on the filename. Use the Browse button to point to other folders as necessary. The file will appear in the Software Video Camera video player, as shown in Figure 15-14.

Figure 15-14: Displaying a video in the video player

4. Click the **Play** button (▶) to start the video. The progression bar moves across the bottom of the view as the video plays, indicating the position in the movie that is currently displayed. You can click and drag the progession indicator to view any portion of the video that you want to see.

5. If you want to interrupt the clip before it finishes, click the **Stop** button (■).

6. You may also set any of the following video/sound player options by clicking the **Properties** button (▤):

Table 15-6: Video/Sound player options

Option	Description
View	Specify the viewing size of the video. Valid choices are Normal, Half Size, and Double Size.
Volume	Make the sound louder or softer.
Speed	Increase or decrease the speed at which the video plays.
Open	Specify a different video file to open in the video player.
Close	Close the current video file.
Copy	Save the current video to a different filename.
Configure	Use the Video Properties window to specify viewing size.
Command	Enter an MCI (media control interface) command. MCI is a standard for multimedia files, and is explained in detail in the Microsoft Video for Windows Developers Kit.

7. Click the **Close** button on the top-left corner of the video player to close the window.

Summary

In this chapter, you learned how to use several RoboHelp tools. You saw how to use the Find tools (Find HTML Help Components and Find HTML Help Files), as well as the HTML Help Registration tool. This chapter also described how to decompile both HTML Help files (with HTML Help Studio) and WinHelp files (with Help-to-Source). Finally, this chapter explained how to use the Software Video Camera to create and view videos.

The next chapter will discuss the unique features of RoboHelp Enterprise.

Chapter 16

Creating WebHelp Enterprise

You already saw in Chapter 1, "Installing RoboHelp," how to install and configure the RoboHelp Enterprise Author and RoboEngine software. In the succeeding chapters, you saw how to plan and create an online help system in HTML Help or WebHelp. You'll now see how to create WebHelp Enterprise by publishing WebHelp to the server and how to take advantage of the many powerful client-server features built into RoboHelp Enterprise.

Why You Should Use WebHelp Enterprise

If you have a small stand-alone online help system or an online help system that ships as part of a product that may not be connected to the Internet or a company intranet, you probably won't need to use WebHelp Enterprise. But if you're creating Internet- or intranet-based online help or you need the strength of RoboHelp Enterprise's features, you should definitely consider creating WebHelp Enterprise.

WebHelp Enterprise supports a number of powerful features not available in other kinds of online help, including natural language search that lets users enter plain English questions to search for information, feedback reports that show how the help is being used, and team development features that allow help files to be merged easily for increased productivity. WebHelp Enterprise also offers increased speed for the navigation tools because the user only downloads the amount of text and data that can be displayed at a single time. For example, if you're displaying a long help topic, WebHelp Enterprise will only download and display a screen of data while HTML Help or WebHelp will download the entire topic (whether it all fits on the screen or not) before displaying it.

What You Need to Use WebHelp Enterprise

The requirements for developing and using WebHelp Enterprise are actually rather minimal. For developing WebHelp Enterprise, you'll need Windows 95 or later and Internet Explorer 4.0 or later on at least a Pentium II 300 MHz with 128 MB RAM. The users of WebHelp Enterprise only need a browser running at least Netscape Navigator 3.0, Internet Explorer 3.0, or another HTML 3.2

compatible browser on Macintosh or Windows 95 or later. (Given the general level of most computers today, these are not difficult requirements.)

Getting Ready to Publish WebHelp Enterprise

There are a few prerequisites to creating and publishing WebHelp Enterprise. First, you must have the RoboEngine software installed and configured on your server as described in Chapter 1, "Installing RoboHelp." You must also know the name of the RoboEngine server and the location to which you're going to publish the WebHelp Enterprise. The server name was specified as part of the RoboEngine setup, but you may need a specific name for the online help you're about to publish.

NOTE: *You must have one product license for each web site you're configuring. You can use the default web site, which is based on the computer's network identification (for example, if the computer is named "BANJO4," the default web site will be \\BANJO4), but this can present security problems because the users will be logging directly in the shared volumes of BANJO4. Talk to your server administrator about setting up web sites using the Internet Service Manager included with IIS.*

The RoboEngine software makes the difference between WebHelp and WebHelp Enterprise systems. RoboEngine's primary function is to collect information about how the online help is used and report on usage statistics through the WebHelp Enterprise reports. It also provides the natural language search features and is the host for the WebHelp Enterprise that your end users log on to.

You can create WebHelp Enterprise from scratch, much like creating a new HTML Help or WebHelp project. When you start a new project within RoboHelp HTML or using the RoboHelp Starter, you select WebHelp Enterprise in the New Project screen (shown as the highlighted option in Figure 16-1).

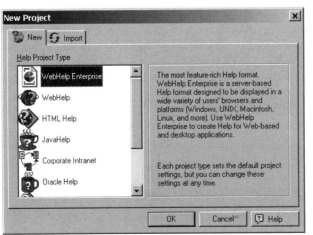

Figure 16-1: The New Project screen

Setting the Primary Target

The primary target setting in RoboHelp HTML determines which features and options are displayed for the project. Opening a new WebHelp Enterprise project will automatically set the primary target to WebHelp Enterprise; however, if you're working with an existing online help system, you'll need to set the primary target in RoboHelp HTML to WebHelp Enterprise, as follows:

1. From the **File** menu, choose **Select Primary Target**, then choose **WebHelp Enterprise** from the submenu. (The primary target will remain WebHelp Enterprise until you change it.)

After you have set the primary target to WebHelp Enterprise, the Enterprise Reports tab appears on the bottom-right corner of the screen, as shown in Figure 16-2.

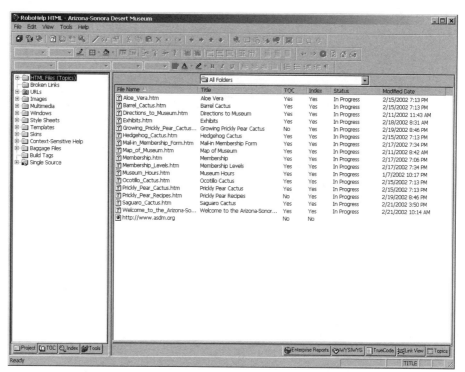

Figure 16-2: The RoboHelp HTML screen showing the Enterprise Project tab

NOTE: *Any online help system can be turned into WebHelp Enterprise fairly easily. HTML Help and WebHelp, being HTML-based already, will have no conversion issues to speak of. You may have some conversion problems with WinHelp ("classic") files, but these are likely to be minimal.*

Connecting to the Server

Regardless of whether you're working with a new WebHelp Enterprise project or converting an existing online help system to WebHelp Enterprise, you need to identify the location of the RoboEngine so RoboHelp knows where to publish the online help files and where to look for the RoboHelp Enterprise reports (described later in this chapter).

To identify the location of the RoboEngine software on the server for the current WebHelp Enterprise project, do the following:

1. From the **File** menu, choose **Project Settings**. Then select the **Server** tab, as shown in Figure 16-3.

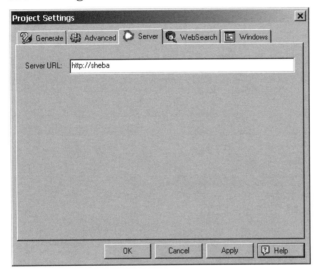

Figure 16-3: The Server tab on the Project Settings screen

2. Enter the name of the server you want to publish files to and click **OK**. (This will remain the location to which you publish the files for this online help project until you change it.) You can enter the server name in three different forms (the http:// is optional in each of the three forms shown):

   ■ Identify the server with its network identification, such as http://sheba or http://P23049RL/museum. (This will only work for computers on the same LAN.)

   ■ Identify the server with a registered domain name, such as http://hedtke.com or http://abcdefghij.com/Product/WebHelp.

   ■ Identify the server by its IP (Internet Protocol) address, such as http://12.34.56.78 or http://98.76.54.32/information.

If you're opening a new project, you can identify the server location as part of the new project setup. Enter the server name in the Server field on the New Project Wizard screen, shown in Figure 16-4 with a sample server entry.

Entering the server name as part of the new project setup sets the server name as the default for all subsequent WebHelp Enterprise projects.

Figure 16-4: The New Project Wizard screen with a sample entry in the Server field

Once the server has been identified, you'll be able to publish the WebHelp Enterprise files to the server and obtain the WebHelp Enterprise reports from the server.

Publishing WebHelp Enterprise

Once you've set up the RoboEngine and identified the server to the WebHelp Enterprise project, you're ready to publish WebHelp Enterprise.

To publish a WebHelp Enterprise project to the server, do the following:

1. Open the WebHelp Enterprise project that you want to publish. (You may also see a dialog box to enter your network name and password if these are required for accessing the server you're publishing to.)

2. From the **File** menu, choose **Publish**, then select **WebHelp Enterprise** from the submenu.

3. If the WebHelp Enterprise files have changed since you last generated them, RoboHelp will ask if you want to generate the help, as shown in Figure 16-5. Click **OK** to start generating the WebHelp Enterprise.

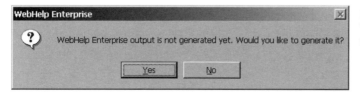

Figure 16-5: The WebHelp Enterprise generation dialog box

NOTE: *If the WebHelp Enterprise files haven't changed since you last generated them, a prompt (not shown) will appear, asking if you want to empty the output folder before generating. Click Yes. Generating the online help deletes the output files created the last time the online help was generated and replaces them with files created from the current source files. These output files are then published to the server. (Any changes you've made to the files outside of RoboHelp will be lost as a result, so be sure that any modified files are copied to another location before you generate online help files again.) RoboHelp will automatically generate the online help as part of the publishing process with the default file locations, but you can do it manually by choosing Generate from the File menu and then selecting the appropriate online help format.*

4. When the WebHelp Enterprise has been generated, the Publish Options screen appears (shown in Figure 16-6). This screen lets you set a few publishing options for the WebHelp Enterprise.

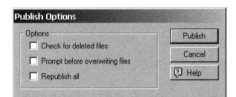

Figure 16-6: The Publish Options screen

Enter information on the screen as follows:

- **Check for deleted files:** Select this option to have RoboHelp check for files that have been deleted from the server location. (This is useful if you're republishing WebHelp Enterprise to this location, but the additional checking time may slow down the publishing process for large help projects.)

- **Prompt before overwriting files:** Select this option to have RoboHelp prompt before overwriting any older online help files that are already on the server. The default option is for RoboHelp to overwrite files without prompting.

- **Republish all:** Select this option to have RoboHelp republish all the online help files to the server without checking to see if the files on the server are newer. The default option is for RoboHelp to check the file dates to see which is the most recent.

 NOTE: *If you leave all the options unchecked, RoboHelp will republish only the new or changed files since the last time this help project was published to this server location.*

5. When you are satisfied with your selections on the Publish Options screen, click **Publish**. RoboHelp starts publishing files to the server location. A status display (shown in Figure 16-7) shows you how the publishing process is going. The publishing process can easily take a few minutes and may take quite a while if there are a very large number of files or you are publishing to a remote server location.

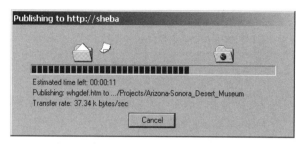

Figure 16-7: The Publishing screen

6. When the files have been published to the server, RoboHelp displays the Publishing Result screen, a sample of which appears in Figure 16-8. The Publishing Result screen shows the total number of files you requested to be published, the number of files actually published, and the time that the publishing process took. These numbers may be different if you have already published the online help files and didn't select Republish All on the Publish Options screen.

7. When you have reviewed the information (you can optionally print the list of published files for audit tracking later), click **Close**.

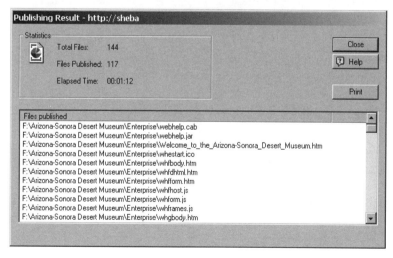

Figure 16-8: The Publishing Result screen

Congratulations! You've published an online help project to the server. You're now ready to view the WebHelp Enterprise on the server.

Copying WebHelp and WebHelp Enterprise to Other Locations

As part of the process of publishing WebHelp Enterprise projects, you may need to copy WebHelp and WebHelp Enterprise projects to other locations, such as:

- An FTP site for quick distribution to other departments
- An HTTP site within the company intranet
- An HTTP site outside of the company intranet that's being used as a mirror site
- A disk drive for distribution, configuration control, or project backup

Smart Publishing Wizard lets you copy entire projects quickly and easily to a specified FTP, web site, or other disk drives.

 NOTE: *Depending on where you're copying files, you may need to get access permissions from your system administrator.*

To use the Smart Publishing Wizard to copy files or folders, do the following:

1. Open your WebHelp or WebHelp Enterprise project and generate.
2. When the help has been generated, click **Publish** on the WebHelp Wizard Result screen (shown in Figure 16-9). This displays the Smart Publishing Wizard - Select Source screen, shown in Figure 16-10.

 TIP: *If you've already generated your files, you can simply go to the Tools screen in RoboHelp HTML and double-click the Smart Publishing Wizard icon ( ).*

Figure 16-9: The WebHelp Wizard Result screen

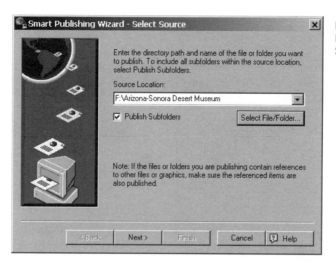

Figure 16-10: The Smart Publishing Wizard - Select Source screen

3. Enter the source for the file or folder you want to publish. Check **Publish Subfolders** if you want to include all the subfolders in the selected folder. When you are satisfied with your entries, click **Next**. The Smart Publishing Wizard - Select Destination screen (shown in Figure 16-11) appears.

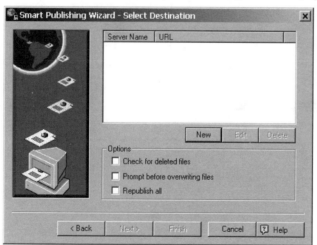

Figure 16-11: The Smart Publishing Wizard - Select Destination screen

4. If there is not already at least one destination appearing in this screen, you'll need to set one up. Click **New** to add a new destination to publish files to. The New Destination screen appears, as shown in Figure 16-12.

NOTE: *You can also select publishing options, just as you did in the Publish Options screen (shown in Figure 16-6).*

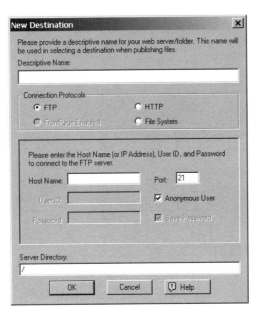

Figure 16-12: The New Destination screen

5. You can set up a destination for FTP, HTTP, a FrontPage-enabled site, or a disk drive. The Descriptive Name is the name that will appear on the Smart Publishing Wizard - Select Destination screen. Depending on the connection protocol you choose, the bottom half of the New Destination screen will show different fields and options. Figure 16-13 shows the New Destination screen with sample entries for a file system destination.

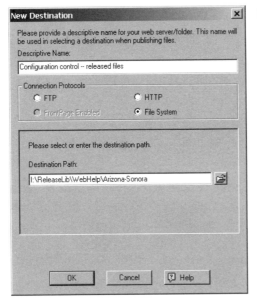

Figure 16-13: The New Destination screen

6. When you are satisfied with your entries, click **OK** to return to the Smart Publishing Wizard - Select Destination screen. Figure 16-14 shows the destination from Figure 16-13 entered and ready to copy a project to.

Figure 16-14: The Smart Publishing Wizard - Select Destination screen with a sample destination

7. Highlight the destination you want to copy the project to and click **Next**. The Smart Publishing Wizard - Publish screen appears, as shown in Figure 16-15.

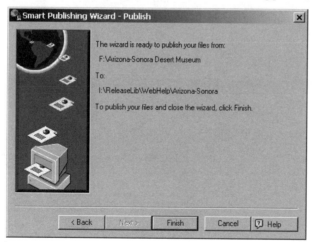

Figure 16-15: The Smart Publishing Wizard - Publish screen

8. If the online help project is open, close it by selecting **Close Project** from the **File** menu. Click **Finish** to copy the project. RoboHelp will copy the files to the destination and then close the Smart Publishing Wizard. When the copying process is complete, the Smart Publishing Wizard will display the Publishing Result screen like the one shown earlier in Figure 16-8.

You can repeat this process to copy files and folders to more than one location. Once you have your locations set up in the Smart Publishing Wizard - Select Destination screen, you can copy the project files to a variety of locations in a matter of minutes.

Viewing WebHelp Enterprise

You can view your WebHelp Enterprise locally to perform such tasks as verifying formatting, testing links and browse sequences, and reviewing content.
To view the WebHelp Enterprise locally, do the following:

1. From the **File** menu, choose **Run** and then **WebHelp Enterprise Preview**. The WebHelp Enterprise Wizard - Limitations screen appears.

2. The WebHelp Enterprise Wizard - Limitations screen is for informational purposes only to let you know that you won't be able to see certain items unless you access the server. Click **OK**.

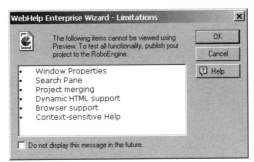

Figure 16-16: The WebHelp Enterprise Wizard - Limitations screen

 NOTE: *You cannot see some window properties—window placement and the Toolbar, Menu, Location Bar, and Status Bar options—when viewing WebHelp Enterprise locally. The server is also necessary for searching, project merging (which is done at run time), DHTML effects, and context-sensitive WebHelp. Some browser-specific problems may also not be compensated for when running locally.*

3. The first screen of the WebHelp Enterprise project appears in the default browser. Figure 16-17 shows the opening page of the Arizona-Sonora Desert Museum project displayed in Internet Explorer.

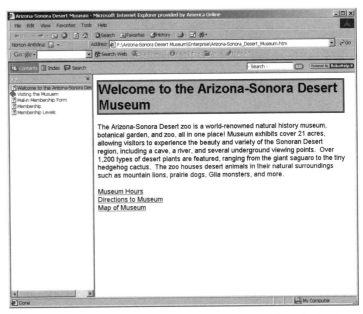

Figure 16-17: The WebHelp Enterprise project opened from the local computer

4. From the main screen, you can navigate the project, check links, and review formatting.

   When you are satisfied with the way the WebHelp Enterprise looks on the local computer, you will need to view the WebHelp Enterprise through the RoboEngine so you can see your help as your end users will see it. Viewing the help through the RoboEngine also lets you test the server-dependent features, such as searching, window customizations, and skins.

   To view the WebHelp Enterprise through the RoboEngine, do the following:

1. From the **File** menu, choose **Run** and then **WebHelp Enterprise with Internet Explorer** or **WebHelp Enterprise with Netscape Navigator.**

 NOTE: *As always, if the project has changed since the last time you generated WebHelp Enterprise, you will be prompted to generate the help first and then to publish the help before running. By accepting these options, you will have the most current version of the WebHelp Enterprise on your server.*

2. If necessary, enter your network name and password to access the server. RoboHelp Enterprise launches the appropriate browser and displays the opening page of the WebHelp Enterprise project, as shown in Figure 16-18.

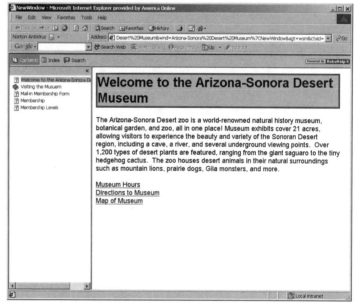

3. From the main screen, you can navigate the project, check links, and review formatting as before. You can also test the server-dependent features, such as searching, window customizations, and skins.

Figure 16-18: The WebHelp Enterprise project opened on the server

Although the differences between Figures 16-17 and 16-18 are slight, you can see that the message at the bottom right of Figure 16-18 shows that this is coming from the local intranet rather than from "My Computer," as was the case earlier. The URL also uses %20 rather than a space, showing that this has been accessed over the net.

All features of the help listed on the WebHelp Enterprise Wizard - Limitations screen as being excluded for local help will be available to you. Depending on your projects, you might also have a newer version of the project locally that hasn't yet been published to the RoboEngine, resulting in different screens and information.

Fine-Tuning the RoboEngine

You saw the basics of installing the RoboEngine and using the RoboEngine Configuration Wizard in Chapter 1, "Installing RoboHelp." This section shows you how to fine-tune RoboEngine for optimal results using the Configuration Manager.

To access the RoboEngine Configuration Manager, do the following:

1. On the server where RoboEngine is installed, from the **Start** menu, select **Programs**, then **RoboEngine**, and then **Configuration Manager** (or just double-click the **Configuration Manager** icon (▣)). The RoboEngine Configuration Manager appears, as shown in Figure 16-19.

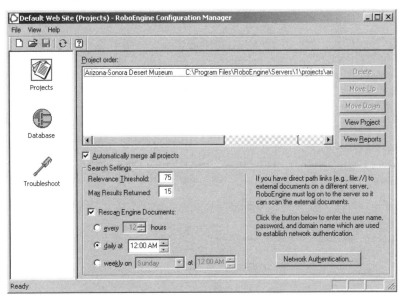

Figure 16-19: The RoboEngine Configuration Manager - Projects screen

2. Enter information in the fields on the RoboEngine Configuration Manager - Projects screen as follows:

   ■ **Project order:** The project field shows the order in which the RoboEngine will search the projects for topics. The first project in the list is the "master" project. If there are identical default topics or context IDs in several projects, the RoboEngine will display the first occurrence it finds. You can change the order of the projects by highlighting a topic and clicking the Move Up and Move Down buttons. You can view the project as published on the

RoboEngine by clicking View Project. This will display the default topic for the project (this has the same results as when you viewed the WebHelp Enterprise project earlier using the WebHelp Enterprise with Internet Explorer or WebHelp Enterprise with Netscape Navigator options). You can view the reports for this project by clicking View Reports. WebHelp Enterprise Reports are described later in this chapter.

- **Automatically merge all projects:** Checking this box (the default option) merges all projects automatically. This option also will override any project merging information that was set for the project in RoboHelp Enterprise Author.

- **Relevance Threshold:** Enter a percentage for the relevance threshold. (The default is 75%.) Generally speaking, the lower the threshold, the more hits will be returned on a question.

 NOTE: *The algorithm for determining relevance is complex. Generally speaking, nouns carry more weight than verbs. For example, the question "When can I visit the museum?" will give much higher results for "museum" than for "visit." You should also note that adjectives only return topics for the nouns they are associated with. For example, the question "Do you have flying lizards?" will give much higher results for topics that contain both "flying" and "lizards" than topics containing "flying insects."*

- **Max Results Returned:** Enter the number of results to return when doing a natural language search on the project.

- **Rescan Engine Documents:** Enter the dates and times you want the RoboEngine to scan documents that are not in your project, such as external HTML files, spreadsheets, Word documents, or PDF files. The default scanning option is daily at midnight. By scanning external documents, they become available to the users when they do a natural language search.

- **Network Authentication:** If you have external documents that are linked from the Search tab to the WebHelp Enterprise project, you need to tell RoboHelp Enterprise where to find them. Click the **Network Authentication** button to display the Network Authentication screen (shown in Figure 16-20). Enter user name, password, and the domain name for the system where the external documents reside. Then click **OK**. (The user name must have read permission on the server.)

Figure 16-20: The Network Authentication screen

3. When you are satisfied with your entries, click **Database** on the left side of the screen. The RoboEngine Configuration Manager - Database screen appears.

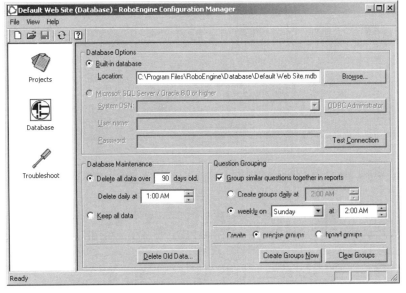

Figure 16-21: The RoboEngine Configuration Manager - Database screen

4. Enter information in the fields on the RoboEngine Configuration Manager - Database screen as follows:

   ■ **Database Options:** The default database is a Microsoft Access database. This will be adequate for smaller WebHelp Enterprise projects, but it may not be powerful enough for WebHelp Enterprise projects with a high volume. If you have Microsoft SQL Server or Oracle 8.0 installed on the server, you can specify your own database by entering the system DSN, the user name, and the password. Clicking the ODBC Administrator button displays the standard ODBC Administrator. You can test the connection to the database by clicking **Test Connection**.

- **Database Maintenance:** The default option is to delete all data over 90 days old; however, you may need to change this if you notice a degradation of system performance when doing natural language searches. On the other hand, if the database is a low-volume database or if the server is powerful enough to handle the volume of searches, you may wish to select the **Keep all data** option and not purge the database at all.

- **Question Grouping:** The default option is to group similar questions in reports. This feature can make reading RoboHelp Enterprise reports easier by grouping similar questions on the report. You can set the time to group questions daily or weekly. You should set this at a time when the system will not be experiencing a high volume. You can choose to create precise groups (the default) of very similar questions or broad groups of loosely related questions. You can click the **Create Groups Now** button to generate groups immediately with all the questions in the database. You can also clear the groups if you wish by clicking the **Clear Groups** button.

5. When you are satisfied with your entries, click **Troubleshoot** on the left side of the screen. The RoboEngine Configuration Manager - Troubleshoot screen appears.

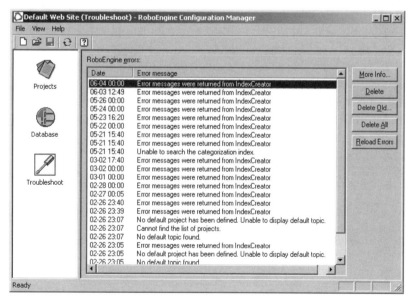

Figure 16-22: The RoboEngine Configuration Manager - Troubleshoot screen

6. The RoboEngine Configuration Manager - Troubleshoot screen is primarily for informational purposes. Error conditions are logged and the messages are displayed on this screen in reverse chronological order. For additional information on a specific error message, highlight the message and click the **More Info** button. Figure 16-23 shows a typical error message in the RoboEngine Error screen.

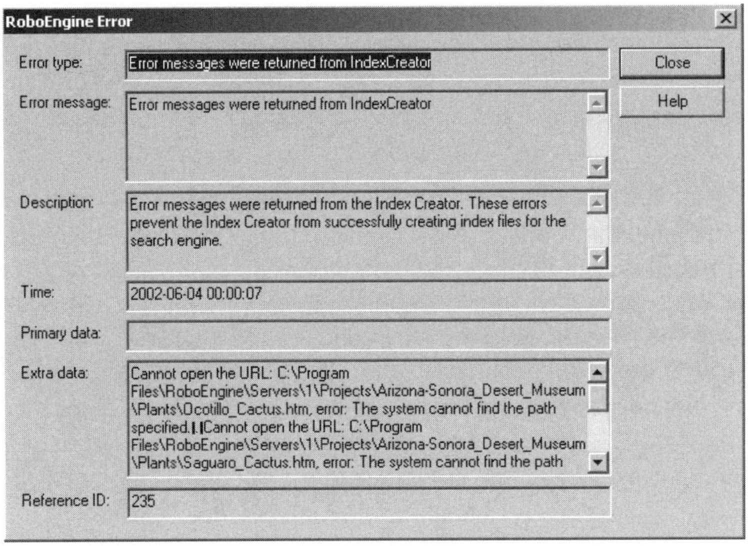

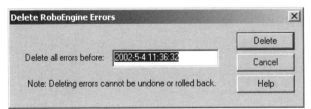

Figure 16-23: The RoboEngine Error screen

Clicking the Reload Errors button reloads the errors from the log and updates the listing on the RoboEngine Configuration Manager - Troubleshoot screen. You can delete an individual error message by highlighting the error message on the RoboEngine Configuration Manager - Troubleshoot screen and clicking Delete. All errors on the list can be deleted by clicking Delete All.

To delete all errors before a given date, click Delete Old. The Delete RoboEngine Errors screen (shown in Figure 16-24) appears. Enter the date and time before which you want to remove all the errors—entered in YYYY-M-D HH:MM:DD with time in 24-hour format—and click Delete to delete all qualifying messages.

Figure 16-24: The Delete RoboEngine Errors screen

Using Natural Language Search

Natural language search is one of the powerful features of WebHelp Enterprise. Natural language search lets you type search questions in plain English rather than in a more stylized fashion that uses Boolean operators. In the sample online help file for the Arizona-Sonora Desert Museum, you could type "What animals are at the museum?" and then see a list of the pages in the online help that have relevant entries.

You can increase the users' options for querying using natural language search by using synonyms. For example, by specifying "zoo" as a synonym for "museum," users will be able to enter either word and see the same list of pages. Synonyms allow the most flexibility for the users because the users don't have to guess which term or phrase is the one used by the online help author.

Because the RoboEngine keeps track of the questions that have been asked, the natural language search becomes more powerful over time. You can run reports to analyze the questions that have been asked to identify the types of questions that users are asking and which questions are going unanswered. With this information, you can update and expand the online help to provide the users with better help.

Natural language search is a built-in feature of WebHelp Enterprise. Once a project is published to the server, natural language search is available.

To view a natural language search, do the following:

1. From the **File** menu, choose **Run** and then **WebHelp Enterprise with Internet Explorer** or **WebHelp Enterprise with Netscape Navigator**. (As described earlier, you must run the project with the RoboEngine on the server rather than locally to take advantage of the natural language search features.)

 NOTE: *As always, if the project has changed since the last time you generated WebHelp Enterprise, you will be prompted to generate the help first and then to publish the help before running. By accepting these options, you will have the most current version of the WebHelp Enterprise on your server.*

2. If necessary, enter your network name and password to access the server. RoboHelp Enterprise launches the appropriate browser and displays the opening page of the WebHelp Enterprise project (shown earlier in Figure 16-18).

3. Click **Search** on the Help toolbar. The Search screen appears.

4. Enter the search question in the question field and click **Go**. As shown in Figure 16-25, RoboEngine responds with the topics that contain information relevant to the question. You can double-click any of the pages in the list to display the topic.

Figure 16-25: The Search window in a WebHelp Enterprise project

You can increase the usefulness of your WebHelp Enterprise project by adding synonyms. Synonyms let the users use similar or related words and phrases in questions.

There are two kinds of synonyms you can use: directional synonyms and synonym groups. A *directional synonym* is a synonym that includes or is included by another term. For example, the sample WebHelp Enterprise project could have "plant" as a directional synonym for "cactus." All cacti are plants, but not all plants are cacti. A *synonym group* identifies synonyms that are to be treated identically when a user enters them as part of question, such as "zoo" and "museum" in the sample WebHelp Enterprise project.

In addition to directional synonyms and synonym groups, you can also exclude words or phrases that would retrieve too many pages or irrelevant information. For this sample help project, for example, you might want to exclude "desert" as a search term because it would retrieve too many entries to be useful. (The natural language search automatically looks for common words such as articles and conjunctions.)

To add directional synonyms, do the following:

1. From the **Tools** menu in RoboHelp HTML, select **Natural Language Synonym Editor.** The Natural Language Synonym Editor opens.

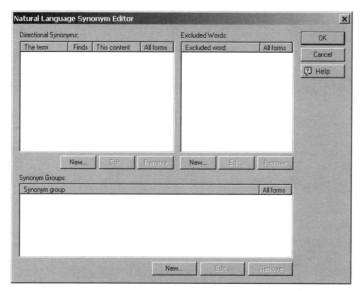

Figure 16-26: The Natural Language Synonym Editor screen

2. Click **New** below the Directional Synonyms window. The New/Edit Directional Synonym screen appears (shown in Figure 16-27 with sample data added).

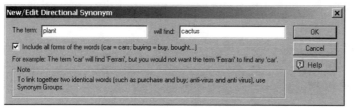

Figure 16-27: The New/Edit Directional Synonym screen

3. Enter the terms in the fields. If you want to find all forms of each word or phrase, click the **Include all forms...** check box. This generally means that the natural language search will find singular and plural forms of nouns and conjugated forms of verbs.

4. When you are satisfied with your entries, click **OK**. The directional synonyms appear in the Directional Synonyms section of the Natural Language Synonym Editor. Figure 16-28 on the following page shows several directional synonyms entered. Click **OK** to save your changes.

TIP: *You can edit an existing directional synonym by double-clicking the entry. The entry appears in the New/Edit Directional Synonym screen where you can make changes to it. To delete an entry, highlight the entry and click Remove.*

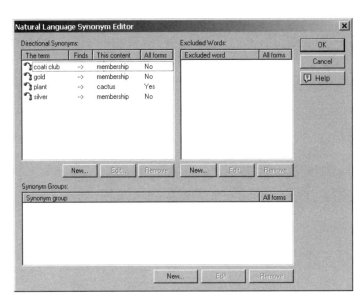

Figure 16-28: The Natural Language Search Synonym screen with sample directional synonyms added

To add synonym groups, do the following:

1. From the **Tools** menu in RoboHelp HTML, select **Natural Language Synonym Editor**. The Natural Language Synonym Editor opens, as shown earlier in Figure 16-26.

2. Click **New** under the Synonym Groups field. The New/Edit Synonym Group screen appears (shown in Figure 16-29 with sample entries already added).

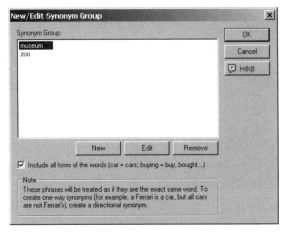

Figure 16-29: The New/Edit Synonym Group screen

3. Click **New** on the New/Edit Synonym Group screen to create a new entry in a synonym group. You can enter as many synonyms as you like in a given synonym group. You can edit or remove a synonym in the group by highlighting the entry and clicking Edit or Remove.

4. When you are satisfied with your entries for the synonym group, click **OK**. Figure 16-30 shows the Natural Language Synonym Editor screen with some sample synonym groups added. Click **OK** to save your entries.

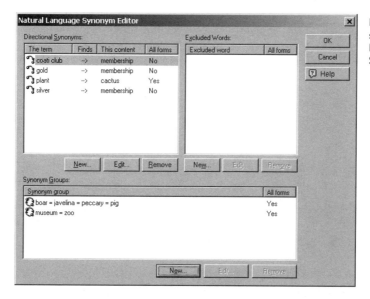

Figure 16-30: Sample synonym groups in the Natural Language Synonym Editor screen

TIP: *As with the directional synonyms, you can edit an existing synonym group by double-clicking the entry. The entry appears in the New/Edit Synonym Group screen where you can make changes to it. To delete an entry, highlight the entry and click Remove.*

To exclude words from your synonym list, do the following:

1. From the **Tools** menu in RoboHelp HTML, select **Natural Language Synonym Editor.** The Natural Language Synonym Editor opens, as shown earlier Figure 16-26.

2. Click **New** under the Excluded Words field. The New/Edit Excluded Words screen appears (shown in Figure 16-31 with a sample entry already added).

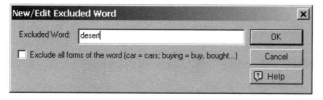

Figure 16-31: The New/Edit Excluded Word screen

3. Enter the word or phrase to exclude. If you want to exclude all forms of each word or phrase, click the **Exclude all forms...** check box. This generally means that the natural language search will exclude singular and plural forms of nouns and conjugated forms of verbs.

4. When you are satisfied with your entries, click **OK**. The excluded term appears in the Excluded Words section of the Natural Language Synonym Editor screen. Figure 16-32 shows a sample excluded word entered in this screen.

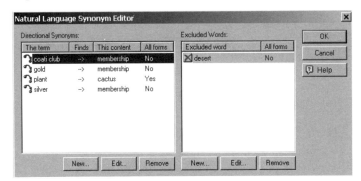

Figure 16-32: The Natural Language Synonym Editor screen with a sample excluded word added

 TIP: You can edit an existing excluded word by double-clicking the entry. The entry appears in the New/Edit Excluded Word screen where you can make changes to it. To delete an entry, highlight the entry and click Remove.

When you are done adding excluded words, click **OK** to close the Natural Language Synonym Editor screen.

 NOTE: All synonyms and excluded words are saved in the project's .SYN file.

Using the WebHelp Enterprise Reports

One of the advantages of using WebHelp Enterprise is that you can monitor how the help is being used and where it needs to be improved. RoboHelp comes with seven WebHelp Enterprise reports for tracking such information as:

■ Which topics are viewed most often?

■ Which questions are most commonly asked?

■ Which questions does the online help fail to answer?

You can use the answers to these and other questions in the reports to fix, enhance, and expand the online help project to provide better help to the users. To run the WebHelp Enterprise reports, do the following:

1. From the RoboHelp HTML window, click the **Enterprise Reports** tab at the bottom of the right pane. RoboHelp prompts you to connect to the server, as shown in Figure 16-33.

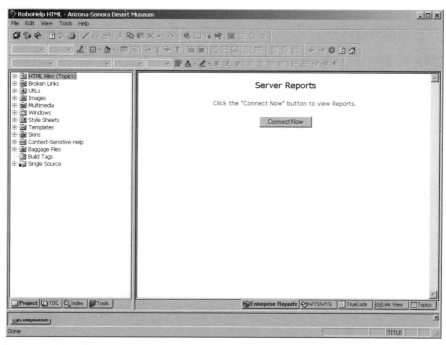

Figure 16-33: The prompt to connect to the server

2. Click **Connect Now**. RoboHelp connects to the server and displays the main report screen, shown in Figure 16-34.

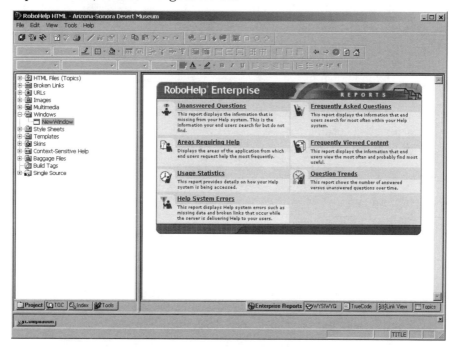

Figure 16-34: The main RoboHelp Enterprise reports screen

3. From the main RoboHelp Enterprise reports screen, you can run any of the seven reports. Each of these reports is described in the following sections.

The Unanswered Questions Report

The Unanswered Questions report lists the questions that are asked by the users that the online help was not able to answer.

From the main RoboHelp Enterprise reports screen, click **Unanswered Questions**. The Unanswered Questions report appears in the right pane. A sample Unanswered Questions report is shown in Figure 16-35.

 NOTE: *You can also generate this report by selecting the report name from the drop-down at the top left of any RoboHelp Enterprise report.*

As you can see in Figure 16-35, the questions are represented visually in the graph, as well as statistically in the report details. You can display the number of times the questions were asked in a bar chart format by selecting the Times Asked option. (An example of the bar chart format is shown in Figure 16-37.)

The questions are grouped according to the Question Grouping options set in the RoboEngine Configuration Manager - Database screen

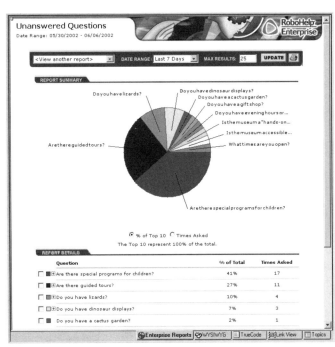

Figure 16-35: The Unanswered Questions report

(shown earlier in Figure 16-21). You can see the specific questions in each question group by clicking the plus sign to the left of the question. The individual questions and their statistics are then displayed below the question group.

You can specify a number of reporting options. You can generate the report for a wide variety of date options. You can also specify the maximum number of results to include on the report. To print the report, click the Printer icon at the upper right of the report screen.

It's possible to remove specific question groups that you don't want to consider by checking the box to the left of the question group and then clicking the Remove Select button at the bottom of the report screen. (The button is not visible in Figure 16-35.)

The Frequently Asked Questions Report

The Frequently Asked Questions report lists the questions that are asked most frequently by the users (whether or not they find an answer in the online help).

From the main RoboHelp Enterprise reports screen, click **Frequently Asked Questions**. The Frequently Asked Questions report appears in the right pane. A sample Frequently Asked Questions report is shown in Figure 16-36.

 NOTE: *You can also generate this report by selecting the report name from the drop-down at the top left of any RoboHelp Enterprise report.*

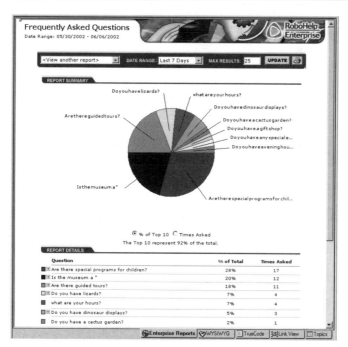

Figure 16-36: The Frequently Asked Questions report

The display options, question grouping, report options, and removal of questions for this report are the same as for the Unanswered Questions report.

The Areas Requiring Support Report

The Areas Requiring Support report lists the topics about which the users most frequently ask questions.

From the main RoboHelp Enterprise reports screen, click **Areas Requiring Help**. The Areas Requiring Support report appears in the right pane. A sample Areas Requiring Support report is shown in Figure 16-37.

 NOTE: You can also generate this report by selecting the report name from the drop-down at the top left of any RoboHelp Enterprise report.

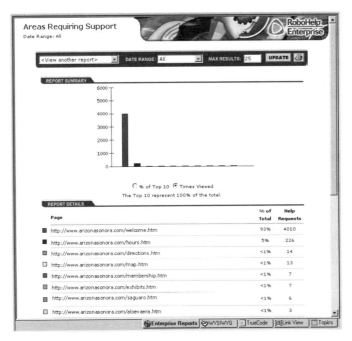

Figure 16-37: The Areas Requiring Support report

The display options, question grouping, report options, and removal of questions for this report are the same as for the Unanswered Questions report.

The Frequently Viewed Content Report

The Frequently Viewed Content report shows how frequently the various topics are viewed by the users.

From the main RoboHelp Enterprise reports screen, click **Frequently Viewed Content**. The Frequently Viewed Content report appears in the right pane. A sample Frequently Viewed Content report is shown in Figure 16-38.

 NOTE: You can also generate this report by selecting the report name from the drop-down at the top left of any RoboHelp Enterprise report.

Figure 16-38: The Frequently Viewed Content report

The display options, question grouping, report options, and removal of questions for this report are the same as for the Unanswered Questions report.

The Usage Statistics Report

The Usage Statistics report provides statistics about how the online help is being accessed.

From the main RoboHelp Enterprise reports screen, click **Usage Statistics**. The Usage Statistics report appears in the right pane. A sample Usage Statistics report is shown in Figure 16-39.

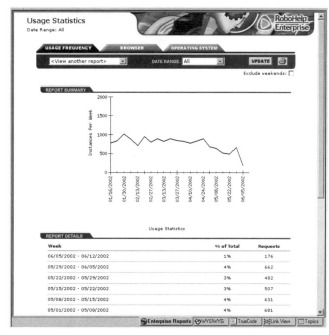

Figure 16-39: The Usage Statistics report

NOTE: *You can also generate this report by selecting the report name from the drop-down at the top left of any RoboHelp Enterprise report.*

The date options for this report are the same as for the Unanswered Questions report. You can also display information on the browsers and operating systems used to access the online help by clicking the appropriate tab at the top of the report.

The Unanswered Questions Trend Report

The Unanswered Questions Trend report shows the percentage of unanswered questions and when they occurred.

From the main RoboHelp Enterprise reports screen, click **Question Trends**. The Unanswered Questions Trend report appears in the right pane. A sample Unanswered Questions Trend report is shown in Figure 16-40.

 NOTE: *You can also generate this report by selecting the report name from the drop-down at the top left of any RoboHelp Enterprise report.*

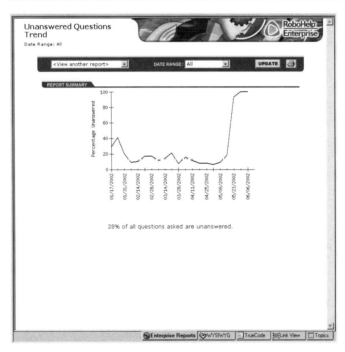

Figure 16-40: The Unanswered Questions Trend report

The date options for this report are the same as for the Unanswered Questions report.

The Help System Errors Report

The Help System Errors report lists the errors that occur in the online help project.

From the main RoboHelp Enterprise reports screen, click **Help System Errors**. The Help System Errors report appears in the right pane. A sample Help System Errors report is shown in Figure 16-41.

 NOTE: *You can also generate this report by selecting the report name from the drop-down at the top left of any RoboHelp Enterprise report.*

Figure 16-41: The Help System Errors report

There is no graph for this report. The date options and removal of individual errors for this report are the same as for the Unanswered Questions report.

Summary

This chapter showed you why and how to use WebHelp Enterprise, how to publish WebHelp Enterprise on your server, how to view WebHelp Enterprise, how to fine-tune the RoboEngine, how to use the natural language search features, and how to analyze your online help projects using the RoboHelp Enterprise reports.

The next chapter will discuss ways for teams to work together to create large online help projects more effectively.

Chapter 17

Developing Large Online Help Projects

In the preceding chapter, you learned how to use WebHelp Enterprise to create web-based online help, how to use the natural language search features, and how to analyze your online help projects using the RoboHelp Enterprise reports. This chapter will show you how to work as a team by using build tags to create and maintain multiple versions of an online help project and by using browse sequences to navigate seamlessly between related sections. The chapter will also discuss some considerations for managing and releasing online help projects.

Using Build Tags

Many large online help projects are released in a complete version to support the primary product and in abridged versions for "lite" versions of the same product. You may also have a primary product that has several add-ons, each of which will require online help to be incorporated as seamlessly as possible. Large corporate clients may also require custom versions of the online help to support a version of the product that has been tailored to fit their needs.

Coordinating multiple simultaneous versions of online help can be difficult. The most common solution is to maintain a separate version of online help for each version you require. The problems with this approach are that it is expensive—maintaining a separate version requires that the same edits must be performed to each version of the same help topic—and slow; once the changes are created for the main version of the online help, the changes must be rippled through all the other versions, resulting in delays. Another approach is to have separate project modules—individual topics or blocks of topics that vary from version to version—but this can be impractical if there are many different modules that need to be assembled to create a version. If you have a large online help project that requires many different versions, the most effective way to manage the changes is to use build tags.

A *build tag* is an internal code assigned to a topic that lets you include or exclude the topic when you compile the online help based on criteria you establish. (This is known as *conditional compiling*.) You can have multiple versions of the same topic—with the same context-sensitive IDs, keywords, and other features—in the source files for an online help project and then include only one of these in the online help.

If you're creating a large online help project from scratch, it's a good idea to create the build tags you know you'll need at the beginning of the project and then assign them to topics as you create them. This gives you an opportunity to set up standards for using build tags and makes sure that individual topics will have the right build tags assigned to them. For example, suppose that the Arizona-Sonora Desert Museum online help has several different versions planned, as follows:

- A general version

- A children's version, with simplified language in some topics and a few added sections with online quizzes and games

- A detailed version with additional botanical and zoological information for students

Each of these versions would require a separate build tag to identify the topics being used. You might have a build tag of MAIN or GENERAL for the general version, KIDS or CHILDREN for the children's version, and DETAILED, EXTENDED, or STUDENT for the student version.

To create build tags, do the following:

1. In the RoboHelp HTML Project Manager, click with the right mouse button on the **Build Tags** folder and select **New Build Tags**. The New Build Tag screen appears.

Figure 17-1: The New Build Tag screen

2. Enter the name of the build tag in the field and click **OK**. Build tags can be up to 32 characters long and are not case-sensitive: "KIDS" is the same as "kids." RoboHelp creates the build tag and adds it to the list of build tags (in alphabetic order) under the Build Tags folder in the Project Manager.

Once you have created build tags, you can assign them to topics. You will most likely want to assign one or two build tags to a number of topics all at once and then fine-tune the build tags for individual topics.

To assign build tags to a group of topics, do the following:

1. Select a group of topics from the Topic pane of the Project Manager. Click the right mouse button and choose **Properties**. The Topic Properties screen appears (shown in Figure 17-2 with several build tags added to the list).

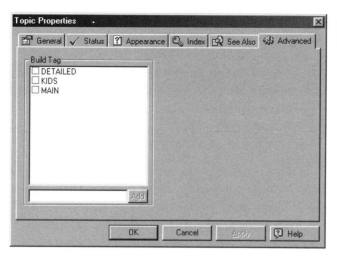

Figure 17-2: The Topic Properties screen with several build tags already entered

2. Check the box for each build tag you want to assign to these topics.

NOTE: *If you discover that you need to add a new build tag, you can do it on the fly in this screen by entering a build tag in the field at the bottom of the screen and clicking Add. RoboHelp adds the build tag to the list and automatically checks the associated box to assign it to the topics you have selected.*

3. When you are satisfied with your selections, click **OK** to close the screen. The build tags you checked are now assigned to the topics.

   Once you have assigned build tags to groups of topics, you can add build tags to individual topics, as follows:

1. Go to the Topic Properties screen for the topic to which you want to assign one or more build tags. The Topic Properties screen for the Welcome topic is shown in Figure 17-3.

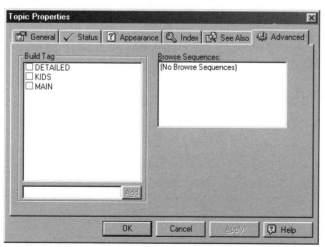

Figure 17-3: The Topic Properties screen for the Welcome topic

2. Check the box for each build tag you want to assign to this topic and uncheck the boxes of any build tags you want to remove from this topic. Because this is the Welcome topic, you'll probably want to check the boxes for all three build tags. You can again add build tags on the fly by entering a build tag in the field at the bottom of the screen and clicking Add.

3. When you are satisfied with your selections, click **OK** to close the screen. The build tags are now assigned to the topic.

When you're done, each topic will have one or more build tags. There will be some topics or groups of topics that have many or all of the build tags assigned to them, some topics with just a couple of build tags, and some topics that only have one build tag. It's important to remember that all topics must have at least one build tag or they won't be selected when you do a conditional compile. For this reason, you may want to create topics using a topic template that has a default build tag and then modify individual topics accordingly. (Topic templates are discussed in Chapter 10.)

Once you have added build tags to your topics, you can do a conditional compile to generate the versions of online help you want, as follows:

1. From the **File** menu, select **Generate**. Then select the type of online help you want to create. The compiler options screen for the type of help you want to create appears.

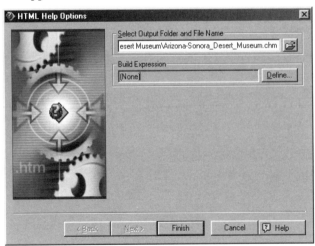

Figure 17-4: The HTML Help Options screen

2. Click **Define**. The Define Build Tag Expression screen appears.

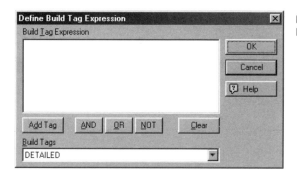

Figure 17-5: The Define Build Tag Expression screen

3. Enter a build tag expression that includes and/or excludes the build tags from the project, either by typing the build tag expression directly in the Build Tag Expression field or by selecting build tags from the drop-down list, clicking Add Tag, and using the AND, OR, and NOT buttons to create a Boolean expression. For example, to include all topics with a build tag of MAIN, you simply enter MAIN in the Build Tag Expression field. To include all topics that have a topic of MAIN or STUDENT, the build tag expression is MAIN OR STUDENT. To exclude topics that have a build tag of STUDENT (and to use everything else), the build tag expression is NOT STUDENT. You can click **Clear** to clear the Build Tag Expression field and start over. Table 17-1 shows some examples of build tag expressions for the sample help file that has build tags of MAIN, KIDS, DETAILED, and MEMBERS_ONLY.

Table 17-1: Sample build tag expressions

Desired functionality	Build tag expression
Include all topics assigned to MAIN	MAIN
Include all topics assigned to either MAIN or KIDS	MAIN OR KIDS
Include all topics that have both the MAIN and KIDS build tags	MAIN AND KIDS
Include all topics assigned to either MAIN or KIDS, but exclude any topics assigned to MEMBERS_ONLY	MAIN OR KIDS AND NOT MEMBERS_ONLY
Exclude all topics assigned to DETAILED	NOT DETAILED
Include all topics assigned to MAIN, except those that are assigned to both KIDS and MEMBERS_ONLY	MAIN AND NOT KIDS AND NOT MEMBERS_ONLY

4. When you are satisfied with your entries, click **OK**. The build tag expression you entered in the Define Build Tag Expression screen appears in the Build Expression field of the compiler options screen, as shown in Figure 17-6.

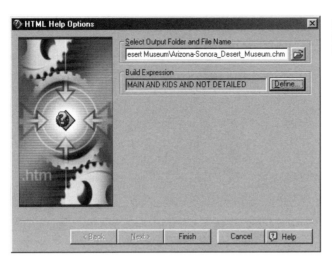

Figure 17-6: The HTML Help Options screen with a sample build tag expression

5. Click **Finish** to continue compiling the online help project as normal.

Once the online help has compiled, be sure to check the results to make sure that you have entered the correct build tag expression. It is very common to have a complex build tag expression that inadvertently includes or excludes topics.

You can find out which topics have a specific build tag by double-clicking the build tag in the Build Tags folder on the Project Manager. RoboHelp displays the Build Tag Properties screen (shown in Figure 17-7) with a list of the topics that are assigned to that build tag. You can display the topic by clicking the Pencil icon or display the Topic Properties screen for the topic by clicking the Hand and Page icon.

If the online help has links, Keyword Link controls, books and pages in the table of contents, or Related Topics controls to topics that have not been included, the links and controls remain active and the topics are included as part of the online

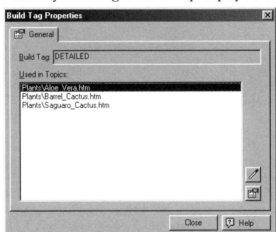

Figure 17-7: The Build Tag Properties screen

help even though the topics were not specifically included by the build tag expression. However, if the topic is directly excluded by the build tag expression, the topics and any links, keywords, table of contents entries, and Related Topics controls do not appear in the compiled help.

Links to external URLs or documents are not affected by build tags: If the topic is included, the link is included. Similarly, external .chm files that are linked to from within an online help project are not affected by build tags. All the information is available from the external topic links, even if the external .chm files also use build tags because build tags only affect the online help project being compiled and not the compiled projects to which it may be linked.

Teams using build tags can write online help modules that can be included conditionally when the help is compiled. By planning for multiple versions of an online help project from the beginning, you can support your company's growth into a variety of markets.

Using Browse Sequences

When you compile your online help project, you can navigate between topics using the table of contents, the index and search features, or the Previous and Next buttons at the top of the topic window. The order in which topics appear is determined by the order in which they're compiled or by their order in the table of contents. You can set up browse sequences that let you move forward and backward within a selected group of topics in a predetermined order.

Browse sequences have many applications. For example, you can set up a browsable range of topics for a single section or module of your online help project, such as the topics in a short training exercise or the steps in a procedure. When the users view the section, they will only be able to browse between the topics in the browse sequence. You can also set up a browse sequence to jump for the topics at a specific heading level, allowing the users to skim the heading topics for entire modules in the online help until they come to the heading topic they need. Figure 17-8 shows how browse sequences work.

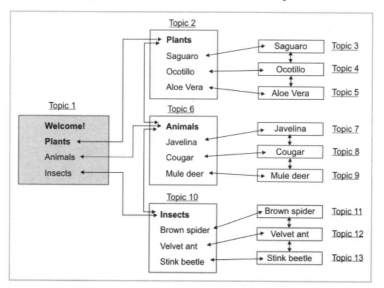

Figure 17-8: How browse sequences work

As you can see from Figure 17-8, the table of contents provides the standard jumps to the referenced heading and detail topics. Your heading topics will also have jumps to relevant detailed topics but not necessarily to other heading topics. Furthermore, when you are scrolling from one topic to the next using the Previous and Next buttons, there are no clear starts or stops to a section—the topics tend to flow into one another. By adding browse sequences at several levels, you can jump from heading topic to heading topic (such as from Plants to Animals to Insects in Figure 17-8) or from Saguaro to Ocotillo to Aloe Vera at the detail level.

It's not necessary to use browse sequences, particularly if you have a relatively small or tightly focused online help project, but they are a valuable tool for large help systems. Browse sequences give the users another logical framework with which to understand the topic matter in a specific section. They let the users page through the online help similar to thumbing through a book looking for a specific chapter and then within a chapter to find a specific page or section.

Browse sequences are of particular importance to team development. Because the online help developed by a team is invariably very large with many sections and modules, browse sequences provide the users with cues for how the information has been structured and an additional method of skimming sections of the online help. Because the browse sequences allow you to cluster related topics, they encourage the users to explore other topics in the same section.

To set up a browse sequence, do the following:

1. From the **Tools** menu, select **Browse Sequence Editor**. The Browse Sequence Editor appears, as shown in Figure 17-9.

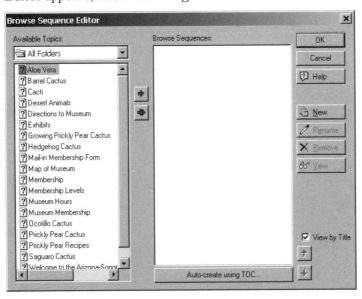

Figure 17-9: The Browse Sequence Editor screen

2. Click **New**. RoboHelp creates a new browse sequence with a default name of Untitled in the Browse Sequences field. Change the browse sequence name to something unique and relevant, such as PLANTS or ANIMALS. If you have several series of plants or animals, you might want to qualify by entering PLANTS-CACTUS and PLANTS-SUCCULENTS. You can also have browse sequence names with numbers, such as PLANTS01 or 3-ANIMALS; however, browse sequence names appear on the online help screen, so it's a good idea not to be cryptic.

3. Add topics to the browse sequence in the Browse Sequences field either by dragging and dropping topics or by highlighting topics and clicking the selection arrow. You can add all the topics displayed in the Available Topics field by clicking the double arrow. By default, all topics are available, but you can select an individual folder of topics from the folders field at the upper left of the screen. The default viewing option is to view topics by their titles, but you can see the actual topic filenames by unchecking View by Title.

   Topics appear in the browse sequence in the order in which they appear on the screen. To rearrange topics in the browse sequence, drag and drop the topic to the desired location or highlight the topic and use the up and down arrow buttons in the lower-right corner of the screen. To delete a topic from the browse sequence, highlight the topic and click **Remove**. To delete the entire browse sequence and start over, highlight the browse sequence and click **Remove**. A sample browse sequence is shown in Figure 17-10.

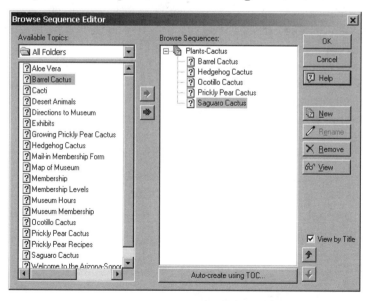

Figure 17-10: A sample browse sequence

4. You can enter and modify as many browse sequences as you like. When you are satisfied with your entries, click **OK**. The first time you enter a browse sequence in your online help project, a message appears that says "Browse sequences have been enabled in your system." Click **OK**.

That's all there is to it! The next time you compile the online help, the browse sequences will appear in a drop-down window in the screen, as shown in Figure 17-11. The topics in the browse sequence are visible above the topic window. The current topic is highlighted on this display, showing the user where he is in the browse sequence.

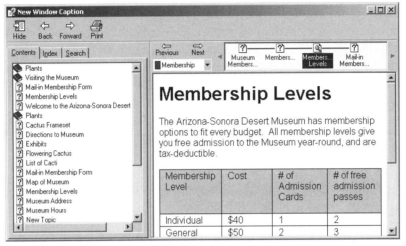

Figure 17-11: The compiled online help showing the browse sequence display and drop-down list

Topics can appear in more than one browse sequence. For example, you might have Saguaro in the PLANTS browse sequence, as well as in the BIRDS-CACTUS-WREN browse sequence. The users only see the topics in the browse sequence they have selected from the drop-down list.

The preceding process showed you how to create browse sequences manually by selecting individual topics or groups of topics in a folder and assigning them to a browse sequence. While you will find this adequate for small online help projects, as well as for fine-tuning browse sequences, it is rather tedious to create dozens or even hundreds of browse sequences for a large online help project. You can use the existing table of contents entries to create a default set of browse sequences and then modify them accordingly.

To create a browse sequence from the table of contents, do the following:

1. From the **Tools** menu, select **Browse Sequence Editor.** The Browse Sequence Editor appears, as shown earlier in Figure 17-9.

2. Click **Auto-create using TOC.** The Auto-create Browse Sequences using TOC screen appears.

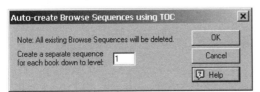

Figure 17-12: The Auto-create Browse Sequences using TOC screen

CAUTION: *Generating browse sequences from the table of contents deletes all previous browse sequences whether generated manually or from the table of contents. You may want to back up your project's source files before using this feature to create the browse sequences.*

3. Enter a number for the depth to which you want to create browse sequences. For example, if you only had a single level of books, you would use the default of 1. If you had three levels of books and topics in your table of contents, you might want to create browse sequences to the first, second, or third level, depending on how detailed the information is and what other navigation tools your users will have in the online help.

4. When you are ready to generate the browse sequences from the table of contents, click **OK**. RoboHelp generates the browse sequences for you. Browse sequences are named using the table of contents book names. Figure 17-13 shows the Browse Sequence Editor after generating browse sequences from the table of contents.

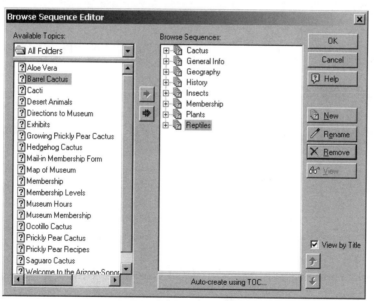

Figure 17-13: Browse sequences generated from the table of contents

TIP: *Because the auto-create feature erases all previous browse sequences, you will probably want to wait until the table of contents is complete or nearly complete, and then auto-create browse sequences using the table of contents and add topics and other browse sequences manually.*

There are several ways to test browse sequences. The most direct is to compile the online help and step through the browse sequences like a user would to see how the browse sequences work. For an overview of the relationships between topics, you can use the Link view to show the browse sequences for a specified topic. Figure 17-14 shows a topic that is part of a browse sequence. The previous and next topics appear above and below the specified topic (and can be reached by clicking on the Previous and Next button below each topic).

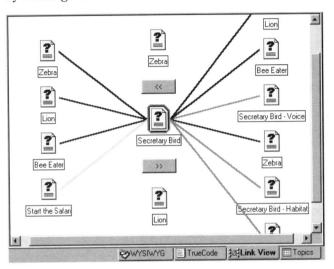

Figure 17-14: Link View showing previous and next topics in a browse sequence

You can also find out which browse sequences a topic is part of by looking at the Advanced tab on the Topic Properties screen.

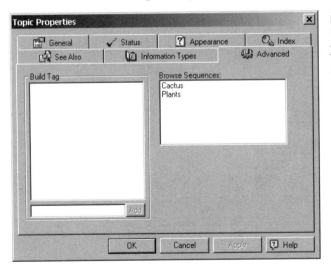

Figure 17-15: Browse sequences for a single topic in the Topic Properties screen

Managing Online Help Projects

The larger the online help project, the more essential good coordination becomes. By coordinating everyone's efforts and providing clear work processes, you can minimize the problems the group is likely to encounter.

Creating a Plan

Good coordination requires careful planning and execution. As you already saw in Chapter 2, a plan identifies who is doing what, when they're doing it, and, to some extent, how. Without a plan, the team will not be nearly as efficient as they could be and there will certainly be coordination problems, overlapping assignments, and topics or even sections that are overlooked.

Establishing Standards

If you are updating an existing online help system, the standards for how to present information are probably already determined, but if you are developing online help from the ground up or you are revamping an existing system, you will need to establish standards. The simplest and most effective way to establish standards is to create standardized style sheets and topic templates, as described in Chapter 10, "Maintaining Consistency with Templates and Skins." These will ensure that information is presented uniformly.

In addition, you should consider setting up a library of commonly used graphics. These can include icons, buttons, windows, and screens, as well as conceptual art that shows tasks, such as sending a form to the printer or emailing a file. Depending on the online help, you may also be able to standardize the phrasing for common procedural tasks so that every time the user is told to open a file or print a document, the language is always the same. Both standard graphics and text blocks should be printed in a simple style guide and kept available online so that the writers and help developers can access it.

Backing Up Your Files

It is invariably the case that a large online help project will be one done on a tight deadline. As a result, you should make sure that all the source files for the project are backed up regularly and reliably.

Backing up is a task that no one really likes to do. It takes time and disk space that you may have difficulty finding, and you don't need to do it 99% of the time. But having a recent backup of your source files is essential; one email virus or hard disk crash can destroy months and even years of combined effort. One good rule of thumb for how necessary it is for you to make backups is to ask yourself "Do I have time to back up the source files at this moment?" If the answer is "no," you should drop whatever you're doing and back up the files.

There are two types of backups you should be making: local backups and network backups. *Local backups* are made by each writer on the team of the files they're working on at the time. They can back up to diskettes, a Zip drive, a CD, or a network drive. Many writers back up individual files to a diskette or a network drive every hour or so as they work on them and then back up all the files in a group or even their entire file directory at the end of the day. *Network backups* are full backups done through the company's network and are usually done once a week by the company's IT department to a backup tape. For this to be most effective, make sure the team members have checked the latest version of their files into the designated location immediately before the backup.

CAUTION: *More than once, IT groups have failed to back up the online help files on schedule, completely, or even at all. It may be prudent to occasionally test IT's ability to respond by asking them to restore a small group of files. (Don't let them know you're testing them, of course.)*

In addition, you should consider periodically creating your own permanent full backups of source files by burning them to CD and storing them offsite in case of fire, theft, or other loss. Also check with the company's legal department: There may be legal requirements to maintain the source code for a product for a certain length of time to fulfill contractual obligations to clients. CDs are a fairly stable means of storing files permanently, as they are moderately sturdy and do not lose magnetic bits as diskettes, tapes, and even hard drives can. Moreover, the ability to read CDs in their current format is commonplace and will probably remain available for the next five to ten years. Many storage and backup systems also have poor backward compatibility so that it can be nearly impossible to restore files from a tape or diskette created with a previous version.

How often you need to back up your files will depend on the amount of change in the files. During development you should probably make a full network backup of all files at least once a week and incremental network backups daily. You should make a permanent offsite archive copy once every two weeks. You should also make a full backup of files immediately prior to a handoff (for example, whenever the online help is released for an alpha release or a beta candidate).

TIP: *If you truly do not have the time and/or the disk space to back up your source files, save the compiled help files. In an emergency, you could use RoboHelp's tools to decompile the online help and use the source files it generates to recreate the project.*

Using a Source Control System

A source control system maintains copies of the source files and establishes a clear chain of ownership. Files are checked in and out from the system (like books in a library), making it harder for two people to make changes on the same file without knowing someone else is working on it. Source control systems also provide historical information about a project by maintaining source files for previous versions. This lets you quickly recreate the online help for a specific product version or even an internal release. Company logos, screen shots of standard screens, generic icons and buttons, and topic text can also be checked into the source control system as a common repository of standardized information. Finally, the source control system also provides a measure of backup protection, as it keeps a copy of any file that's checked out. If you need to recover from changes you've made, you can revert to the original file quickly and easily.

If the developers are using a source control system to maintain their source code, explore the possibility of using it to store online help project files. You may even be able to arrange to have the engineer in charge of the source control system do much of the work for checking files in and out for you.

Tracking Topic Status

RoboHelp provides several handy tools for assigning and tracking work for each team member. You can use the Topic Status features to track information on a topic's priority, status, and estimated hours for each topic, as well as identify which topics are assigned to which writers. This information can be used to create and refine performance statistics and metrics and provide an audit trail of the work being done.

To enter status information for a topic, do the following:

1. Click with the right mouse button on a topic and choose **Properties**. When the Topic Properties screen appears, select the **Status** tab (see Figure 17-17 on the following page).

2. Information about the file name, its location, size, creation date, and last modified date appear on the top of the tab. Enter information as follows:

   ■ **Status:** Select one of three options from the drop-down list: In Progress (the default), Ready for Review, or Complete.

   ■ **Priority:** Enter a numeric priority. (RoboHelp sorts the priority numbers, but you will have to assign the relative importance for priorities.)

   ■ **Hours:** Enter the number of hours for this topic. This can be used as an estimated or a final number of hours.

   ■ **Comment:** Enter any comments about the topic, such as who made changes to it when.

■ **To Do List:** Check off the boxes for each task as they're completed.

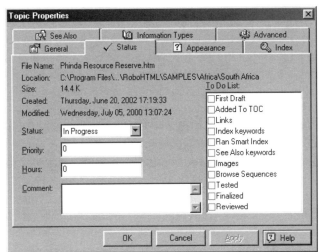

Figure 17-16: The Status tab in the Topic Properties screen

3. When you are satisfied with your entries, click **OK**. RoboHelp saves the topic status information you've entered.

You can enter or change topic status information for groups of topics by selecting the group of topics in the Topic List, right-clicking, and selecting Properties. Make the changes, and click OK to update the information for the selected topics.

Once you have entered the topic status, you can run any of several reports to tabulate and use the information, including the reports shown in Table 17-2.

Table 17-2: Reports that show topic status

Report	Description
Project Status report	Shows the total number of topics in your project, estimated development time to author all topics, and the total number of topics in progress/ready for review/complete
Topic Properties report	Shows detailed information on properties for each topic
Topics by Priority report	Shows a list of topics by priority

For more information on reports, see Appendix B.

You should print a Project Status report for each writer on the team on a regular basis as a measure of work accomplished and tasks left to do. The Topics by Priority report will be helpful for whittling down the remaining high-priority tasks.

Releasing the Finished Online Help

The final steps in releasing online help are about the same as the steps for releasing a printed document. You need to test the final version, check for spelling and grammar errors, and make sure that the online help complies with company standards for look and feel. In addition to the usual tests applied to any documentation, online help also requires some additional tests prior to release.

First, check for broken links within the online help. You can do this by opening the Broken Links folder in the Project Manager and seeing the broken links listed there. If you have a number of broken links, you may want to print the Broken Links report. (The Broken Links report is shown in Appendix B.)

After you have resolved any broken links, use the Unreferenced Topics report (also shown in Appendix B) to identify any topics that cannot be reached by the user with jumps, popups, table of contents entries, keywords, See Also links, aliases, or context-sensitive help.

 NOTE: *It is possible that you may want to hide information in the online help as an unreferenced topic, such as a help change log in a beta version of a help file. Accessing this topic could be done by entering a specific map ID or by searching for a key phrase using the full-text search.*

Several other reports, including the Unused Keywords and Duplicate Map IDs reports, are also useful tools for testing.

Prepare a CD or handoff directory of all the files that are necessary to make the online help work and create a ship list that lists them. Be sure to include the following files in your handoff:

- The compiled online help file(s)
- Any supporting files, such as DLLs, AVIs, MPGs, and related programs, used specifically by the online help
- Any external files, such as external .chm files, that are referenced by the online help (the External Topics report identifies these files for you)
- Any redistributable files necessary for running the online help in the format in which it is being released (the REDISTRB.TXT file on the RoboHelp CD lists the redistributable files included with RoboHelp)

Closing the Project

Once the handoff has been made and the product is in production, you should do the following to close down the project:

1. Create a backup of all source files and supporting files. If you're using a source control system, check this in as the released version for this product. Also burn two CD copies of the source and supporting files for archival purposes. Keep at least one of these off site.

2. Print any reports that you or the team members may need to track and audit the work flow.

3. Schedule a postmortem analysis meeting with the members of the team. In this meeting, identify the successes and failures of the project. Discuss the various problems that occurred and identify ways in which the next online help project can be more efficient.

4. If possible, everyone should go home early and come in late the next day.

Summary

This final chapter has discussed ways in which you and your team can work more effectively. You saw how to use build tags to create and maintain multiple simultaneous versions of a project and how to use browse sequences to improve navigation for the users. The chapter also discussed a number of the issues related to managing large online help projects and showed you some of the tools RoboHelp provides to make tracking work and testing a project easier. The chapter closed by showing you how to release an online help project and close down a project.

File Extensions

RoboHelp HTML creates output files in a variety of formats, depending on the output type that you choose. Most of the time, the RoboHelp HTML program manages the files without your intervention. However, you may need to identify the different file types by their extensions. The following table lists the most common RoboHelp HTML output file types.

Extension	Output type	Description	Comments
*.ali	HTML Help	Stores alias information for window-level context-sensitive help	See Chapter 12, "Creating Context-Sensitive Help"
*.brs	HTML Help, WebHelp, WebHelp Enterprise	Stores browse sequence information	See Chapter 17, "Developing Large Online Help Products"
*.chm	HTML Help	Compiled help file that is delivered to the users	See Chapter 4, "Creating Your First RoboHelp HTML Project" and throughout this book
*.css	HTML Help, WebHelp, WebHelp Enterprise	Cascading style sheet	See Chapter 6, "Formatting Text, Paragraphs, and Topic Pages"
*.glo	HTML Help, WebHelp	Glossary file	Glossary entries can be automated with a wizard accessed through the Glossary tab at the bottom of the left-hand pane.
*.h, *.hh	HTML Help, WebHelp, WebHelp Enterprise	Map files used in creating context-sensitive help	See Chapter 12, "Creating Context-Sensitive Help"
*.hhc	HTML Help, WebHelp, WebHelp Enterprise	Table of contents file	See Chapter 9, "Getting Organized Using Folders, Tables of Contents, and Indexing Tools"
*.hhk	HTML Help, WebHelp, WebHelp Enterprise	Index file	See Chapter 9, "Getting Organized Using Folders, Tables of Contents, and Indexing Tools"
*.hhp	HTML Help	HTML Help version of the master project file (.mpj) generated only if you are creating HTML Help output	This file is an interim file created by RoboHelp. You should not need to access this file directly.

Extension	Output type	Description	Comments
*.hht	HTML Help, WebHelp, WebHelp Enterprise	Help Template	See Chapter 10, "Maintaining Consistency with Templates and Skins"
*.hlp	HTML Help	Compiled WinHelp file. If your project links to a WinHelp file, the file must be shipped along with the .chm.	See Chapter 5, "Linking Topics Together"
*.hpr	HTML Help, WebHelp, WebHelp Enterprise	Preferences used by single-source output	This file is created by RoboHelp. You should not need to access this file directly.
*.htm	HTML Help, WebHelp, WebHelp Enterprise	Topic files written in HTML	See Chapter 4, "Creating Your First RoboHelp HTML Project" and throughout this book
*.ldb	HTML Help, WebHelp, WebHelp Enterprise	Lock file used internally by RoboHelp	This file is an internal RoboHelp file and should not be changed or edited manually.
*.lng	HTML Help, WebHelp, WebHelp Enterprise	Language file (only created when you change the language in your project)	This is a text file that contains the labels for various portions of RoboHelp output. If you want to change the language, you can edit the .lng file in a text editor.
*.mpj	HTML Help, WebHelp, WebHelp Enterprise	The main project file	See Chapter 4, "Creating Your First RoboHelp HTML Project" and throughout this book
*.phr	HTML Help, WebHelp, WebHelp Enterprise	Phrase list, created by the Smart Index Wizard	See Chapter 9, "Getting Organized Using Folders, Tables of Contents, and Indexing Tools"
*.ppf	HTML Help, WebHelp, WebHelp Enterprise	A file that contains information about your project and is automatically updated as you work	This file is an internal RoboHelp file and should not be changed or edited manually.
*.skn	WebHelp, WebHelp Enterprise	Skin file. A project may have several skins associated with it.	See Chapter 10, "Maintaining Consistency with Templates and Skins"
*.stp	HTML Help	Stop list file. This file contains the words that you want to omit from full-text search.	Stop list entries can be entered in the Project Settings window Advanced tab under Advanced Localization Settings.
*.txt context file	HTML Help	Always called context.txt, this is the file that contains the text-only topics created by the What's This? Help Composer.	See Chapter 12, "Creating Context-Sensitive Help"

Extension	Output type	Description	Comments
*.txt log file	HTML Help, WebHelp, WebHelp Enterprise	The log file has the same name as the project (such as Arizona-Sonora_Desert_Museum.txt) and records information about the project as it's being compiled.	This file is created by RoboHelp. You should not need to access this file directly.
*.wlf	HTML Help, WebHelp, WebHelp Enterprise	Words to ignore list created in the Smart Index Wizard	See Chapter 9, "Getting Organized Using Folders, Tables of Contents, and Indexing Tools"
*.xml	HTML Help, WebHelp, WebHelp Enterprise	The support files for skins, WebSearch, and WebHelp Enterprise output (TOC, index, glossary, and full-text search).	See Chapter 9, "Getting Organized Using Folders, Tables of Contents, and Indexing Tools"

Appendix B   *Reports*

In addition to the Enterprise reports described in Chapter 16, RoboHelp can generate the reports in the following table. These reports are covered in this chapter in alphabetical order.

Report	Description	Page number
Broken Links	Lists the links that point to topics that don't exist	394
Duplicate Map IDs	Lists map IDs that are used more than once	394
External Topics	Lists only those links that point to topics outside of the current project	395
Glossary	Lists all glossary entries	396
Images	Lists all graphic images (.jpg, .gif, .bmp)	397
Index	Lists all index entries	398
Map IDs	Lists all map IDs, including the duplicates	400
Project Status	Lists the status of each topic. Topic status must be entered manually.	401
See Also	Lists the topics included in each See Also category	402
Style Sheet	Lists the topics that use each style sheet	403
Table of Contents	Lists the TOC entries and associated topics	404
Topic Properties	Lists the topics along with any combination of properties that you specify	405
Topic References	Lists the topics and their associated links, TOC entries, and index entries	407
Topics by Priority	Lists the topics in order by priority number. Priority numbers must be entered manually	408
Unreferenced Topics	Lists the topics that do not have links from other topics, TOC entries, or index entries	409
Unused Files	Lists the files that exist in the project directory but are not included anywhere in the project	410
Unused Index Keywords	Lists the index keywords that do not have any associated topics	411
Used Files	Lists all the files used by the project	412

Broken Links Report

The Broken Links report displays any links that jump to topics that RoboHelp cannot locate.

To generate this report, follow these steps:

1. From the **Tools** menu, choose **Reports** and then **Broken Links** to display the report, as shown in Figure B-1.

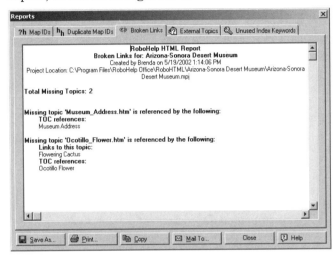

Figure B-1: The Broken Links report

2. You can save, print, copy, or mail the report by clicking any of the buttons across the bottom of the report window.

3. Click **Close** to close the report window.

Duplicate Map IDs Report

The Duplicate Map IDs report displays any map IDs that appear in more than one topic. When creating context-sensitive help, duplicate map IDs will cause unexpected links and should be removed.

To generate this report, follow these steps:

1. From the **Tools** menu, choose **Reports** and then **Duplicate Map IDs** to display the report, as shown in Figure B-2 on the following page.

2. You can save, print, copy, or mail the report by clicking any of the buttons across the bottom of the report window.

3. Click **Close** to close the report window.

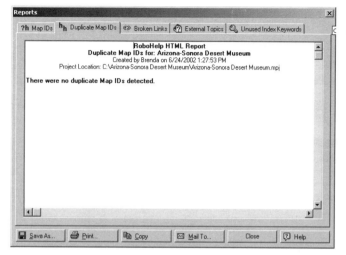

Figure B-2: The Duplicate Map IDs report

External Topics Report

The External Topics report displays links to files outside of the project, such as URLs.

To generate this report, follow these steps:

1. From the **Tools** menu, choose **Reports** and then **External Topics** to display the report, as shown in Figure B-3.

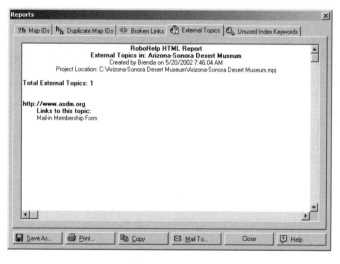

Figure B-3: The External Topics report

2. You can save, print, copy, or mail the report by clicking any of the buttons across the bottom of the report window.

3. Click **Close** to close the report window.

Glossary Report

The Glossary report displays either a list of the glossary entries or a list of the entries and their definitions.

To generate this report, follow these steps:

1. From the **Tools** menu, choose **Reports** and then **Glossary** to display the report, as shown in Figure B-4.

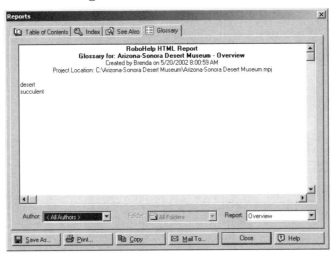

Figure B-4: The Glossary report, Overview option

2. To display the definitions for each glossary entry, as shown in Figure B-5, choose **Detailed** from the Report pull-down menu.

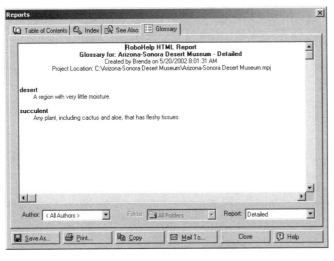

Figure B-5: The Glossary report, Detailed view

NOTE: *The Author pull-down menu is a placeholder for future functionality and has not yet been implemented as of RoboHelp HTML 2002 release 2.*

3. You can save, print, copy, or mail the report by clicking any of the buttons across the bottom of the report window.

4. Click **Close** to close the report window.

Images Report

The Images report displays an alphabetic list of the images and topics in which each image appears. You can display the Images report in order by image or topic.

To generate this report, follow these steps:

1. From the **Tools** menu, choose **Reports** and then **Images** to display the report in order by image name, as shown in Figure B-6.

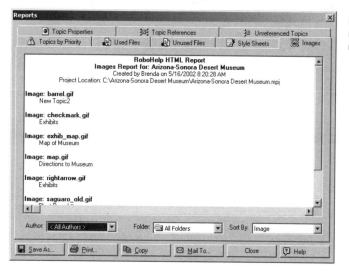

Figure B-6: The Images report, sorted by image name

2. To display the Images report in order by topic, as shown in Figure B-7, choose **Topic** from the **Sort By** pull-down menu.

 NOTE: *The Author pull-down menu is a placeholder for future functionality and has not yet been implemented as of RoboHelp HTML 2002 release 2.*

3. You can limit the images included in the report to just those in a single folder by choosing the folder name from the Folder drop-down menu. For example, choose the Plants folder to see a report that contains only the topics and images in that folder.

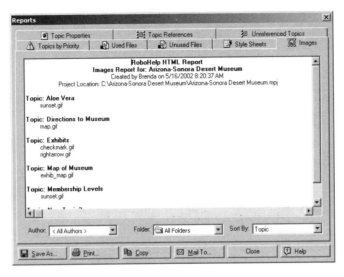

Figure B-7: The Images report, sorted by topic

4. You can save, print, copy, or mail the report by clicking any of the buttons across the bottom of the report window.

5. Click **Close** to close the report window.

Index Report

The Index report displays a list of the index keywords or the index keywords with their associated topics. You can view the keywords in order by index keyword or topic.

To generate this report, follow these steps:

1. From the **Tools** menu, choose **Reports** and then **Index** to display the list of index keywords, as shown in Figure B-8.

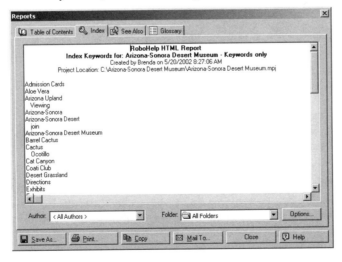

Figure B-8: The Index report, keywords only

2. To change the Index display, click the **Options** button to display the window shown in Figure B-9.

Figure B-9: Index report options window

3. Specify the format of the Index report by choosing one of the following options:

   ■ Keywords displays only the keywords and subkeywords.

   ■ Keywords and Topics displays the index keywords in alphabetical order and the topics associated with each keyword.

   ■ Topics and Keywords displays the topics in alphabetical order and the keywords associated with each topic.

4. Index keywords may be entered in topics or may be stored in the index file. In the **Show** area, select whether you want the report to include the index file keywords, topic index keywords, or both.

5. Click **OK** to apply your changes to the Index report. For example, the report in Figure B-10 shows the topics and keywords.

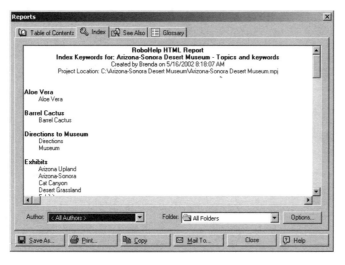

Figure B-10: Index keywords in order by topic

NOTE: *The Author pull-down menu is a placeholder for future functionality and has not yet been implemented as of RoboHelp HTML 2002 release 2.*

6. You can limit the keywords included in the report to just those in a single folder by choosing the folder name from the Folder drop-down menu. For example, choose the Plants folder to see a report that contains only the topics and keywords in that folder.

7. You can save, print, copy, or mail the report by clicking any of the buttons across the bottom of the report window.

8. Click **Close** to close the report window.

Map IDs Report

The Map IDs report displays all map IDs associated with the project.

To generate this report, follow these steps:

1. From the **Tools** menu, choose **Reports** and then **Map IDs** to display the report, as shown in Figure B-11.

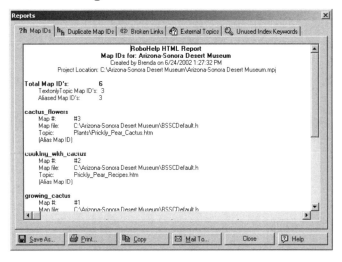

Figure B-11: The Map IDs report

2. You can save, print, copy, or mail the report by clicking any of the buttons across the bottom of the report window.

3. Click **Close** to close the report window.

Project Status Report

The Project Status report displays information about the topics for which you've entered status information. Status information includes estimated time and specifies which of several predefined tasks have been completed. You must enter the status information manually in the Topic Properties window for each topic. RoboHelp HTML does not automatically track this for you.

To generate this report, follow these steps:

1. From the **Tools** menu, choose **Reports** and then **Project Status** to display the report, as shown in Figure B-12.

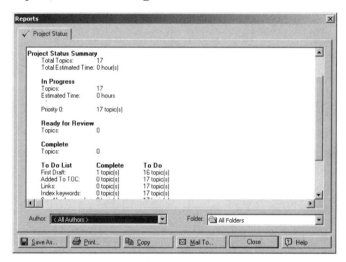

Figure B-12: The Project Status report

NOTE: *The Author pull-down menu is a placeholder for future functionality and has not yet been implemented as of RoboHelp HTML 2002 release 2.*

2. You can limit the topics included in the report to just those in a single folder by choosing the folder name from the Folder drop-down menu. For example, choose the Plants folder to see a report that contains only the topics in that folder.

3. You can save, print, copy, or mail the report by clicking any of the buttons across the bottom of the report window.

4. Click **Close** to close the report window.

See Also Report

The See Also report displays a list of the See Also keywords (also called A-Links). You can display just the keywords or the keywords with their associated topics.

To generate this report, follow these steps:

1. From the **Tools** menu, choose **Reports** and then **See Also** to display the report, as shown in Figure B-13.

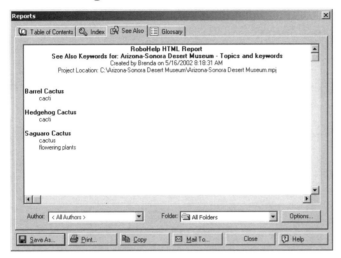

Figure B-13: The See Also report

2. To change the display, click the **Options** button to open the window shown in Figure B-14.

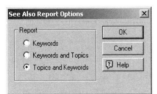

Figure B-14: See Also Report Options window

3. Specify the format of the See Also Report by choosing one of the following options:

   ■ Keywords displays only the See Also keywords.

   ■ Keywords and Topics displays the keywords in alphabetical order and the topics associated with each keyword.

   ■ Topics and Keywords displays the topics in alphabetical order and the keywords associated with each topic.

4. Click **OK** to apply your changes to the See Also report.

NOTE: *The Author pull-down menu is a placeholder for future functionality and has not yet been implemented as of RoboHelp HTML 2002 release 2.*

5. You can limit the topics included in the report to just those in a single folder by choosing the folder name from the Folder drop-down menu. For example, choose the Plants folder to see a report that contains only the topics in that folder.

6. You can save, print, copy, or mail the report by clicking any of the buttons across the bottom of the report window.

7. Click **Close** to close the report window.

Style Sheet Report

The Style Sheet report displays a list of the style sheets and their associated topics or a list of topics and their associated style sheets.

To generate this report, follow these steps:

1. From the **Tools** menu, choose **Reports** and then **Style Sheets** to display a report that shows all the topics associated with each style sheet.

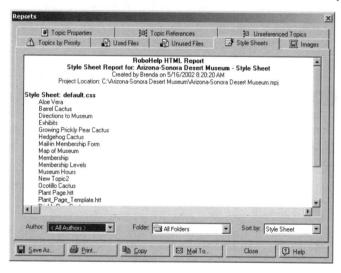

Figure B-15: The Style Sheets report, sorted by style sheet

2. To display the report in order by topic, as shown in Figure B-16, choose **Topic** from the **Sort by** pull-down menu.

 NOTE: *The Author pull-down menu is a placeholder for future functionality and has not yet been implemented as of RoboHelp HTML 2002 release 2.*

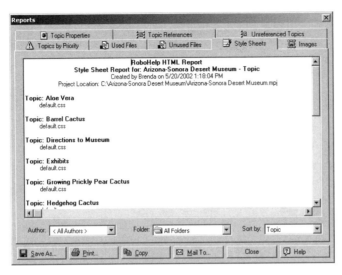

Figure B-16: The Style Sheets report, sorted by topic

3. You can limit the topics included in the report to just those in a single folder by choosing the folder name from the Folder drop-down menu. For example, choose the Plants folder to see a report that contains only the topics in that folder.

4. You can save, print, copy, or mail the report by clicking any of the buttons across the bottom of the report window.

5. Click **Close** to close the report window.

Table of Contents Report

The Table of Contents report lists the books and pages in your table of contents. You can also display the document and folder to which the TOC entry points.

To generate this report, follow these steps:

1. From the **Tools** menu, choose **Reports** and then **Table of Contents** to display the report, as shown in Figure B-17.

NOTE: *The Author pull-down menu is a placeholder for future functionality and has not yet been implemented as of RoboHelp HTML 2002 release 2.*

2. To display the documents to which each entry is linked, as shown in Figure B-18, choose **Detailed** from the **Report** pull-down menu.

3. You can limit the topics included in the report to just those in a single folder by choosing the folder name from the Folder drop-down menu. For example, choose the Plants folder to see a report that contains only the topics in that folder.

4. You can save, print, copy, or mail the report by clicking any of the buttons across the bottom of the report window.

5. Click **Close** to close the report window.

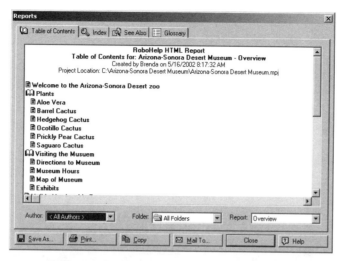

Figure B-17: The Table of Contents report, Overview mode

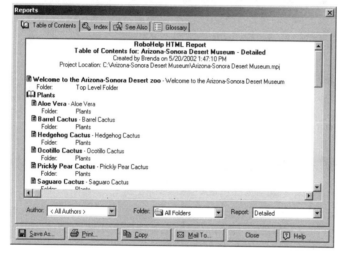

Figure B-18: The Table of Contents report, Detailed view

Topic Properties Report

The Topic Properties report lists all of the topics in the project and can display any combination of the following properties for each topic:

- Folder
- Bookmarks
- Status
- Priority
- Time
- Completed to do's
- Comment

- Links to the topic
- Links from the topic
- Table of contents
- Index entries
- Info types
- Style sheet

To generate this report, follow these steps:

1. From the **Tools** menu, choose **Reports** and then **Topic Properties** to display the report, as shown in Figure B-19.

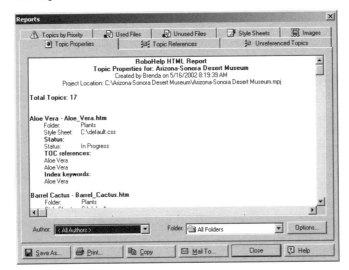

Figure B-19: The Topic Properties report

2. To change the Topic Properties display, click the **Options** button to display the window shown in Figure B-20.

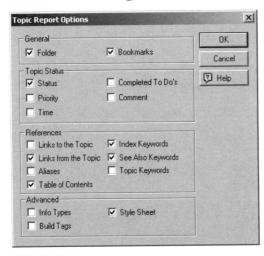

Figure B-20: Topic Report Options window

3. Select the information you want included in the report. Then click **OK** to close the option window and display the report with your changes.

4. You can limit the topics included in the report to just those in a single folder by choosing the folder name from the Folder drop-down menu. For example, choose the Plants folder to see a report that contains only the topics in that folder.

5. You can save, print, copy, or mail the report by clicking any of the buttons across the bottom of the report window.

6. Click **Close** to close the report window.

Topic References Report

The Topic References report lists links, TOC entries, index entries, and hotspots for each topic.

To generate this report, follow these steps:

1. From the **Tools** menu, choose **Reports** and then **Topic References** to display the report, as shown in Figure B-21.

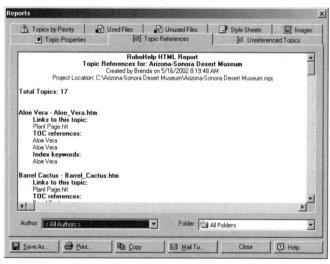

Figure B-21: The Topic References report

2. You can limit the topics included in the report to just those in a single folder by choosing the folder name from the Folder drop-down menu. For example, choose the Plants folder to see a report that contains only the topics in that folder.

3. You can save, print, copy, or mail the report by clicking any of the buttons across the bottom of the report window.

4. Click **Close** to close the report window.

Topics by Priority Report

The Topics by Priority report lists topics by their topic priority. The priority must be set manually in the Topic Properties window for each topic.

To generate this report, follow these steps:

1. From the **Tools** menu, choose **Reports** and then **Topics by Priority** to display the report, as shown in Figure B-22.

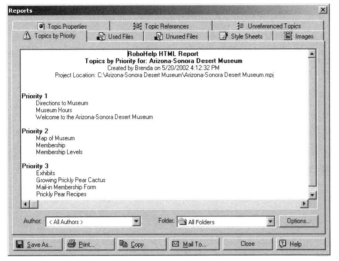

Figure B-22: The Topics by Priority report

2. To change the Topics by Priority display, click the **Options** button to display the window shown in Figure B-23.

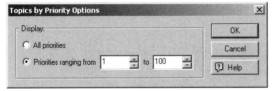

Figure B-23: Topics by Priority Options window

3. To limit the report to only certain priorities, enter numeric values in the two boxes next to **Priorities ranging from**. Or you can click **All priorities** to show all topics. Topics which have not yet been assigned a priority will be listed as priority 0. Click **OK** to close the option window and display the report with your changes.

NOTE: *The Author pull-down menu is a placeholder for future functionality and has not yet been implemented as of RoboHelp HTML 2002 release 2.*

4. You can limit the topics included in the report to just those in a single folder by choosing the folder name from the Folder drop-down menu. For example, choose the Plants folder to see a report that contains only the topics in that folder.

5. You can save, print, copy, or mail the report by clicking any of the buttons across the bottom of the report window.

6. Click **Close** to close the report window.

Unreferenced Topics Report

A project can normally be referenced in any or all of the following ways:

■ Link from another topic

■ Link from a table of contents entry

■ Link from an index entry

The Unreferenced Topics report lists those topics that are not referenced in any of these ways. You can also limit the Unreferenced Topics report to any one of the above categories. For example, you can list only topics that have no index entries or only topics that have neither index nor table of contents entries.

To generate this report, follow these steps:

1. From the **Tools** menu, choose **Reports** and then **Unreferenced Topics** to display the report, as shown in Figure B-24.

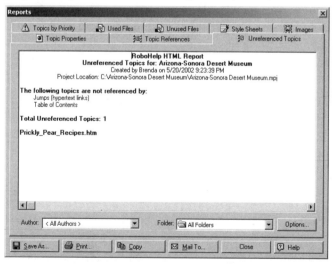

Figure B-24: The Unreferenced Topics report

2. To change the Unreferenced Topics display, click the **Options** button to display the window shown in Figure B-25.

Figure B-25: Unreferenced Topics Options window

3. Select the category of unreferenced topics you want to view. If you click more than one category, only topics that meet all of the criteria will be displayed. For example, if you choose both Table of Contents Entries and Index Entries, only topics that lack both types of links will be included in the report. Topics that have links from the TOC (but not the index) will not be included.

NOTE: *The Author pull-down menu is a placeholder for future functionality and has not yet been implemented as of RoboHelp HTML 2002 release 2.*

4. You can limit the topics included in the report to just those in a single folder by choosing the folder name from the Folder drop-down menu. For example, choose the Plants folder to see a report that contains only the topics in that folder.
5. You can save, print, copy, or mail the report by clicking any of the buttons across the bottom of the report window.
6. Click **Close** to close the report window.

Unused Files Report

The Unused Files report lists the files in your project directories that are not used anywhere in the project. This may happen, for example, when you import an image into a topic, and then later delete the image or the whole topic. The image file itself remains in the directory but no longer appears in the RoboHelp project manager. You'll have to generate this Unused Files report, and then delete the files outside of RoboHelp.

To generate this report, follow these steps:

1. From the **Tools** menu, choose **Reports** and then **Unused Files** to display the report, as shown in Figure B-26.

NOTE: *The Author pull-down menu is a placeholder for future functionality and has not yet been implemented as of RoboHelp HTML 2002 release 2.*

2. To display the report in order by filename, choose **File Name** from the **Sort by** pull-down menu.

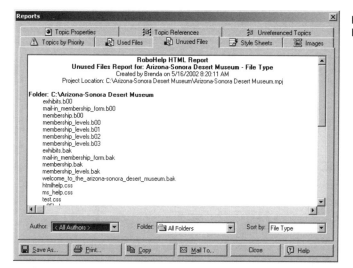

Figure B-26: The Unused Files report

3. You can limit the files included in the report to just those in a single folder by choosing the folder name from the Folder drop-down menu. For example, choose the Plants folder to see a report that contains only the files in that folder.

4. You can save, print, copy, or mail the report by clicking any of the buttons across the bottom of the report window.

5. Click **Close** to close the report window.

Unused Index Keywords Report

The Unused Index Keywords report displays the index keywords that are not associated with any topics. These keywords will also appear in bold in the RoboHelp Explorer Index Designer.

To generate this report, follow these steps:

1. From the **Tools** menu, choose **Reports** and then **Unused Index Keywords** to display the report, as shown in Figure B-27 on the following page.

2. You can save, print, copy, or mail the report by clicking any of the buttons across the bottom of the report window.

3. Click **Close** to close the report window.

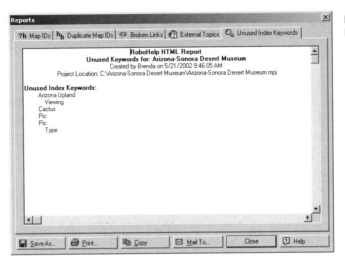

Figure B-27: The Unused Index Keywords report

Used Files Report

The Used Files report lists the files used in the project.
    To generate this report, follow these steps:

1. From the **Tools** menu, choose **Reports** and then **Used Files** to display the report, as shown in Figure B-28.

Figure B-28: The Used Files report

2. To display the report in order by file name, choose **File Name** from the **Sort by** pull-down menu.

NOTE: *The Author pull-down menu is a placeholder for future functionality and has not yet been implemented as of RoboHelp HTML 2002 release 2.*

3. You can limit the topics included in the report to just those in a single folder by choosing the folder name from the Folder drop-down menu. For example, choose the Plants folder to see a report that contains only the topics in that folder.

4. You can save, print, copy, or mail the report by clicking any of the buttons across the bottom of the report window.

5. Click **Close** to close the report window.

Index

Index

About the CD

There are two programs included on the companion CD-ROM:

- The 15-day demo of RoboHelp Office 2002
- The 7-day demo of RoboDemo

RoboHelp Office 2002 is the version described in this book. RoboDemo is an exciting new product for generating animated interactive software tutorials quickly and easily. (For more information on RoboDemo, be sure to check out the eHelp web site at http://www.ehelp.com.)

Installing the RoboHelp Office 2002 Timed Demo

To install the 15-day demo of RoboHelp Office 2002, do the following:

1. Insert the companion CD in your computer's CD-ROM drive.
2. If you have Autorun enabled for the CD-ROM drive, the RoboHelp Office 2002 setup program will start automatically. Otherwise, click **Start | Run**, then type [*d*:**setup.exe**], and click **OK**. (Replace *d* with the appropriate drive letter.)
3. Follow the RoboHelp Office installation instructions.

Installing the RoboDemo Timed Demo

To install the 7-day demo of RoboDemo, do the following:

1. Insert the companion CD in your computer's CD-ROM drive.
2. Click **Start | Run**, then type [*d*:**setuprd.bat**], and click **OK**. (Replace *d* with the appropriate drive letter.)
3. Follow the RoboDemo installation instructions.

 CAUTION: *By opening the CD package, you accept the terms and conditions of the CD/Source Code Usage License Agreement.*

Additionally, opening the CD package makes this book non-returnable.

CD/Source Code Usage License Agreement

Please read the following CD/Source Code usage license agreement before opening the CD and using the contents therein:

1. By opening the accompanying software package, you are indicating that you have read and agree to be bound by all terms and conditions of this CD/Source Code usage license agreement.

2. The compilation of code and utilities contained on the CD and in the book are copyrighted and protected by both U.S. copyright law and international copyright treaties, and is owned by Wordware Publishing, Inc. Individual source code, example programs, help files, freeware, shareware, utilities, and evaluation packages, including their copyrights, are owned by the respective authors.

3. No part of the enclosed CD or this book, including all source code, help files, shareware, freeware, utilities, example programs, or evaluation programs, may be made available on a public forum (such as a World Wide Web page, FTP site, bulletin board, or Internet news group) without the express written permission of Wordware Publishing, Inc. or the author of the respective source code, help files, shareware, freeware, utilities, example programs, or evaluation programs.

4. You may not decompile, reverse engineer, disassemble, create a derivative work, or otherwise use the enclosed programs, help files, freeware, shareware, utilities, or evaluation programs except as stated in this agreement.

5. The software, contained on the CD and/or as source code in this book, is sold without warranty of any kind. Wordware Publishing, Inc. and the authors specifically disclaim all other warranties, express or implied, including but not limited to implied warranties of merchantability and fitness for a particular purpose with respect to defects in the disk, the program, source code, sample files, help files, freeware, shareware, utilities, and evaluation programs contained therein, and/or the techniques described in the book and implemented in the example programs. In no event shall Wordware Publishing, Inc., its dealers, its distributors, or the authors be liable or held responsible for any loss of profit or any other alleged or actual private or commercial damage, including but not limited to special, incidental, consequential, or other damages.

6. One (1) copy of the CD or any source code therein may be created for backup purposes. The CD and all accompanying source code, sample files, help files, freeware, shareware, utilities, and evaluation programs may be copied to your hard drive. With the exception of freeware and shareware programs, at no time can any part of the contents of this CD reside on more than one computer at one time. The contents of the CD can be copied to another computer, as long as the contents of the CD contained on the original computer are deleted.

7. You may not include any part of the CD contents, including all source code, example programs, shareware, freeware, help files, utilities, or evaluation programs in any compilation of source code, utilities, help files, example programs, freeware, shareware, or evaluation programs on any media, including but not limited to CD, disk, or Internet distribution, without the express written permission of Wordware Publishing, Inc. or the owner of the individual source code, utilities, help files, example programs, freeware, shareware, or evaluation programs.

8. You may use the source code, techniques, and example programs in your own commercial or private applications unless otherwise noted by additional usage agreements as found on the CD.

 CAUTION: *By opening the CD package, you accept the terms and conditions of the CD/Source Code Usage License Agreement.*

Additionally, opening the CD package makes this book non-returnable.